Studio Magicae:
A Journal of Practical
and Theoretical Magic

Edited by Alex Criddle

Studio Magicae: A Journal of Practical and Theoretical Magic Vol. 1 No. 1
Copyright: © Alex Criddle, 2022

Cover illustration "the Magus" and details by Ina Auderieth (inurath.com)
Cover layout by Ben Havlicek

ISBN: 979-8-9861326-0-0

studiomagicae.com
twitter.com/studiomagicae
facebook.com/studiomagicae
instagram.com/studiomagicae

Contents

Introduction:
The Meaning of Magic

Alex Criddle

Welcome to the inaugural issue of *Studio Magicae: A Journal of Practical and Theoretical Magic*. I take it you have some interest in the topic or else you wouldn't be here. First, a bit about the journal. This is an open access journal. All articles can be read online at studiomagicae.com. It is also interdisciplinary and is meant to promote dialogue between practitioners and scholars and include the perspective of both. I've met many scholars who are quite knowledgeable regarding indigenous magical practices or occult phenomena but who have never actually practiced the subject matter and thus have a one-sided perspective. I've also met many practitioners who don't understand why what they are doing has the results that follow which could be understood if they understood the broader framework. It's my hope that journal will be of benefit to both.

Why this form? I've always loved academic journals. To me, they feel like a small library. I get a sampling of a dozen people's styles of thinking and ideas—often from people I would not otherwise have stumbled across. Some of my favorite thinkers have been discovered by browsing issues of various journals and coming across an author's work in a compilation. My hope is that this occurs for you as well.

Similarly, I hope to pull from many different magical traditions as the journal continues to grow. I think there is something useful in encountering unfamiliar ways of thinking and experiencing the world.

A final tenet, at least for me, is that this is playful in nature. Scholarly and seriousness are not mutually exclusive to being playful. I play with ideas in a scholastic way all the time. For many people, some sort of playful energy is key to seeing results from magic. We are fundamentally playful creatures and to me this is a form of play. Many of my magical beliefs are playfully held. Reading the articles in this issue kicked both my practical playfulness and my idea playfulness into full gear.

Why the name *Studio Magicae*? It's Latin for study of magic and here we will study and practice magic.

Why use the term magic?

Despite the claims of a number of anthropologists disavowing the word as meaningless, I find it useful for the very reasons they would argue it is meaningless. It covers a very broad range of phenomena that spans every tradition. Spells? Magic. Astrology? Magic. Spirit veneration? Magic. Art? Magic. Science? Magic.[1]

Dean Radin proposes three categories of *real* magic:

1. Force of will: associated with spell-casting and other techniques meant to intentionally influence events or actions
2. Divination: associated with practices such as Tarot and mirror-gazing

---

1   Dean Radin has taken a scientific approach to magic in his fascinating book *Real Magic*.

Frater U.D. makes a useful distinction between the science of magic and the art of magic that I find worth quoting here:

"First of all, the terms 'art, and "science', are important here. Often the term 'occult science' is used, but the occultist (or occult scientist) generally defines ''science, quite differently than the 'exact' or 'natural scientist', does. In the attempt to earn the recognition of orthodox schoolbook science, many occultists (and even magicians) have tried to use the word 'scientific' to describe their discipline. This is only true as long as magic uses scientific methods. In technical jargon, it's 'empirical' or 'empirically scientific,' which applies to everyday practical magic at least. This means that magic first aims at what is visibly successful. On the other hand, the term 'art' refers to the more intuitive area of magic that includes 'fine instincts' and feelings in general, as well as the sensitivity for subtle energies (such as those involved in the various types of clairvoyance). Dreams and visions also fall under the "art" aspect of magic, but thought and the knowledge of correlations, on the other hand, belong to the 'science' aspect." See Frater U.D. *High Magic: Theory and Practice* (Llewelyn, 2005), 10.

3. Theurgy: involves methods for evoking and communi-
    cating with spirits.

This is far from an exhaustive list or categorization of what magic
is. All of that, and anything else labeled magic, is what I am interested
in. And magic is a thread that runs through everything. A more fundamental level might be that magical *consciousness* is a theme in all types.
There's a certain way of being in the world that exists that I will return
to.

What is the Meaning of "Magic"?

What do we mean when we talk about magic? Ariel Glucklich gives
a concise history of the meaning of magic through four answers. First,
early anthropologists such as Edward Tylor and James Frazer argued
that magic does, or at least tries to do, what science does but not as
well.[2] Second, later social scientists decided to ask instead of "what does
magic do?" "what is the function of magic in social and psychological
contexts?" Third, and more recently he says, the question has been
rephrased to "what does magic mean?" by those interested in the symbolic interpretation of magic and its elements. Fourth, there is the "naive
insider's view" that magic does what it claims to do. It starts or stops the
rain, heals people, etc. by controlling powers that are predictable and
useful which are not accessible to most.[3] All of these questions are valid
approaches to magic. But they do not individually encompass even a
portion of the experience that is out there.

Some scholars, such as Glucklich and Susan Greenwood, do approach the idea of magical consciousness. Magical consciousness is a
certain way of being with the world, approaching the world, living with
the world, and participating in reality. It is exploring the nature of reality
and playing with it in acts of co-creation and co-participation, a topic

---

2   See James G. Frazer's *The Golden Bough* and Edward Burnett Tylor's
The Origins of Culture.

3   Ariel Glucklich, *The End of Magic* (Oxford University Press, 1997),
9-10.

which Becca Tarnas will pick up in her article.

The philosopher Jean-Paul Sartre undertook the task of making sense of magic. He suggested that "magic" described a particular way in which someone is able to be conscious of something (i.e. magical consciousness). Magic isn't something that we impose onto the world, it is something out there that we encounter. It reveals structural features of consciousness and its mode of existence in this world. For Sartre the elements that are key to understanding magic—emotions, imagination, and language—are also fundamentally a part of the existential matrix from which our own essence arises.[4] In other words, magic arises from the same place as our very essence.

Sartre also thinks that the term magic "is the one that best expresses a situation in which both mind and world are gripped and transformed by a power that is wholly other to either of them."[5] When confronted with "the magical aspect of . . . human situations" we can either deny it and return to hide behind the ephemeral 'rational' or deterministic superstructures or "the consciousness seizes upon the magic as magic, and lives it vividly as such" and embrace the co-creation of reality that we are afforded.[6]

Whatever tradition it might come from, one of magic's fundamental projects is the same: making sense of experience and reality and exploring relationships between things as they exist in our and other realities. Magical consciousness is a particular way of interacting with the world and, by most definitions, changing the world around us.

A fundamental problem when talking about magic is that someone's understanding of it is shaped by the culture they grew up in and their life experiences. For some magic is equivalent to the fantasy world of Harry Potter with all its spells and correct wand waving,[7] video game characters shooting fireballs from their hands, or forcing people to do what you

---

4   Jean-Paul Sartre, *Sketch for a Theory of the Emotions* trans. Philip Mairet (Routledge, 2015 [1962]), 56-58.

5   Hannu Poutiainen, "Tractatus Logico-Magicus: A Definition of Magic in Three Throws of the Die." *Correspondences* 7, no. 2 (2019): 305–337, 326.

6   Jean-Paul Sartre, *Sketch for a Theory of the Emotions*, 56-58.

7   I, like many other people, am still waiting for my acceptance to Hogwarts.

want. For others magic is something not to be touched or acknowledged and is relegated to those souls who have been led astray. And still others experience magic as an every day part of their life.

Our understanding of magic has been warped and shaped by the media we consume, the people we interact with, and other contextual features of our lives. Whether or not someone "believes" in magic largely comes down to how they conceptualize it. For the Abrahamic religions, healing someone with God's power is not magic, yet the act is theurgical—invoking God and his angels to heal the individual. That is not magic because, since the inception of the Greek form of the word—referring to the *other* Zorastrians with their secret knowledge—magic has been used as the scapegoat. What the Abrahamic religions are doing is the will of God, what *they* are doing is of the devil. If we remove the insinuated *other* from magic, what is it?

Magic as an Art and Science of Change

On a broad view, magic is an art of change. I happen to like Aidan Wachter's version: "The change or changes it involves can be many and various, complex or simple—a change of state, from one thing to another, a change of meaning, a change of mind, identity, heart, soul, or spirit. Often it is the art of changing outcomes." He characterizes it as "wading into the Field" and "altering its flows".[8]

Perhaps the most famous and touted in the Western occult works today is Crowley's "Magic is the science and art of causing changes to occur in conformity with Will."[9] Others, such as Israel Regardie and Francis King, have expanded on Crowley's definition: "Magic is the science and art of using states of altered consciousness for causing changes to occur in conformity with will."[10] Or perhaps you have seen Dion Fortune's "Magick is the art of causing changes in consciousness

---

8   Aidan Wachter, *Weaving Fate: Hypersigils, Changing the Past, and Telling True Lies* (Red Temple Press, 2020), 17.

9   Aleister Crowley, *Magick in Theory and Practice* (Dover Publications Inc., 1976 [1929]), XII.

10   See Frater U.D. *High Magic*, 9.

in conformity with the Will." Or even Donald Michael Kraig's "Magic is the art and practice of causing change in accordance with will, using methods not currently accepted by science."[11] Frater U.D. added that "Magic is the Science and Art of causing Change, on a material as well as a spiritual level, to occur in conformity with Will by altered states of consciousness."[12]

At the core of it, it would seem, is change: whether enacting physical changes, spiritual changes, mindset changes, etc. Even if one's goal is simply to figure out what is out there (or to figure learn everything, as my impossible goal is) it involves a change in one's base knowledge and likely in their interactions with the world. As such it is a process and any magical act could be perceived as a theory of change or a theory of that process.[13]

This quest for figuring out how things connect, for making sense of things is fundamental to human existence. Christopher Bache astutely explains that the journey is not new to us. We are all explorers, but we are not the first. We are part of a cooperative enterprise with other seekers who have come before us. Each generation begins again, building on their ancestors' shoulders. We each get introduced to the journey at different stages in life and with different sets of skills, and in some respects, we are all beginners in some area or another.[14]

As such, this journal will include articles from people in all stages of their journey—people with decades of experience in their subject, people with a few years of experience, or perhaps decades in another field of magic and are just dipping their toes into another. Each can provide a unique insight into the practices and theories of magic, both historical and contemporary.

A purely intellectual approach to magic would produce only limited results. Experiences of magic expand our worldview. Critical reflection then clarifies and evaluates the experience. It allows us to approach our

---

11   Donald Michael Kraig, *Modern Magick: Eleven Lessons in the High Magickal Arts* (Llewellyn, 1988).

12   Frater U.D., *Secrets of the German Sex Magicians* (Llewellyn, 1995).

13   See Arthur M. Young's *The Reflexive Universe* for a theory of process or change that is quite interesting.

14   Christopher Bache, *LSD And The Mind of the Universe: Diamonds from Heaven* (Park Street Press, 2019), 50.

experiences and understand why they occurred the way that they did. It finds patterns and creates narratives for us to explain and understand our experiences.

Historically (and presently), theories of the world were fragmentary in nature, confined to the area in which they originated. Yet, for some reason, these fragments are sometimes still vehemently defended as the whole. In my mind, unless *everything* and *every possible experience* is included in the worldview, that view is fragmentary at best, and *cannot* be defended as the whole of experience. And, as such, we will include any and all descriptions of, explanations for, and experiences of magic here. There are significantly more magical practices and traditions out there that we don't know about individually than we do.

Some people might mistake magic as a "comforting delusion" as an escape from facing the so-called truths of materialism. Magic isn't just an escape. It's not a desire to escape physical reality into some assumed make-believe world with fairies, goblins, and demons. Instead, it is taking a hold of reality, recognizing that we are co-creators of our reality to an extent, and awakening more deeply to our embodied experience— playing a more active role in our emergence from it.

All of our experiences are shaped in some way by where we are at the time of the experience: our physical, emotional, and spiritual status among other things. Magic enables us to alter all three to some degree. And as such is inherently participatory and co-creative.

Articles in this Issue:

As **Becca Tarnas** explains in her article, if we approach astrology as a co-creative practice we can shape the archetypes' expressions in our lives and potentially even the archetypes themselves. It becomes a dance between you and the cosmos and you get a say in whether it is a waltz, a tango, a ballet, or a belly dance.

If you are unsure of where to begin in understanding astrology and its practical applications, **Sadalsuud**'s article is the place to start. It is, perhaps, the best introduction to astrology that I have come across in its ease of use and insight. Let him be your guide into the foray of the planets' role in magic.

The way we understand magic in the past, which shoulders of ancestors we are building on, and how our concepts have developed through time is of paramount importance to understanding where we are today and how to act moving forward.

Hereward Tilton elucidates early modern theurgical techniques in the context of Christian anti-magic polemics and looks at an under-appreciated aspect of the Rosicrucian tradition: The Gold and Rosy Cross's invoking planetary spirits using animated statues and bells.

The oft-overlooked intent behind astrological practices in Rosicrucianism is found in the Gold and Rosy Cross's gnosticism. He also discusses how inspirationist tendencies in Rosicrucianism are reactions to the mechanistic science of the Enlightenment which had discarded divine inspiration as a path to scientific knowledge.

Chris Bennett then explores the role of cannabis in ancient Jewish magical practices making the case for it and other psychoactive substances' widespread usage in Jewish magic and alchemy.

Christian Swenson then does an incredible analysis of the architecture of one of Mormonism's most important buildings and its significance for understanding Mormonism's forgotten relationship to astrology. There exist many parallels between early Mormon leaders' cosmological beliefs and the philosophy of Rudolf Steiner.

Jack Chanek puzzles out the role of the ritual of the Fires of Azrael in Dion Fortune's novel *The Sea Priestess*. He makes a solid case for the importance of the ritual and of it's connection to Solomon's temple and the sea temple featured in the novel.

Antero Alli presents his paratheatre manifesto, "Undoing the World". At first glance, one might wonder why this is a part of a journal on magic. It fits perfectly. Culture is a form of magic. Magic is a ritual, sometimes performed with other people, an audience and other times performed alone. Or in groups. The way Alli describes paratheatre and its influences is a form of performative magic. He also guides us on the integration of ritual into daily life.

Saul Mondriaan offers an incredible insight into the relationship between magic and hypnosis. He guides the reader on a journey through his own experience, techniques of hypnosis, practices for the magician to utilize and offers insights into how to integrate it.

Finally, **Ina Auderieth** graciously allowed me to use her artwork on the cover of this issue and offers her thoughts on the role of art in rituals and practice, tarot, and the inspiration for her piece "The Magus".

Each of these articles has been written by individuals who are people who have shaped my thinking and the way I interact with the world. I hope these articles provide as much pleasure and food for thought as they did for myself.

Let's explore the world and play with magic together.

Works Cited

Bache, Christopher. *LSD And The Mind of the Universe: Diamonds from Heaven* (Park Street Press, 2019).

Frater U.D. *High Magic: Theory and Practice* (Llewelyn, 2005).

Frater U.D. *Secrets of the German Sex Magicians* (Llewellyn, 1995).

Frazer, James G. *The Golden Bough: A Study in Magic and Religion* (Macmillan, 1935).

Glucklich, Ariel. *The End of Magic* (Oxford University Press, 1997).

Greenwood, Susan. *The Nature of Magic: An Anthropology of Consciousness* (Berg, 2005).

Kraig, Donald Michael. *Modern Magick: Eleven Lessons in the High Magickal Arts* (Llewellyn, 1988).

Poutiainen, Hannu. "Tractatus Logico-Magicus: A Definition of Magic in Three Throws of the Die." *Correspondences* 7, no. 2 (2019): 305–337.

Radin, Dean. *Real Magic: Ancient Wisdom, Modern Science, and a Guide to the Secret Power of the Universe* (Harmony Books, 2018).

Sartre, Jean-Paul. *Sketch for a Theory of the Emotions* trans. Philip Mairet (Routledge, 2015 [1962]).

Tylor, Edward Burnett. *The Origins of Culture* (Harper Torchbooks, 1958).

Wachter, Aidan. *Weaving Fate: Hypersigils, Changing the Past, and Telling True Lies* (Red Temple Press, 2020).

Young, Arthur M. *The Reflexive Universe: Evolution of Consciousness* (Doubleday, 1976).

Astrology as Participatory Spirituality

Becca Tarnas

Astrology is an ancient practice that has flourished in many cultures around the globe, and has evolved and diversified to bring forth numerous branches within the astrological tradition. In essence, astrology is the discipline of observing the significant correlations between planetary movements and the unfolding of human events in individual lives, relationships, communities, and throughout history.[1] Astrology is a spiritual way of knowing, and can be approached as a spiritual practice. The archetypal dynamics of astrology indicate that we live in a radically participatory, co-creative universe that is saturated with divine intelligence and care.

The branch of astrology known as archetypal astrology—pioneered by the cultural historian Richard Tarnas, in conjunction with his work with Stanislav Grof on non-ordinary states of consciousness and psychedelic psychotherapy—recognizes that the correlations observed between

---

1   This essay has been revised and adapted from the article "Iridescent Infinity: Participatory Theory and Archetypal Cosmology," published in 2016 in *Archai: The Journal of Archetypal Cosmology*, Issue 5, *Saturn and the Theoretical Foundations of an Emerging Discipline*. To read the original article, please visit: https://archetypalprism.files.wordpress.com/2014/07/becca-tarnas-e28093-iridescent-infinity-e28093-archai-issue-5.pdf.

human affairs and planetary dynamics is of an archetypal character.[2] The planetary bodies in our solar system each correlate with a different archetype, a character with a spectrum of interrelated qualities that can be observed through their multivalent manifestations in human experience. Planetary archetypes are functionally similar to the archetypes as understood by the depth psychological tradition, yet are also comparable to the pantheon of gods and goddesses central to many ancient cultures. Such archetypes can be understood through a variety of philosophical lenses, as they exhibit qualities comparable to Platonic Forms or Ideas, Aristotelian universals, Freudian instincts, Jungian psychological archetypes, and Whiteheadian eternal objects, to name a few, as well as the mythic deities of ancient religious traditions.

The archetypes are not thought to be imposed structures projected upon the physical spheres, but rather, "cosmic perspectives in which the soul participates." As the archetypal psychologist James Hillman writes:

> They are the lords of [the soul's] realms of being, the patterns for its mimesis. The soul cannot be, except in one of their patterns. All psychic reality is governed by one or another archetypal fantasy, given sanction by a God. I cannot but be in them.[3]

From the archetypal astrological perspective, the cosmos is structured and ordered according to these primordial principles, which permeate every level of being, from the depths of the psychic interior to the interrelational dynamics of worldly and cosmic events. Archetypal astrology is a continuously ongoing, universally visible form of synchronicity, what Jung describes as a meaningful coincidence between an inner and outer event.[4]

---

2   Richard Tarnas, *Cosmos and Psyche: Intimations of a New World View* (New York: Viking, 2006), 68-69.

3   James Hillman, *Re-Visioning Psychology* (New York: Harper Perennial, 1992), 169-170.

4   C. G. Jung, "On Synchronicity," in *The Structure and Dynamics of the Psyche*, vol. 8, *The Collected Works of Carl Gustav Jung*, trans. R. F. C. Hull, ed. H. Read, M. Fordham, G. Adler, and W. McGuire, Bollingen Series XX (Princeton, NJ: Princeton University Press, 1973), p. 520, §969; Tarnas,

Archetypal astrology can be understood as a way of spiritual knowing, a form of what the transpersonal theorist Jorge Ferrer calls "participatory knowing."[5] There are many ways of knowing beyond the intellectual knowledge of the mind: the body has its own somatic and sensual ways of knowing, the heart has emotional, relational, and empathic ways of knowing, the soul has imaginal, intuitive, and visionary ways of knowing.[6] Astrology too can be recognized as a form of participatory knowing. The techniques of astrology are first grounded in an understanding of astronomical and mathematical data, which is then blended with what Hillman calls "the archetypal eye"[7]—the capacity to read symbolically, to perceive archetypal qualities as they manifest in actions, events, conversations, art, politics, dreams, visionary and mystical experiences, and so forth. In the practice of astrology, human participation in the archetypal realm occurs not only in the archetypal manifestations in our daily lives, but also in our very cognition and interpretation of astrological correlations. Using astrological practice, we can observe archetypal manifestations occurring simultaneously in multiple realms of experience—in individual human beings and world events—irrespective of whether individuals are aware of the archetypes' participation in their lives. From this perspective, one could say that every moment is a participatory event co-created with the archetypes.

If astrology is approached as a co-creative practice, or even as a spiritual discipline, one's engagement with the archetypes can shape, to a certain extent, the archetypal manifestations in one's life, or even the expressions of the archetypes themselves. With greater awareness of the planetary movements and archetypal combinations, the individual human participant can co-create a more emancipated reality through their own conscious participation. I want to emphasize that such participation is a *co*-creation, and is neither exclusively subject to the independent free will of the human nor solely to the fundamental principles of the plan-

---

Cosmos and Psyche, 61.

5   Jorge N. Ferrer, *Revisioning Transpersonal Theory: A Participatory Vision of Human Spirituality* (Albany, NY: State University of New York Press, 2002), 121.

6   Ferrer, *Revisioning Transpersonal Theory*, 121.

7   James Hillman, "Why 'Archetypal' Psychology?" in *Loose Ends* (Zurich, Switzerland: Spring Publication, 1975), 139.

etary archetypes, but rather a constantly shifting relationship between these agential entities. It implies both a level of responsibility on the part of the human being, and a trust in the ultimate, dynamic creativity of the archetypes. This ongoing co-creative participation with archetypal reality can be approached as a spiritual practice, a daily engagement with the sacred forces at play within our lives and in our cosmos.

The primary aim of most contemplative spiritual traditions is not actually to have mystical experiences of the divine, but rather to be liberated by greater spiritual knowledge and to overcome self-centeredness.[8] The practice of astrology can be an aid in this journey, because by understanding one's astrological complexes and owning one's psychological projections, one can become more self-aware and self-reflexive. Furthermore, by observing the correlation between your own experiences and the movement of the planets, one can recognize that one's life is not encapsulated within the self but is embedded in, and participating with, the larger experience of the cosmos. When we see the manifestations of the archetypes in realms beyond the individual, or even the human, we can recognize that spiritual meaning pervades the cosmos, and is not exclusive to the connection between humanity and the divine alone. Rather, the cosmos itself seems to be alive, aware, and participating with and between the human and the divine mystery.

The aim of astrology, as with other spiritual traditions, may not be to have a mystical experience of the divine, but such experiences can provide a deeper and more profound understanding of the archetypes in their multivalent complexity. Keiron Le Grice, an archetypal astrologer and depth psychologist, intimates the great power of such an encounter:

> In deep psychological exploration, or in heightened moments of openness, receptivity, and inspiration, one can have a direct encounter with the archetypal realm in all its unbridled power and intensity, an experience that is distinguished by a sense of the numinous——of mystery and awe, of tremendous power rising through the body, of intense religious affect, of emotional arousal, of tingling nerves, of soaring moral uplift, of demonic strength or even evil, or of overwhelming beauty and a sense of rightness or truth. In such moments, it seems

---

8   Ferrer, *Revisioning Transpersonal Theory*, 127.

that one has truly stepped into the realm of the gods.[9]

Beyond even the magnificence and power of what one has encountered, to recognize the astrological correlations between such a direct experience of the archetypes and the significant positioning of the planets at that time can deepen the profundity of such revelations.

The apt naming of the planets and luminaries—from the Sun and Moon, to Mercury out through Saturn—by the peoples of numerous ancient cultures indicates that they perceived a clear connection between the archetypes as planets and the archetypes as gods, although the names of the gods and planets together varied from culture to culture. In a discussion of archetypes and gods, Hillman alludes suggestively to their cosmic status in the very metaphor he chooses to describe them:

> By setting up a universe which tends to hold everything we do, see, and say in the sway of its cosmos, an archetype is best comparable with a God. And Gods, religions sometimes say, are less accessible to the senses and to the intellect than they are to the imaginative vision and emotion of the soul.[10]

From ancient gods to psychological complexes, the archetypes seem to have pervaded human consciousness in their multivalent expressions since the dawn of our species. From this perspective, archetypal astrology can be seen as a spiritual path, discipline, or tradition: one of many religions participating in the great mystery of divinity. The practice of astrology calls upon each of us to participate more fully in the spiritual unfolding of our lives, as we learn to become ever more conscientious co-creative partners in the great dance with the primordial archetypes.

---

9   Keiron Le Grice, *The Archetypal Cosmos: Rediscovering the Gods in Myth, Science and Astrology* (Edinburgh, UK: Floris Books, 2010), 169.
10   Hillman, *Re-Visioning Psychology*, xix-xx.

Works Cited

Ferrer, Jorge N. *Revisioning Transpersonal Theory: A Participatory Vision of Human Spirituality*. Albany, NY: State University of New York Press, 2002.

Hillman, James. *Re-Visioning Psychology*. New York: Harper Perennial, 1992.

———. "Why 'Archetypal' Psychology?" In *Loose Ends*. Zurich, Switzerland: Spring Publication, 1975.

Jung, Carl Gustav. "The Psychology of the Child Archetype." In *The Archetypes and the Collective Unconscious*. 2nd edition. Vol. 9, part 1 of *The Collected Works of Carl Gustav Jung*. Translated by R.F.C. Hull. Edited by H. Read, M. Fordham, G. Adler, and W. McGuire. Bollingen Series XX. Princeton, NJ: Princeton University Press, 1968.

Le Grice, Keiron. *The Archetypal Cosmos: Rediscovering the Gods in Myth, Science and Astrology*. Edinburgh, UK: Floris Books, 2010.

Tarnas, Richard. *Cosmos and Psyche: Intimations of a New World View*. New York: Viking, 2006.

Sadalsuud's Guide to Reading Your Own Natal Chart

Sadalsuud

Introduction

So! You got a hold of your own natal chart and you're staring at it in all of its highly inscrutable resplendence. What does it mean? You probably searched the internet and found either extremely basic (and unfair) significations like "Taurus likes to eat" or "Scorpios are treacherous". Interpreting a natal chart is a complex and nuanced task which cannot be easily learned from one or two blog posts. And unfortunately, most of the first hits you'll find for online astrology searches tend to overreach, say too little, or is just plain wrong.

This guide exists to solve that problem for you. It is a condensation of the past six years of my astrological study, synthesizing multiple schools of astrological thought. It will teach you the basics of how to read your own chart and give you solid grounding to read charts for other people, too.

Who I Am

I am Sadalsuud (@sadalsvvd on twitter). I am a programmer-skeptic turned programmer-astrologer. I've been working professionally in software for a decade and studying astrology for the past six. I initially started studying astrology reluctantly in order to learn more about the astrological correspondences in my equally secular, skeptical tarot practice.

I figured I would learn the planets' meanings and then never think about it again. No such luck: instead, I was staggered by just how much this hokey-looking astrology book could tell about myself that simply shouldn't be possible.[1] My curiosity (and furious incredulity) led me further down the rabbit hole in order to understand why it works at all, and now I spend my spare time building astrological software focused on making it easier to conduct studies with astrology as well as perform financial prediction.

Now, I can read natal charts at a glance and tell people many details about themselves I shouldn't be able to, such as core psychological stumbling blocks, the nature of their romantic lives, or what their home environment growing up was like. Occasionally I am wrong, because I am human, and always learning more about the intricacies of astrology, but my "hit rate" for natal chart reading is far above chance and has been for years. This has less to do with me and more with the fact that astrology works, and anyone can learn to do it.

Astrology has given me genuine insights that resolved years of internal conflict, made me more tolerant and understanding, increased my understanding of how people work, and built an awe in me for the deeply mysterious nature of reality. I could have gotten there quicker if I had what you have now: a synthesis of the broad landscape of astrological practice, written for people who know absolutely nothing about astrology but are curious enough to try it out.

What You'll Learn

I believe that when learning astrology, a vivid demonstration of practice is more effective than pages of theory. Therefore, this is going to be a whirlwind guide to the practice of astrology. We're going to cover how to read these parts of your chart, in order:

---

1   This book was Joanna Martine Woolfolk's *The Only Astrology Book You'll Ever Need*.

- Planets, which describe the different parts of your experience
- Signs, which describe the flavor and tone of those experiences
- Houses, the area of life planets in their signs inhabit
- Aspects, a set of angles between the planets which describe the relationships between them
- An example chart reading
- A few fun extra tidbits

You'll be learning a blend of both traditional and modern astrology that I have found to be effective in quickly identifying cogent parts of the natal chart that relate to people's character and lived experience.

This guide will be concise and dense. You'll want to come back to each section as a reference. In the first section, I'll cover the raw information you need to piece together your chart. Feel free to skim past descriptions that don't apply to it. In the second section, I'll describe a systematic way to read a natal chart using all the information from the reference. Be patient with the process; the full picture that describes you does not become clear until you understand and synthesize all of the components. Once you do, however, it is unbelievably specific and precise.

Part One: Meet Your Chart

If you haven't already, go and make a natal chart.[2] This is a geocentric, 2D picture of the sky at the time of your birth. Let's learn how to read it! (Don't worry if the astronomical bits make your eyes glaze over; understanding how the shapes rotate isn't very important for the type of astrology we're doing.)

I'll use this example chart for the purposes of demonstration:

------

2   This is the site I'll use for this article: https://www.astro.com/cgi/chart.cgi.

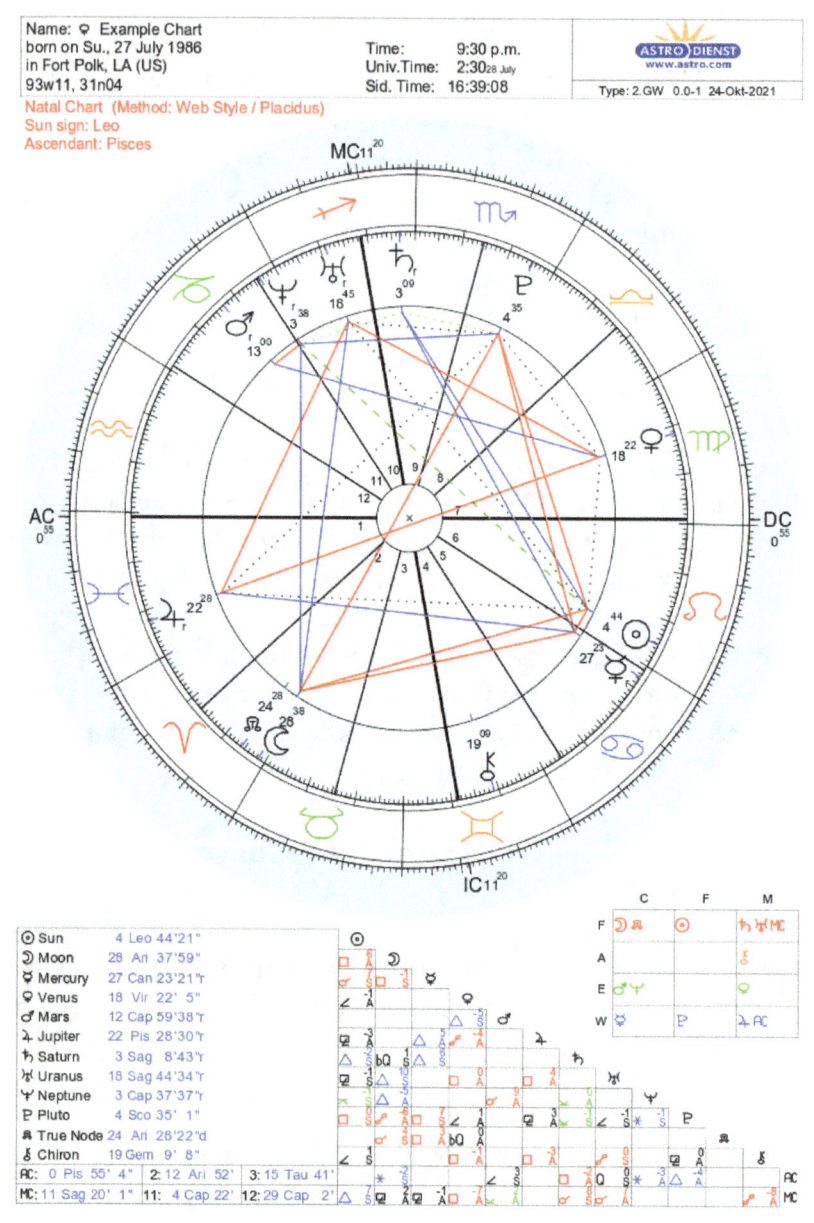

Name: ♀ Example Chart
born on Su., 27 July 1986
in Fort Polk, LA (US)
93w11, 31n04

Time: 9:30 p.m.
Univ.Time: 2:30₂₈ July
Sid. Time: 16:39:08

ASTRO DIENST
www.astro.com
Type: 2.GW 0.0-1 24-Okt-2021

Natal Chart (Method: Web Style / Placidus)
Sun sign: Leo
Ascendant: Pisces

There are a number of terms for this diagram: horoscope (this is what a horoscope actually is), natal chart, birth chart, or nativity. We sometimes refer to the owner of the nativity as the "native".

The ring of 12 glyphs around the wheel is the zodiac, and each of the glyphs demarcates a sign of the zodiac. These signs represent 30°

sections of the sky, not the literal stars, so there's no Ophiuchus here.[3] Modern astrologers mostly work with planets, although some also work with stars. Here's a list of the signs with their glyphs, names, and mode/element combinations (we'll cover all that soon):

1. ♈ - Aries - Cardinal Fire
2. ♉ - Taurus - Fixed Earth
3. ♊ - Gemini - Mutable Air
4. ♋ - Cancer - Cardinal Water
5. ♌ - Leo - Fixed Fire
6. ♍ - Virgo - Mutable Earth
7. ♎ - Libra - Cardinal Air
8. ♏ - Scorpio - Fixed Water
9. ♐ - Sagittarius - Mutable Fire
10. ♑ - Capricorn - Cardinal Earth
11. ♒ - Aquarius - Fixed Air
12. ♓ - Pisces - Mutable Water

The "AC" symbol means **ascendant**, or **rising**, and it indicates the exact degree of the zodiac that was on the horizon at the time of your birth. In this chart, since the AC is in Pisces, that makes the ascendant, or **rising sign**, Pisces.

Since the ascendant marks the horizon, any planets below it were not visible at the time of your birth, and any planets above it were in the sky. Imagine if you were taking a picture of someone out in a field far away; that's the perspective of the natal chart. If the Sun (☉) is above the horizon/AC in your chart, you have a **day chart**, and if it's below, you have a **night chart**, which affects how to read some components of the chart. We'll come back to that later once we've got our grounding.

The black lines with numbers inside represent the **houses**, with the

---

3   The zodiacal constellations in the sky were originally associated with various star myths which were used to find omens in the motion of the stars, but as skygazers compiled their observations of the motions of the planets across the stars, they structured the sky into 12 divisions of 30°. These zodiac signs do take their names from the constellations because their qualities are associated with the myths belonging to their respective constellations, but they represent sections of sky, rather than the stars themselves.

first house starting under the AC, moving counterclockwise, and ending with the twelfth house above the AC. The glyphs inscribed within the zodiac wheel and in one of the twelve houses are the various planets, luminaries (the Sun and Moon), asteroids, and important points in your natal chart. For shorthand, I refer to them all as "bodies", "planets", or "placements". The red, blue, green, and dotted lines you may see between the placements in your chart show **aspects**, which are sets of meaningful angular distances between placements.

Those are the basics. That's all you need to know to get into the meat and potatoes: interpretation.

The Planets: The Gods

Let me be upfront: astrology's interpretive framework is most effective if we, for the sake of matching the extremely archetypal nature of astrological delineations, assume a polytheistic perspective. Every culture's theological history has their own gods they assign to the planets and stars. For the sake of our highly secular era, we moderns say that astrologers observed *correlations* between placements and constructed their myth frameworks around them, but that does not help us get inside their heads. To do so, we have to embrace the planets as gods, at least in concept.

Gods claim domain over certain activities and areas of our lives; they rule concepts like love, virtue, wisdom, war, time. They rule things: banks, athletes, clergypeople, movies, cows. They rule moods: austerity, exuberance, fury, lust, curiosity. Gods are all-encompassing entities within their archetypes, which helps us interpret natal charts with more depth and nuance. It enables us to broach the psychological, spiritual, mythical, and mundane all at once. If religiosity or heathenry makes you ick, don't worry—it doesn't get in the way all that much.

Throughout this guide you'll find "mundane" definitions attached to some sets of interpretations. People often find that parts of their lives match with the mundane meanings of planets and signs so they are included for curiosity's sake.

The Ascendant (AC)

Do you know your birth time? Is it really accurate, like birth certificate accurate? Parents are notorious for misremembering birth charts and sending astrologers and their clients into disarray. The ascendant defines the structure of your entire natal chart and it moves one degree roughly every 4 and a half minutes. That means being off by just an hour, depending on what you previously thought your birth time was, can change the shape of your entire chart. The most important thing is that your ascendant stays within the same sign, and the ascendant takes 2.25 hours[4] to go through each sign.

If you don't know your birth time at all, don't fret—you can still interpret a lot, but there will be some key pieces missing. If you cannot retrieve your birth time and get desperately curious, you can hire an astrologer to perform a rectification, whereby they can determine your birth time from the timing of events throughout your life.

As for the ascendant itself, it is considered to be the energetic imprint upon your body at the exact moment you took your first breath outside of the womb. It represents a union of body, soul, and the immediate energetic dynamic of the moment represented by the planets. The sign of the ascendant tends to color our personality and expression, but often in a way that is so innate as to be unconscious. When I ask people if they relate to their ascendant's qualities, they often reply in a, "Oh huh, yeah, I guess I do do that", sort of way. I find that the ascendant often describes our autopilot, instinctive reactions to new situations, and how we unconsciously present ourselves to other people. It also plays a major role in the first impression and "vibe" others get from us.

Its expression is easily colored by any planets aspecting it, especially by conjunction (when planets are immediately next to each other). As you read the descriptions of the planets, note where they are in your chart and see what other planets they make connections to by the blue, red, and green lines (the dotted ones, if present, are minor and can be ignored).

---

4   Due to the obliquity of the ecliptic against the earth, the different signs take shorter and longer times to rise, but it doesn't make a significant difference for now.

Sun (☉), ruling Leo (♌)

The Sun is very misunderstood by popular astrology. "Sun sign" astrology is the type of daily "horoscope" "astrology" you'll find in the newspaper (or Yahoo's homepage), which is simply language using the Barnum effect against the overly credulous for profit.

The Sun is identity, mission, drive, innate vitality. It describes the fundamental nature of who you consider yourself to be and your purpose as an archetype. I like to describe it as if you wrote an autobiography about yourself, the themes of the Sun's sign would factor heavily into it.

The Sun's placement in your natal chart will show where your core egoic sense of self is rooted. It describes personal aspirations, desires, strengths, and weaknesses.

Moon (☽), ruling Cancer (♋)

The Moon is comfort and instinct. It's the nature of the mind. Its placement shows what we need to feel secure, and also how we feel insecure. It shows our instinctive emotional reaction to experiences which will also blend with the nature of the ascendant. The Moon also rules the body, and shows our relationship to food, family, and nurturing instincts and needs.

Note that the Moon moves on average 13.2° per day, or 1° every two hours, which means that if you don't know your birth time (or it is wrong), and your Moon is near the edge of a sign, your Moon may actually be in that other sign.

Mercury (☿), ruling Gemini (♊) and Virgo (♍)

Mercury is intellect and insight. This differs from the Moon's emotional nature of the mind—Mercury is how your intellect functions. Mercury describes how we think, learn, speak, and teach. Being a joker (literally, mercurial), Mercury also describes the nature of our sense of humor. It shows, fundamentally, how we engage with information.

Venus (♀), ruling Taurus (♉) and Libra (♎)

Venus is affection and value. Venus is the flavor of experience we require to build bonds of affection and love. It can describe how we woo and like to be wooed, even extending into the realm of sextrology, but alas, we don't have time to explore that sultry topic here. It also describes the types of things we value aesthetically such as leisure activities, taste in art, and fashion sense.

Mars (♂), ruling Aries (♈) and Scorpio (♏)

Mars is initiative, drive, aggression, impulse. It shows how we go about getting shit done, and collaborate with people. It shows the engine of the personality that drives you forward toward tasks, goals, projects, and foes to conquer. It shows where we are competitive and how we tend to deal with conflict. It shows how we get the things we want.

Jupiter (♃), ruling Sagittarius (♐) and Pisces (♓)

The planets before have had to do with the essential nature of you, your personality, and your direct experience. Modern psychological astrologers call these the "personal planets", because their placements are wrapped up in the egoic self. Jupiter is the first of the two "transpersonal" planets, which describe a relationship to the greater whole of the world around us.

Jupiter is empowerment, growth, expansiveness, exuberance, confidence, faith. It indicates sources of luck, good will, and wisdom in our lives. Its placement describes the nature of all of these things, and also shows the things we personally tend to have wisdom about, but also experience great confidence and reward in exploring.

Saturn (♄), ruling Capricorn (♑) and Aquarius (♒)

Saturn is the slowest of the seven traditional planets that were known to the ancients, and the last planet that is visible to the naked eye in our solar system. Saturn rules time, and all that it implies. Saturn is limitation, restriction, duty, responsibility, diligence, hard work, discipline. Saturn shows the things in our life that we feel called to structure, discipline, and regulate. Saturn also shows the way in which we accomplish that, and as ruler of material forms, Saturn also shows how and what we tend to construct and build.

Uranus (♅)

Now we are entering the realm of the outer planets. The outer planets are often called "generational" planets because they move so slowly. Uranus takes 84 years to make a full cycle. They are less like gods and more like aliens, adding a transcendent dynamic wherever they go. You can broadly interpret the meaning of the outer planets by house and aspect, but they are especially impactful if they closely aspect any of your inner planets. More on all of that later.

Uranus is associated with the myth of Prometheus who stole fire from Zeus to give to the humans. He was an intellectual trickster god, and is related to liberation, eccentricity, revolution, unpredictability, acceleration, and in my personal opinion, essential human life-improving utilities. Uranus' location in the natal chart shows where we experience unpredictable changes and unexpected events, and in aspect to other planets it accelerates them, quickening them with Uranus' genius. Incidentally, Uranus is also associated with astrology and astrologers, so if you find that Uranus is prominent in your chart, astrology may be for you.

You'll notice that Uranus doesn't rule any signs. Because the outers were discovered after the traditional scheme of rulership was established, the rulership of the various planets is contentious. I do think that the outer planets have strong affinities with certain signs, but I find the traditional rulership scheme more useful. Feel free to play around with Uranus as a co-ruler of Aquarius, the most commonly chosen rulership.

Neptune (♆)

I always have trouble thinking of ways to describe Neptune at first, but that's very fitting. Neptune is the planet of the ethereal, sublime, nondual, mysterious, hidden, foggy, unclear, haunting, divine. Neptune's placement in the chart indicates where and how we experience sudden inexplicable losses but also where we feel near-spiritual draws to manifest visions impossible from planes unimaginable. Neptune carries a strong call toward the divine and sublimative experiences which can manifest as an interest in the occult, meditation, or alcohol, sex, drugs, and rock and roll.

Neptune is generally considered to have affinity with/co-rulership of Pisces.

Pluto (♇)

Pluto is a planet of incredible intensity and transformation. Pluto is associated with nuclear power, which is appropriate: it is a crucible, indicating heavy themes of creation through destruction, domination, control, obsession, and survival at any cost. It can show where we experience fixation or sometimes paranoia, but also serves as an incredibly powerful engine of change. It shows our most potent, destructive personal force and how they can be utilized or abused, as nuclear weapons or nuclear power.

Pluto is generally considered to have affinity with/co-rulership of Scorpio.

Chiron (⚷)

Chiron's themes are best conveyed by its myth. Chiron was a centaur who was deeply respected for his kindness, civility, and knowledge of hunting, medicine, and prophecy. He taught many Greek heroes, including Heracles (Hercules). He was accidentally wounded by one of Heracles' poisoned arrows in a fight against wild centaurs. Despite his great healing skills, he could not heal himself, and because he was immortal, could not be relieved of his pain through death. As a way to die, he offered to sacrifice his immortality for Prometheus' freedom from Zeus's punishment to have Prometheus shackled to a rock and have his liver torn at by eagles every day. Zeus agreed, and as Chiron was dying, Zeus recognized his noble nature and placed him into the sky as the constellation Centaurus.

Because of his myths, Chiron is associated with the core wounds we experience, often in childhood. These become wounds that never

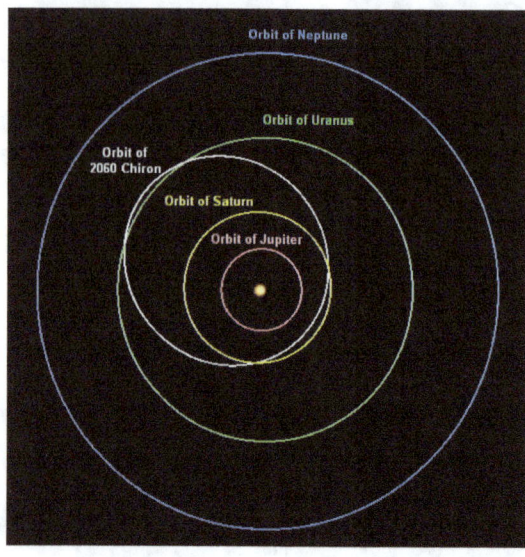

Chiron's Orbit

heal, but from which we gain deep wisdom and the ability to help others who are suffering in ways we suffer. Often, Chiron's placement by sign and house strongly suggest the nature of a core wound, but also the nature of the strength that can grow from it.

In terms of Chiron's position in the solar system, it is unusual. Its elliptical orbit connects the orbits of Uranus, the first outer planet, and Saturn, the last traditional planet. This, along with Chiron's transference by Zeus into the stars, suggests its themes of transcendence, but also bringing the transcendent down into our reality. Barbara Hand Clow calls Chiron the "rainbow bridge" between the inner and outer planets.

Being an asteroid only recently discovered in 1977, Chiron does not rule any sign, and its affinity is still debated among astrologers.

The Nodes (North ☊ / South ☋)

The Nodes are not actual physical stellar bodies, but rather the two points where the plane of the ecliptic (the plane that all bodies in our solar system more or less move along in circular revolutions) and the oblique orbit of the Moon meet as it travels around the earth. The point that the Moon moves upwards is the North Node, and the point that the Moon passes as it moves downwards is the South Node.

The Nodes are a complicated topic in astrology because their interpretation varies between various styles of astrology. This is an extraordinary simplification, but:

- evolutionary astrology (which focuses on the idea of reincarna-

The Moon's Orbit and the Line of Nodes

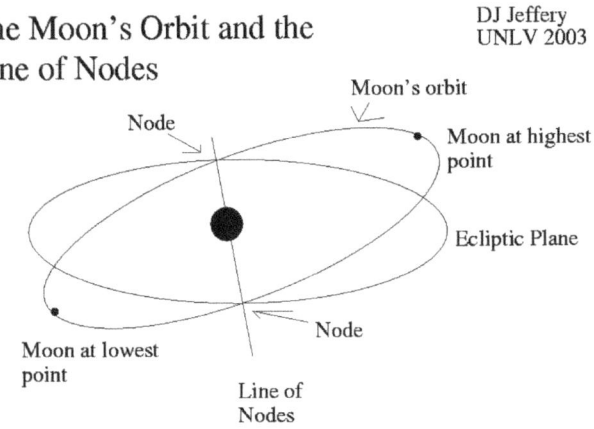

DJ Jeffery
UNLV 2003

The line of nodes rotates westward 19.4 degrees per year due the gravitational perturbation of the Sun on the Earth-Moon system.

tion and using astrology to navigate our present lifetime) often describes the Nodes as "karmic" points with the North Node being our destiny, and the South Node being the karmic debt we bring into this lifetime.[5]

- jyotish (sometimes called Vedic) astrology from India describes the North Node (or Rahu, the dragon's mouth), as a point of endless desire and fixation and hunger for new experience in the material, and the South (or Ketu, the dragon's tail), as a point of material dematerialization and loss to force spiritual development.[6]

- psychological astrology often describes the Nodes as representing the relationship between the solar and lunar impulses within the self and the lifelong struggle we experience learning about the themes of our Nodes' axis.[7]

When dealing with conflicting or subtly different interpretations, I like to blend them. The Nodes are a combination of not just the Sun and Moon but also the earth, since without the earth, there would be no

---

5   Deva Green, "Evolutionary Astrology: What the Moon's Nodes Mean in Your Chart," August 25, 2014, llewellyn.com.

6   Komilla Sutton, "Rahu Ketu: The Shadow Planets," komilla.com.

7   Anne Whitaker, "The Moon's Nodes in Action," 2015, astro.com.

lunar orbit and thus no Nodes. For me, this reflects why the nodes are sometimes described as "manifestation" points where we experience vast changes that seem to operate on the physical, spiritual, and emotional levels all at the same time. The nodal axis (the signs and houses that the Nodes straddle in your chart) describes the dynamics in our lives that we often have strong awareness of as major life lessons. The North Node represents where we often have fixations, fascinations, and can devote a great deal of energy pursuing, while the South Node represents those natural talents and fixations which in this life are so well-developed as to become crutches. We often find ourselves automatically embodying the shadow expressions of the South Node's house and sign, while pursuing the talents and skills of the North Node's house and sign. If the Nodes are in close aspect to any other placements in the chart, the themes and dynamics described by those planets and their connections to the Nodes will be especially impactful and present throughout life. (You'll learn about signs, houses, and aspects in the following sections.)

The Nodes are tricky to describe, but many people, when learning more about their own Node placements, often react very strongly to the themes they delineate. If you'd like to learn more about the Nodes, I highly recommend *Astrology for the Soul* by Jan Spiller.

Transits, Retrogrades, and Stations

Astrology doesn't stop at the fixed picture of your natal chart. It can also be used to forecast—and if you're good enough, specifically pre-dict—your life experiences as the planets continue moving through the sky and make contact with the locations of where your natal placements were at the time of your birth. While a proper treatment of forecasting and prediction is far beyond the scope of this guide, I'll occasionally refer to transiting planets throughout, which means "when the moving planets in the sky make aspects to the placements in your natal chart".

Just like the planets are moving now, they were moving at the time of your birth. And because of our geocontric perspective, planets rhythmi-cally appear to slow down until they come to a complete standstill called **stationing**, and then reverse direction, moving in reverse or apparent **retrograde**. This is due to the relative speed of the earth versus other planets. As we pass by a slower planet (or are passed by a faster planet),

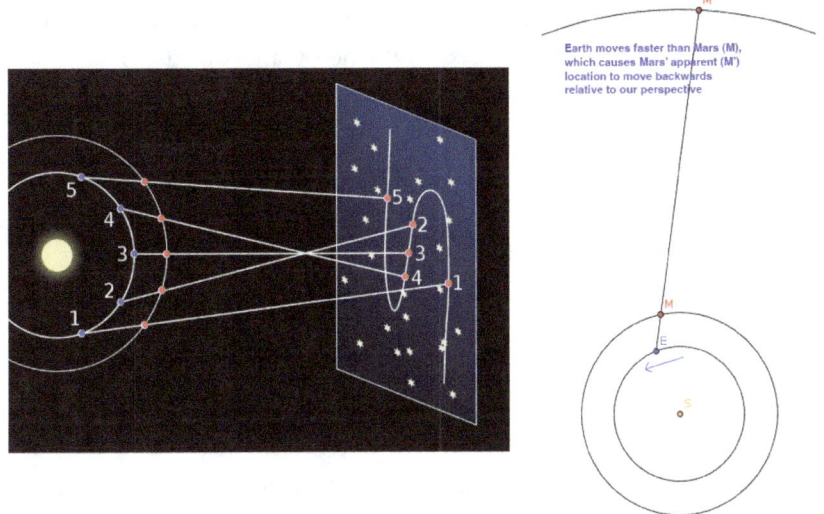

Earth moves faster than Mars (M), which causes Mars' apparent (M') location to move backwards relative to our perspective

the other planet appears to stop moving and retrograde. This is best explained with a couple diagrams as seen above.

You can identify retrograde planets in your chart by the little "r" next to them. Interpretively, the speed of a planet affects its expression, particularly when a planet is stationing or retrograde. Retrograde planets tend to function in a way that reflects their backwards status: they tend to blossom later in life, have a tendency to double back and "check their work", so to speak, or to express themselves with some hesitancy. Despite the bad rap that retrograde planets get, they also have unique perspective and abilities that arise from their tendency to look back, reconsider, contemplate, ponder, and redo things. People with many retrograde planets sometimes exhibit "retrograde characteristics" very literally, such as being very interested in the past, memory, history, frequently experiencing l'esprit d'escalier, or working in careers that involve retrograde activities such as editing, fact-checking, and verification work (especially Mercury retrograde).

Stationing planets, due to their stillness, are thought to cast an especially strong "gaze" upon whatever they look at, and thus have an outsized influence in the natal chart. When a planet is stationing before turning retrograde it's said to be **station[ing] retrograde**, and when it is stationing before turning direct, it's said to be **station[ing] direct**. A stationing planet can also be said to be in the transitory state between direct and retrograde motion, or vice versa, and reflects a "turning inward" or "turning outward" to respective direct or retrograde motions. This is a subtle distinction, but regardless, stationed planets in the natal chart are often express themselves very strongly.[8]

The Signs: A Modal, Elemental Approach

There are twelve signs with endless characteristics which can seem like a lot, but we'll start by breaking them down through two classifications: modes and elements.[9] As we describe the modes and elements of the sign, keep in mind that we are not talking about literal people but the archetypal expression and behaviors of these signs. If it helps, you can imagine these descriptions of the modes, elements, and signs as describing someone with all of their placements in these modes, elements, or signs.

Modes

There are three "modes", or modalities, for each of the signs: cardinal, mutable, and fixed. They describe the general rhythmic nature of how this sign accomplishes tasks through time.

The cardinal signs are Aries, Cancer, Libra, and Capricorn. They are focused on initiating expressions of energy and initiative pointed in a specific direction. Cardinal signs like to come up with project ideas, champion initiatives, and seek out challenges. Their general energetic dynamic is full of bursts of inspiration and effort that seek to drive change into the world. "Strike while the iron is hot" is an apt phrase for cardinal signs.

The fixed signs are Taurus, Leo, Scorpio, and Aquarius. They are consistent, persistent, and slow to change. Fixed signs express a rigid insistence on the field of experience they have accustomed themselves

---

8   For more information on stationing planets see Ray Grasse, "Tectonic Triggers: The Hidden Power of Station Points (Part 1)," 2015, astro.com.

9   There's another term for elements and modes: triplicities and quadruplicities. A triplicity is a group of 3, so there's 4 triplicities of the elements, and a quadruplicity is a group of 4, so there's 3 quadruplicities of the modes. I constantly forget which 4 and 3 goes where, so I use the terms elements and modes instead.

to. Because of this, they can be quite stubborn and afraid of change, but when they finally do, these signs bring just as much consistent application of effort that they did to their old patterns. "Slow and steady wins the race" is an apt phrase for fixed signs.

The mutable signs are Gemini, Virgo, Sagittarius, and Pisces. They are flexible, curious, and constantly changing. Mutable signs have vast interests in equal degrees, which lead them to acquire a wide array of shallow knowledge and skills in a variety of topics. Mutable signs get bored quickly and require constant stimulation. "A jack of all trades is a master of none, but oftentimes better than a master of one" is an apt phrase for mutable signs.

Elements

There are four elements, modeled after the traditional Greek elements: fire, earth, air, and water. The elements broadly describe the traits and tendencies of the signs in terms of their polarization toward purpose, material concerns, abstract ideas, and emotional depth.

For the fire signs Aries, Leo, and Sagittarius, purpose is most real. They are motivated by proving themselves, by success, by recognition and fame. They are filled with great energy, and often work until they burn out and crash. They seek out excitement and high degrees of stimulation. Moderation is difficult; everything is urgent and important. Self-individuation is key, although they tend not to want to spend time in self-contemplation because they perceive all of the action as being on the outside.

For the earth signs Taurus, Virgo, and Capricorn, the material world is most real. They are motivated by securing resources whether for survival, business, or pleasure. They innately gravitate towards organizing time, space, or people. They are physically skilled in various arts such as construction, craftwork, or dance and martial arts. They are hard workers and have a deep appreciation for the relationship between sustained effort and success.

For the air signs Gemini, Libra, and Aquarius, ideas are most real. They are motivated by abstract ideals and interests, and love exchanging information. They spend their time discussing, sharing, calculating, analyzing, debating, and exchanging ideas. They are highly social although aloof; getting too close to the emotional side of things is uncomfortable for their detached natures.

For the water signs Cancer, Scorpio, and Pisces, emotions are most real. They are motivated by passion, feeling, and connection. Memory, legacy, sentiment, family, and deep bonds are important. They are emotionally adept and often make for incredible artists and healers. Their shadow side can be the deep quagmire of subjective feeling and distorted vision, with those closest to them warping their lens on life.

The Signs

Now that we've covered the structure behind the signs, we can describe them using this framework and add in more of the nuance associated with each sign. As you read, identify which signs the placements in your chart fall under. Try to combine the nature of the planet with the nature of the sign, and consider if this synthesis matches your own experience of your personality and inner world. We'll go over examples of how to do this.

(Bonus: notice how the permutations of modality and elements create a loop: this is both beautifully symmetrical but also important to astrology's aspect system, which we will cover soon.)

Aries (♈) — Cardinal Fire, ruled by Mars (♂)

As a cardinal fire sign, Aries is concerned with tight bursts of extremely powerful, focused, purpose-driven, competitive energy. As the first sign of the zodiac, Aries echoes the themes of personal agency, existence, and identity. Aries is highly competitive and aggressive, and reflects the Mars' archetypal association with war and outright conflict and martial achievement. While there aren't many opportunities for the lamentations of our enemies in modern civilization, Aries energy expresses itself as extreme ferocity and desire to win in the world of sports, business, and play.

Taurus (♉) — Fixed Earth, ruled by Venus (♀)

As a fixed earth sign, Taurus is concerned with the slow accumulation and enjoyment of physical resources. Taurus likes to take its time, and as the more physical manifestation of Venus' aphroditic nature, has a love for beautiful sensual experiences. This includes fine food and drink, spending time with the aesthetic side of nature, and physically sensorious experiences such as massage or yoga. Taurus is generally very even-keeled and patient, though also possessive of the experiences and people in their lives and resistant to change.

Gemini (♊) — Mutable Air, ruled by Mercury (☿)

As a mutable air sign, Gemini is concerned with the wide-ranging connection of ideas and friendships. Gemini loves to talk, and echoes the highly social side of its ruler Mercury. This sign likes connecting ideas and meeting a wide variety of people. As part of its mutability and mythic association with twins, Gemini often has a "split brain" nature where it is simultaneously perceiving and thinking along two processes of thought at the same time, leading this sign to surprise itself when one of these processes becomes dominant. These factors, combined with an airy intellectual detachment that can find playing with ideas more interesting than actual problem-solving, leads to Gemini's bad reputation in popular astrology among non-Mercurial types.

Cancer (♋) — Cardinal Water, ruled by the Moon (☽)

As a cardinal water sign, Cancer is concerned with the emotional, familial world of the heart and hearth. It is fundamentally a nurturing sign, often prone to great capacity for empathy and work in healing and caring professions. Highly sensitive, the myth of the crab is appropriate: Cancer will often use its pincers to defend itself and lash out at those who try to attack them, but most especially those they care about. The shadow side of a natural emotional intelligence is a tendency to use emotional manipulation as a weapon. Cancer often has a reputation as being demure, quiet types, but this belies the wild side of Cancer signified by the changing, mysterious nature of the Moon. Cancer is just as capable of excessive demonstrations of impulsive, feral energy directed in emotional directions as any other cardinal sign.

Leo (♌) — Fixed Fire, ruled by the Sun (☉)

As a cardinal fire sign, Leo is concerned with personal creativity and selfhood. It is a sign of steady, radiant warmth as indicated by its ruler, the Sun. Leo is fundamentally concerned with giving life to things, just as the Sun enables life on earth to grow. Leo is a childlike sign, and loves to play (especially pretend) and is dispositionally cheerful, but can also be petulant or egotistical. This sign has an innate appreciation for the value of the self and the importance of reputation, but also how the self can be a vehicle for transformation through play-acting which eventually becomes reality.

Virgo (♍) — Mutable Earth, ruled by Mercury (☿)

As a mutable earth sign, Virgo is concerned with being helpful through the application of incisive discernment and dextrous proficiency. Virgo is the more practical, tactical expression of Mercury, where knowledge and information are bent toward the practical and material. Virgo sees exceptional detail in everything and understands the depth of nuance that pervades all things. The flipside of this can be excessive rumination, unhelpful nitpicking, and having trouble being in the moment. Also being of the archetype "The Virgin", Virgo tends toward the upright and "clean" in its presentation, although its incisive, analytical view usually sees too much to have any claim of actual innocence.

Libra (♌) — Cardinal Air, ruled by Venus (♀)

As a cardinal air sign, Libra is concerned with fairness, harmony, and beauty. Libra is the abstract, intellectual and aesthetic side of Venus, especially the loquacious and light socialization of small talk, manners, and delightful company. This sign desires equilibrium and harmony in all things, but especially its connections with others. Libra can be a powerful force for championing causes for the underprivileged and oppressed, often concerned with law, politics, and government. However, their fixation on doing things in social matters can lead them toward fickle gossip, aversion to deeper connection, and petty social deception. This sign's glyph representing a set of scales also reflects the Libran tendency to spend much time deliberating and weighing options before making a choice.

Now that we have reached the seventh sign and the first sign to oppose a sign we know, I can point out that Libra opposes Aries in the zodiac, highlighting the figurative and literal opposition between their themes and goals.

Scorpio (♏) — Fixed Water, ruled by Mars (♂)

As a fixed water sign, Scorpio is concerned with deep, powerful emotional intensity. This sign intuitively understands the potency of penetrating mysteries to reveal what is hidden. Scorpio is a natural secret seeker and keeper, and often forms intense, almost obsessive bonds with others. This intensity allows Scorpio to go further than others will, reflecting the subtler aspects of Mars' martial practice in terms of the desire, curiosity, and incisive perspective required to find the secret weaknesses of the enemy. As one of Mars' signs, Scorpio can easily externalize their enemies and lower themselves to acts of subterfuge and silent destruction, or they can find and transmute the true enemy within themselves, enabling them to reach great heights. Scorpio is fundamentally a sign of power which can be devoted toward incredible constructive or destructive purposes.

Scorpio opposes Taurus.

Sagittarius (♐) — Mutable Fire, ruled by Jupiter (♃)

As a mutable fire sign, Sagittarius is concerned with striving, finding, and sharing what it considers to be the truth. Ideals and aspiration are essential to Sagittarius, as well as personal freedom, exploration, and optimism. Sagittarius is highly interested in matters of philosophy, law, and higher truths. It's also one of the most direct and blunt of the signs, valuing truth and its expression very highly, although sometimes in a manner that lacks nuance or hurts feelings. Sagittarius loves to express what it has found to be true, and is often a bit of a proselytizer. This sign also needs, with great urgency, to pursue its true passions and interests, or it suffers greatly.

Sagittarius opposes Gemini.

Capricorn (♑) — Cardinal Earth, ruled by Saturn (♄)

As a cardinal earth sign, Capricorn is concerned with personal achievement, authority, and traditionalism. Capricorn has a natural understanding of life's limitations and the hard work required to build and preserve structures. This sign is motivated toward personal responsibility, obligation, and duty, although this can come with pessimism, cynicism, or an overemphasis on decorum and formalisms. Capricorn is a consummate workaholic and overachiever, though they can be frozen by their fear of failure or burn out from overwork. Family values and their preservation is also a strong theme for Capricorn, as they have an innate connection to the value and power of longstanding structures.

Capricorn opposes Cancer.

Aquarius (♒) — Fixed Air, ruled by Saturn (♄)

As a fixed air sign, Aquarius is concerned with freedom, experimentation, and social welfare. It is a complex sign, also ruled by taciturn Saturn, which expresses its understanding of duty in loyalty to society at large. Aquarius loves people, but being a detached air sign, has difficulty with close individual connections. It's extremely open-minded and will hear anything out, except for the hills-to-die-on it has chosen where it refuses to budge. This sign can be brilliant but eccentric, even veering into extreme, rebellious behavior in its shadow expression.

Aquarius opposes Leo.

Pisces (♓) — Mutable Water, ruled by Jupiter (♃)

As a mutable water sign, Pisces is concerned with sensitivity, compassion, and vulnerability. Pisces lacks the psychic boundaries of other signs and merges itself with others almost unconsciously. Pisces can be a powerful healer through its sheer compassionate presence, but it can also entangle with others and lose its own identity in them. Pisces is frequently considered dreamy, but they are not spacey—rather, Pisces is often consuming vast amounts of information from their experience and environment which enables their powerful intuition.

Pisces opposes Virgo.

Now that we have a picture of the signs, you might have synthesized them with the nature of the planet and related it to your own experience. If it's still too abstract, no worries—we will do an example reading for our example chart, which should demonstrate the approach to reading your own chart.

The Aspects: A Network of Energy

Aspects are specific degree angles between the planets. In your chart, they're represented by the blue, red, green, and dotted lines. The different aspects describe the type of essential nature of the interaction between the two planets. There are generally two types of aspects: easy/flowing/harmonic aspects and difficult/hard/dynamic aspects.

The types of aspects are often described as unilaterally good or bad, but the effects of any single aspect cannot be considered without looking at the aspects around the entire chart, which represents a network of energy between the planets. Too many "positive" and flowing aspects can make someone so internally flowing that they never reflect, come off as disconnected from reality or egotistical, and often get struck hard by life into adulthood unless they manage to utilize that inner harmony instead of coasting on it. Meanwhile, a ton of difficult aspects often create extraordinarily strong people who go on to do incredible things, although it often comes as the result of difficult experiences and hard inner work.

Regardless, there are no "good" and "bad" charts, as they do not describe the limits of human potential—they only describe its essential flavor. I use the terms "harmonic" and "dynamic" to describe their flexible and contextual nature.

Use the following graphic to help you visualize what aspects your different placements are making to other placements. Each aspect on this diagram is 30° apart. So if you mentally overlay the conjunction point of this diagram on a planet in your chart, then a planet 30° away in either direction would be making the semisextile aspect, 60° away the sextile, 90° away the square, 120° the trine, 150° the quincunx or inconjunct, and 180° (directly across) the opposition.

Since each sign is also 30° wide, a shortcut is to just count the number of signs from the reference planet to another planet: 1 sign is a semi-

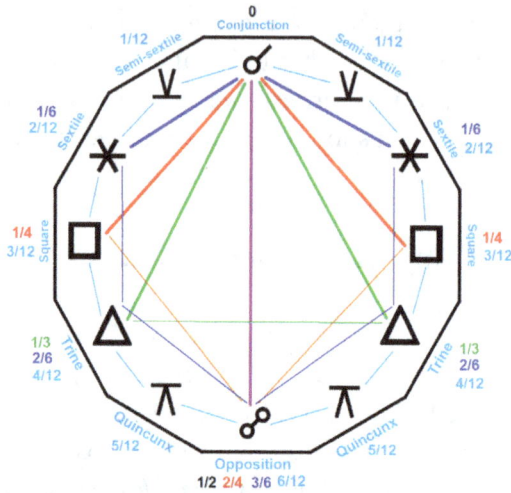

sextile, 2 signs is a sextile, 3 signs is a square, 4 signs is a trine, 5 signs is an inconjunct, and 6 signs is an opposition. One scenario you need to watch out for using this shortcut is when a planet is very close to the end of a sign, while the other is very close to the beginning of a sign. For instance, in our example chart, the Moon is at 28° Aries while Pluto is at 4° Scorpio. Scorpio is technically 5 signs away which would be an inconjunct, but because the Moon is at the end of Aries, the two planets are roughly 174° apart which is much closer to an opposition than to an inconjunct.

This is a little confusing at first, but the more you practice identifying aspects, the faster you will get. It helps to imagine the aspect lines going from each planet in turn and where they land in each sign. For instance, imagine two lines from the Moon at 28° Aries going to 28° Aquarius and 28° Gemini; if there were planets there, the Moon would be making an exact sextile to them.

While I mentioned the semisextile for the example, we will leave it aside in practice, as its influence is often too benign and minor to be noticeable in comparison to other aspects. There are many other minor and more esoteric aspects but their expression is almost always more subtle in comparison to most of the primary 30°-based aspects here.

If you generated a chart from astro.com, then at the bottom of your chart you can find a grid that shows the aspects between planets which can help you identify them on the chart.

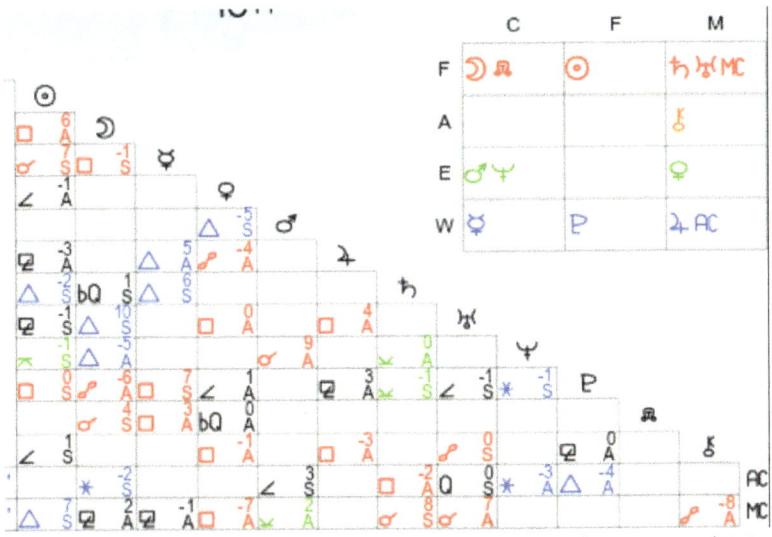

The top-left most one shows a square between the Sun and Moon, the next row's two cells show a conjunction between the Sun and Mercury and a square between the Moon and Mercury, and so forth.

I personally find this view a little hard to read. There is another view on astro.com's chart page: you can hit "Additional tables" to open up a PDF file which has a tabulated view of your chart, including the aspect grid below:

Orbs

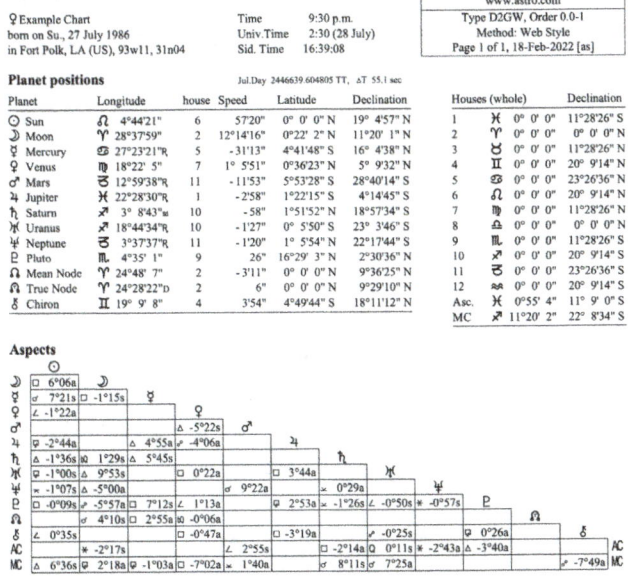

Keep in mind that all aspects have an "orb", or allowable distance for the aspect to be in effect. For instance, a planet at 25° Cancer trine a planet at 20° Pisces would be considered to be within 5° of orb of trine. An aspect of 1° or less is considered "exact" or sometimes "partile", though the true exactitude of an aspect is 0°. I sometimes call this a "perfect" aspect (give or take 15'). The tighter an aspect, the more significant and pronounced the relationship between the planets forming it is.

There are no standard maximum orbs, and it varies widely with multiple systems. I use a 10° orb for conjunctions, oppositions, about 7° for everything else, but I spend most of my time discussing aspects 3° and under.

The Neutral Aspect, the Conjunction

The **neutral aspect** is the **conjunction** (0°)—the combination of two or more things, merging, fusion, union, reunion, cycles with endings that become beginnings. The ancient astrologers considered this configuration to be special, and did not consider it an aspect, but we refer to it as one for convenience's sake. The flavor of this aspect depends entirely on the planets that have become conjunct. When conjunct, planets blend their purposes and become intermingled. If you have close conjunctions, it can sometimes be difficult to tease out the separate functions and expressions of the planets involved because they are so unified.

Harmonic Aspects

The **harmonic aspects** are:

- The **trine (120°)**—the perfect slope, flowing, harmonious, easy. This aspect is natural talent, instinct, and intuition. It describes an effortless flow between the nature of the two planets it connects, one which can be so effortless as to be taken for granted early in life. Trines ease the function between two planets to the point that impressions and reactions associated with one planet immediately flow and activate the nature of the planet connected by trine.

- The **sextile (60°)**—amiable friends, natural sympathy, latent potential, waiting to be developed. The sextile is generally compatible energy, a mutual understanding. A friend that's there to cheer you on but doesn't do much to help. However, this fair weather dynamic can be developed into a powerful force if intentionally practiced and honed.

Dynamic Aspects

The **dynamic aspects** are:

- The **square (90°)**—conflict, competition, enemies, harsh sensations, arguments, impulses, fears, misunderstanding. The square is one of the most pronounced and difficult aspects, representing a deep antipathy between the two planets. These placements do not want to understand each other, but they must in order for the impasse to resolve. Squares are often points of internal tension and difficulty that require personal transformation over a lifetime.
- The **inconjunct (150°)**—tension, irritation, dis-ease, agitation, nervous energy. The inconjunct is an uncomfortable aspect between planets, suggesting a complete lack of familiarity between the two. There is often a constant energetic tension going between the two planets, stimulating and urging them both toward some aim. The inconjunct is a minor aspect, but I find that in very close aspect (3°) it has a pronounced and outsized presence in the natal chart.
- The **opposition (180°)**—literal opposition, rivals, apexes, peak moments, respect, presence, power struggles. The opposition represents the complete and total, well, opposite. The two planets are at a true impasse, and do not fight directly but instead tug on their human. Oppositions often manifest as internal dilemmas between two modes of being or areas of life that are important. Those with significant oppositions find themselves having to toggle back and forth between expressing each planet until they find a creative solution to satisfy both needs. Sometimes, one planet is

stronger than the other and dominates the competition.

Aspects Parallel Elemental Relationships

It helps to note the relationship between aspects and the signs. Recall how each sign is opposed to another, forming 6 pairs. This diagram from Chris Brennan, an esteemed Hellenistic astrologer, shows the five traditional aspects (conjunction, sextile, square, trine, and opposition) from ancient astrological practice. We also considered the inconjunct (or "quincunx"), but left the semisextile aside for its relatively benign nature which makes it difficult to notice.

Recall our discussions of the modes and elements. Notice how

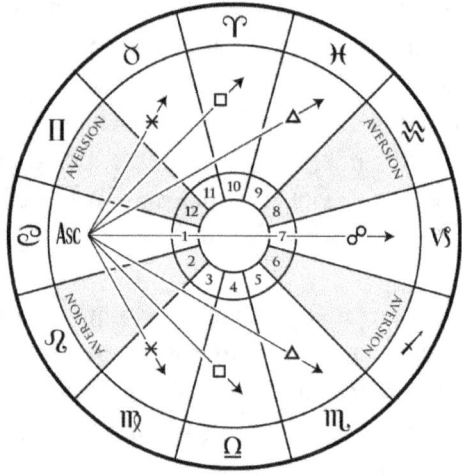

sextiles from earth or water signs only reach other earth or water signs, suggesting mild sympathies of friends. The same is true for fire and air signs. This reflects the doctrine of astrological elemental compatibility; earth and water signs tend to get along well, fire and air signs tend to get along well, but the two groups often don't mix well, requiring adjustment and adaptation. This applies both within the personality and between people. If you have behaviors and emotional patterns within your personality that seem to be at odds even though you don't have planets that are making direct aspects, you may have conflicting elements in your chart. (Another way to think about this is in terms of sign-based squares/oppositions/inconjuncts—both doctrines describe the same phenomenon.)

Notice how trines from each element only reach the two signs of the same element, those of a deeply similar nature. Harsh squares are only formed between signs of the same mode (cardinal, mutable, or fixed) while reaching across element groups suggesting the competitive and unsympathetic nature of the aspect. Inconjuncts are made between signs that share neither mode nor element, suggesting their fundamentally alien, irritating, and discomforting nature.

Another layer of depth you can optionally add is the traditional Hellenistic **sign-based aspects**. Like modern practitioners, the Hellenistic astrologers considered the precise angles to be aspects, but also held that simply having a planet in any sign as many degrees away as the aspect's degrees represents that relationship. So if you had your Moon at 2° Aries but your Sun at 28° Leo, you would still have a sign-based trine between your Sun and Moon. This makes sense, as these planets' expressions will still be fundamentally compatible in signs of the same element.

Interpretation

As you look at the aspects between the different planets in your chart, consider your own experience. Take special note of:

- Clusters of planets—3 or more within 10° is considered a "stellium", and the three planets act especially strongly together
- Multiple planets aspecting the same planet
- Very tight aspects
- Aspects between planets that are close to the ascendant/descendant or midheaven/imum coeli axis

Think about each planet in each sign and how your experience relates to its description. These descriptions are terse, so don't be afraid to let your imagination or intuition guide you; each sign and planet is a massive archetype with many perspectives and flavors on the same core themes. Then look at what aspects that planet makes. Consider the other planet's expression, and the nature of the aspect, and how that may present itself in your life or psychology.

For some people it can be as literal as a dynamic fixated on the opposition between work and love showing up in the natal chart as Saturn opposite Venus. For others, a Mars square Moon can make the emotions volatile, quick-tempered, and defensive, as Mars' combative and fiery nature casts a harsh square to the heart of emotion and safety instincts, the Moon. Meanwhile, a flowing trine between Mercury and Mars can suggest a sharp wit and the ability to handle (Mercury, hands, dexterity) knives (Mars, weapons, blades) uncannily well.

More than most aspects, squares and oppositions show us where we have complex inner dynamics and where difficult life experiences tend to appear for us. Squares are resolved by finding a mutual language for the planets involved to cooperate while oppositions are resolved by finding ways to appease both planets, either alternately or simultaneously. This can be difficult to handle in isolation, and often one of the planets involved in harsh aspects has a sextile or trine to another planet. I think of this as a "valve" for excess energy to vent out of, and often recommend that clients engage in activities represented by the "vent planet" when the tension produced by the harsh aspects involved grow unbearable.

The Houses: The Realms of Experience

We are almost done with the blunt information consumption. This is the last part before synthesis: the houses. The houses are a mathematical method of dividing the celestial sphere into 12 parts which describe various areas of experience in our personal lives.

If you look on your natal chart, you will see the AC marks a thick black line, the horizon. The AC is also the beginning of the first house, stretching counterclockwise until the next cone with the house number inscribed into the middle. Thus, houses one through six are under the horizon, while houses seven through twelve are above the horizon.

The best way to understand what is actually happening is with a visualization as shown on the next page.

Don't worry if this overwhelms you at first. It's not necessary to have an intuitive grasp of what the houses look like in 3D space (though it can help)—all you have to understand is that they divide the sky, and that their relative placements have meaning.

First, though, we must talk about what a "Placidus" is.

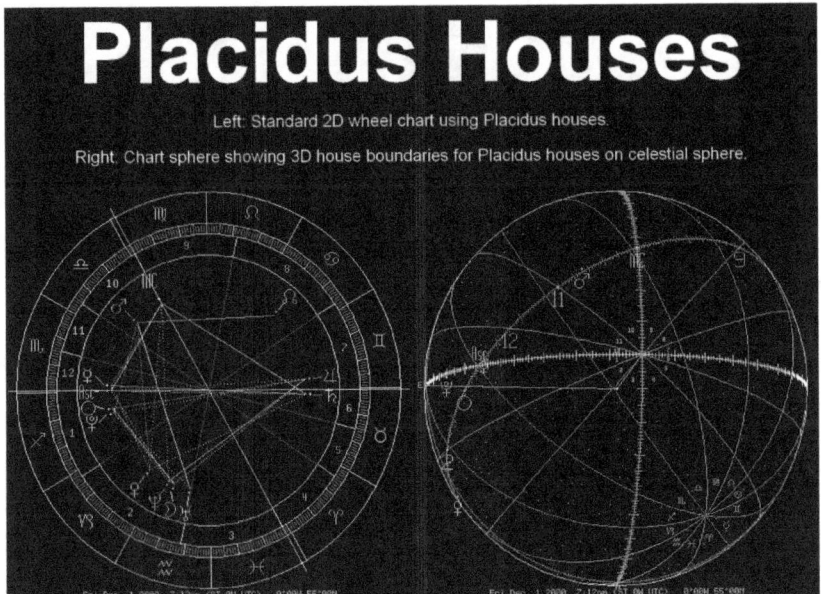

House Systems

Since the houses are a mathematical method of dividing the sky, this suggests there may be multiple methods—and there are. The default mode that astro.com generates a chart in is "Placidus", a house system named after 17th century astrologer Placidus de Titis.[10]

There are dozens of house systems, but Placidus is the most popular. This only means that it's popular—nothing more, nothing less. There are many others that are relatively unexplored or forgotten completely, which could give us new perspectives and techniques. One which has been brought back, all the way from the Hellenistic era, is whole sign houses (WSH). With whole sign houses you simply match each house to each sign, so whatever sign your ascendant is in, your first house begins at 0° of that sign.

---

10 Technically, Placidus de Titis did not invent the system, which was widely acknowledged (including by Placidus) as created by Claudius Ptolemy, a highly influential second century astronomer who later explored astrology, mostly from a mathematical perspective.

Here is our example chart, but in WSH:

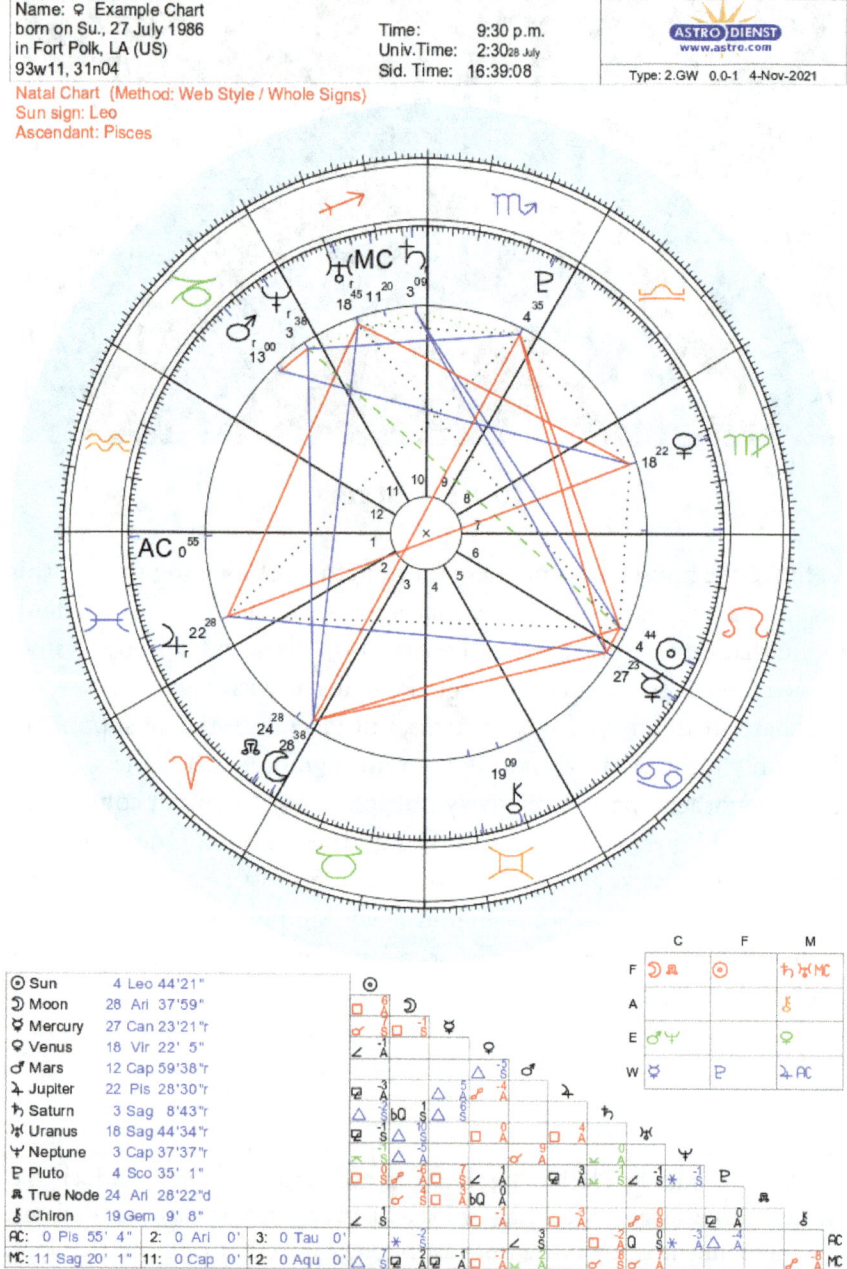

To turn on whole sign houses, first go to the Extended Chart Selection page.

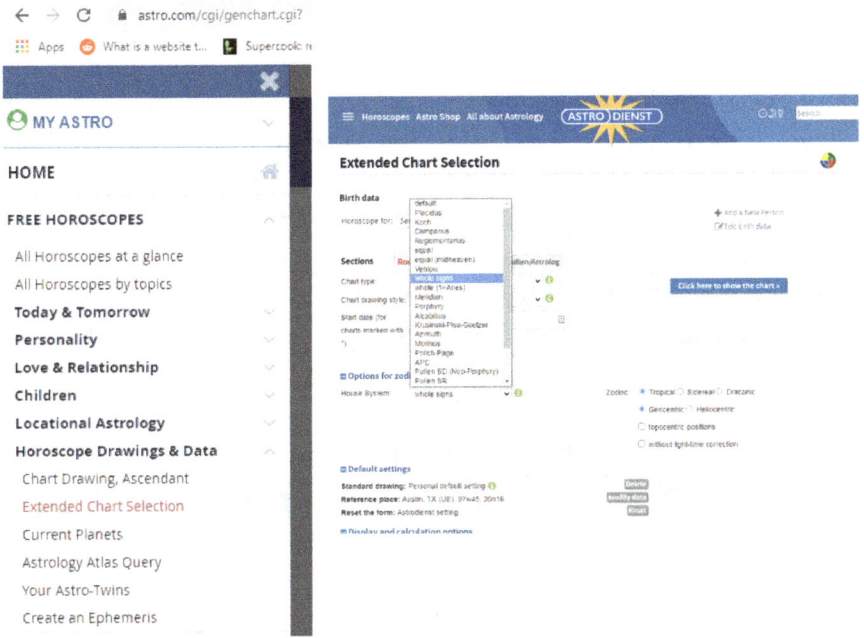

You may need to create an account to access this; I highly recommend it, as astro.com is free for up to 100 charts, and then after that has a very inexpensive yearly fee.

Once at the Extended Chart Selection page, under Options for zodiac and houses > House System, select whole signs. Then just hit "Click here to show the chart".

Depending on where you were born, your Placidus houses may look very different from your whole sign houses. What to do?

One rationale and solution put forward is that whole sign houses come from times when class mobility and lots in life were much more fixed, and so astrology was designed more for the direct, mundane, and concrete results in life. Meanwhile, the more modern Placidus which accounts for our exact location on earth, is tied more intimately to ourselves and our perspectives. Placidus may reflect the highly subjective perception of one's own experience, despite the actual mundane experiences in life being associated with the whole sign house chart.

It's difficult to say—I personally have key placements that switch houses, and I have also had many times where I felt like I was experiencing the elements of those placements in both houses, both subjectively and in the real world. There are other areas of astrological practice where we can apply a fine discriminating eye to the efficacy of house systems, but the world of highly subjective natal subject isn't one of them.

I personally like whole sign house because it enables a number of powerful predictive techniques, but I swap between house systems every now and then as a matter of practice. To start, I recommend you read through the descriptions of the houses and reflect on how the planets might manifest in them between Placidus and whole sign house. Once you have a bit of a sense of which one resonates more, just pick that one and stick with it for a while. You can always come back to the other one (or any of the other dozens) later.

Origins and Functions

The houses are where the abstract, archetypal depth psychology language of planets, signs, and aspects meet concrete lived experience. Because the houses are defined by the sign the ascendant is in, the birth time is very important. However, because the meanings of the houses are so specific, they can enable one to make educated guesses about what time someone was born, which is a rectification technique. The point is, if you're not sure of your birth time, you may need to do some detective work to see which houses seem to logically pair with your signs.

Each house, similar to signs and planets, is a vast archetype enveloping a wide array of things and experiences. For instance, the first house rules both outlook on life as well as acne. The seventh house rules contracts, public enemies, marriage, and sunset.

The house meanings as defined in modern astrology generally combine multiple conceptual sources, including but likely not limited to:

- "mundane"/real world associations with the sign (9th house ruling churches)
- traditional astrology (3rd house ruling religious observance)
- affinity qualities from the sign whose number matches the house (5th house ruling "fun" as relates to Leo, the 5th sign)
- psychological astrology (Mars in the 3rd means you have a sharp

tongue)
- depth astrology (12th house ruling the grieving process).

Each house is such a large idea that it helps to have core concepts behind each of them. For natal astrology, I personally find Dane Rudhyar's metaphor from *The Astrological Houses: The Spectrum of Individual Experience* concept of the houses as symbolically describing the cycle of life from birth until death (and continuing again) to be extremely useful, and you will notice allusions to this idea throughout the descriptions of the houses.

The houses are not just grab-bags for archetypal concepts—each individual house has its own quality which affects the planets in the houses, and similar to the interweaving system of sign modes, elements, and aspects, the houses have their own analogous quality which becomes apparent as you elucidate the meanings of the houses. We'll do this after covering the individual houses.

The presence of planets within a house indicate what area of life that planet tends to operate most actively within. In very brief summary:[11]

- The Sun's placement by house shows where the core sense of personal identity and mission is centered
- The Moon shows where we seek comfort, nourishment, and safety, but also how we provide it for others
- Mercury shows where our curiosity leads us, what we usually want to talk about, and what domains we frequently travel
- Venus shows where we find beauty, relationships, companionship, leisure, pleasure, and where the sensual and/or sexual impulses are deployed
- Mars shows where energy, motivation, aggression, initiative, and sometimes conflict is generated
- Jupiter shows where we experience success, blessings, joy, wisdom, and where we tend to "preach" our experiences
- Saturn shows where we experience limitation, responsibilities,

---

11   I would like to emphasize that this is an incredibly brief summary, and each planet has so many more significations that pair with each house in complex and fascinating ways.

and restrictions, but also discipline, focus, and pragmatic insight.

- Chiron shows where we experience core wounds and become teachers.
- The North Node shows where we experience significant learning and personal development.

You can also identify the outer planets' roles by house, though their effects tend to be lessened unless they are making a close aspect to inner planets which connects their influences to the rest of the chart.

- Uranus shows where we experience sudden and unexpected changes, strokes of brilliance, rebellious impulses, and technological competence.
- Neptune shows where we experience fantasies, delusions, irrational fears, spiritual yearnings, and sometimes dreams coming true.
- Pluto shows where we experience intensity, secrecy, paranoia, obsession, control, and a survival mentality.

The planets may express themselves most actively in the houses they are placed in but their operations are not restricted to only that house. The aspects between the planets also connect the planets' themes. For instance, Mars in the fifth house opposing Saturn in the eleventh house can indicate that there is a direct conflict between one's desire to work on personal projects, or, perhaps, have recreational sex (Mars: energy, drive; 5th house: hobby projects, sex) and obligations to one's social group (Saturn: obligations, restrictions; 11th house: social groups, clubs).

If you have no planets in a house, that is called an "empty house". Having an empty house isn't a bad thing, and by definition everyone has at least one or two.[12] It also does not mean that you won't have experiences related to that house. For instance, having an empty seventh house doesn't mean you'll be alone forever; it only means that relationships are not emphasized as a life theme in your chart. But throughout your life as the planets transit the various houses of your chart, they will bring their significations and concerns into those houses, as will other events such

---

12 Technically, if you are working with asteroids or other stellar bodies, you may have no empty houses due to how many objects can populate the sky.

as retrogrades, eclipses, new and full moons, and conjunctions between planets.

There is another layer of richness to be found in the rulership system. Each planet rules the houses whose signs start at their cusps. That is, if your second house starts in the sign Gemini, then Mercury rules your second house. Mercury's sign, position, received aspects, and general nature will describe how the second house is experienced, but aspects that Mercury receives from transiting planets will trigger events related to the second house (as well as whichever house starts in Virgo). This means that houses are not only related to one another by aspects cast between planets in the houses they occupy, but also by aspects formed between planets ruling houses. For instance, in a whole sign chart with a Gemini rising, having Mercury conjunct Mars means that your 1st (Gemini) and 4th (Virgo) houses are related to your 11th (Aries) and 6th (Scorpio) through that conjunction.

If you are using whole sign houses, rulership is simple. Each house has one sign and one ruler. If you're working with Placidus, the houses begin at the Ascendant instead of 0° of the sign. This means that houses often have more than one sign within them, and if the house is large enough, it can "intercept" a sign, or completely enclose a sign between two other ones such that it does not touch either edge of the house. It's common to say that the house is "co-ruled" by two or more planets, in the proportion matching the proportions of the signs that they rule. Intercepted signs are rarer, and interpretively they are considered to be a "suppressed" energy in that house, and since the opposing house must also have an intercepting sign, the axis that is intercepted becomes a theme that must be explored and discovered over time through life.[13]

As you read about the meanings of the houses, think about the ways in which each of your placements might describe your lived experience of that house's themes. Follow aspects to other planets in other houses and see if you can identify what relationship it describes in your life.

---

13   For decent information on intercepted signs, see: Cal Garrison, "Intercepted Signs," November 13, 2019, mountaintimes.info and Bernie Ashman, "What Do Planets in Intercepted Signs Mean?" January 8, 2018, llewellyn.com. However, keep in mind that not all astrologers agree on how to interpret intercepted signs, and with whole sign houses there are no intercepted signs. Use your life experiences and judgment.

Take note of houses that are particularly packed with placements. Take note of houses containing planets making especially exact aspects. Look at the house rulers and see what aspects they make to other planets, and ponder how the nature of the aspect between them could describe the dynamic between the themes associated with the houses they rule.

Finally, let's talk themes of the houses. I have given them single word summaries as a mimetic aid, but just like the planets and signs, the houses are vast archetypes with infinite forms of expression. As you read their descriptions, think about how these themes relates to the involvement of the planets and signs you've identified in your experience.

House Meanings
The First House: Identity

The first house begins with the ascendant, the first moment of direct union between your body, soul, and the world outside of the womb. It represents the themes of that first burst of awareness into existence: consciousness and awareness of self, preceding everything else. Fittingly, the first house's themes are self-determination, outlook on the world, personal style and fashion, as well as awareness of the self as an identity, all of which will be described by the sign and the ruler of the sign.

Because the first house begins at the ascendant which is a special point, the ruler of the ascendant is particularly important in describing one's overall vitality, health, and character.

The Second House: Possession

After awareness of self comes awareness of the self as a thing that has stuff. For a newborn, this is the body. Eventually, this becomes my stuff, my toys, my room, my money, my career, my reputation, my friendships, my connections, my power, my strength, my my my. The second house reflects the perspective of ownership, even for abstract concepts such as social connections, personal fortitude, reputation, or knowledge. This house shows our relationship to possessions, and also shows how we tend to acquire them, both in terms of the sorts of things acquired as well the ways we tend to go about acquiring them.

The Third House: Environment

Extending beyond the domain of me and mine is the immediate environment: the people around us and the space around us. This includes our friends, siblings, family, and our local neighborhood. This house has to do with all things within our orbit, such as the local coffee shop we visit, and the people we spend the most time with. Bridging the gap between ourselves and others in our immediate environment involves communication: conversations, writing, recurring small-scale publishing (such as your local newspaper). It also frequently requires short-distance travel, such as one's daily commute or the walk we take to the local library. Historically, the third is also associated with religious observance, worship, sacred places, temples, and priesthood, from a time when religious experience was deeply intertwined with local community.

The Fourth House: Foundations

After recognizing the beings around us we recognize what home means as a concept, as a family, as well as in its most literal sense of the places we grow up in. The ancient Hellenistic astrologers called the fourth the "subterraneous" or "underground" place, since it marks the lowest section of the chart.[14] It is the foundation of our selves in all sense: the place we are born, the country we live in, the parents that raise us, the house we grow up in, and the sort of home we tend to replicate for ourselves as adults, although usually in more developed forms than what we experienced in childhood. The fourth house generally shows our deepest, most intimate roots related to our familial upbringing, experiences in youth, and most sentimental feelings. The nature of the sign in the fourth house often describes the flavor of experience of growing up, and planets often describe the influences most prominent in our youth. As the lowest part in the chart, the fourth house is also associated with topics that are secret or hidden. This especially includes family secrets,

---

14   In whole sign house you will have the separate Imum Coeli, or IC, which opposes the Midheaven, or MC, in one of the lower houses, typically the 4th. In Placidus, the IC will mark the beginning of the 4th house.

but also treasure, both literal and figurative such as buried gold or occult wisdom.

The Fifth House: Play

Once we have foundations, we can build upon them. The fifth house is fundamentally the house of creativity and rewards (the Hellenists even called it the place of Good Fortune). In modern psychological astrology the fifth shows where we create whether as artwork, side hustles, or children. This house relates to the times and spaces where we get to play, on our own terms and for our own needs, during those moments of respite away from the obligations of work, chores, family, and society. The noodling riffs on a guitar we do for fun, the side gig that we dream will become a career one day, and just lounging around are all fifth house themes. These and other fifth house activities can lead to great luck and bounty, and the fifth house is correlated with windfalls, rewards, success, and sudden fortune. However, games can also be lost, and another theme of this house is financial losses, especially in games of chance. Finally, this house also relates to the themes creativity and play in the carnal senses of both recreational sex and reproductive sex. Thus, the fifth also rules romance, love affairs, pregnancy, motherhood, and children.

The Sixth House: Materiality

After we have played games, opened chests and strewn toys everywhere, comes time for the necessary conclusion: cleaning it all up. The sixth house is the house of handling the aftermath of what vital forces have come before. Here is where we deal with the limits of the real world. Bedtime approaches. There are only so many hours in a day and only so much energy in your body. This implicates health and its maintenance, the structure of our daily routine, and also those we work with, especially our employees as extensions of how we utilize our personal resources. This house also covers activities of space: reorganizing, moving things, building things, tinkering, and working with the hands. This house generally shows the way in which we tend to structure these activities and handle the small repetitions of life. The sixth can also give hints about the nature of work and career by examining any planets within it and the ruler of the house. Traditionally, the sixth house also rules small domesticated pets like cats and dogs.

The Seventh House: Other

The seventh house is the first time we peek outside of confines of our own world and ego. This house is about meeting the Other, truly encountering and grappling with the existence of another being, and the implications of living in collaboration and exchange with them. The last six houses have dealt exclusively with our own experience—the seventh marks the beginning of what I call the "external" or "exterior" houses. Each of the six external houses opposes the previous six "internal" or "interior" houses, and they all deal with the same themes, but above the horizon they deal with where we meet the experiences of the Other.

More specifically, the seventh house rules significant relationships with others. This is generally any sort of committed relationship, formal or not, including romantic partners, business partners, and truly close friends. The sign on the seventh house tends to show either the types of people we attract, or the role we play in our partners' lives. Because the descendant's sign is opposing the ascendant sign which is an integral part of our spirit, and that each opposing sign on an axis contains a fundamentally shared essence, the descendant can show us where we disown part of our own nature and instead project them onto our experience of those closest to us. In its healthiest function, the seventh house can show us how our own polarity can be reintegrated into our psyches and embodied healthily in full recognition of what is ours and what is theirs. This allows us to see each other as we truly are, and go even further together.

The Eighth House: Burden

Opposing the second house of possessions, the eighth house holds other people's possessions. While "Burdens" is a foreboding word for a house, it is fairly accurate to this house's significations: death, and taxes. Death because you inherit other's possessions, and taxes because in most countries, part of your income is actually another's possession: the state.

More broadly, this is the house of other's stuff in general. It includes your partner's money and furniture, your family's emotional burdens, and your best friend's secrets. People with significant 8th house placements sometimes work in careers having to do with other people's stuff or inheritance, such as accounting, tax software, real estate, or funeral and mortuary services, to name a few. This house can also be related to themes of familial, ancestral, and epigenetic trauma that we have nonetheless taken on, or can show how we interact with others' deepest burdens.

The Ninth House: Kingdom

Opposing the third house of environment is the ninth house of governmental power, institutions of higher learning, and organized religions. It also rules foreign cultures, wisdom, and publishing. The ninth house is like the expansive, externalized, authority-driven version of the third house's themes. If your local community church is the third, then the entire Catholic Church is the ninth. If your local library is the third, national publishing companies are the ninth. If your local school is the third, colleges and academic journals are the ninth. The ninth shows our relationship to religion, faith, and authority. It also shows our orientation toward institutionalized education and the general cultural mores of society at large. Having to do with the wide arm of governmental power and law, the ninth house also extends to the national community and diplomacy with fellow countries. The ninth often signifies encounters with other cultures, and having many planets in the ninth or its ruler be very prominent can sometimes point to experiences involving foreign countries and people, even extending to marrying a foreign spouse and possibly living abroad.

The Tenth House: Work

If you are using Placidus, the tenth house begins at the midheaven. If you are using Whole Sign House, the Midheaven is a separate point which is usually, but not always, in the tenth house. The tenth house and the midheaven share general significations, but the midheaven functions as a locus point where those topics are especially important.

The tenth house is the very height of the chart, and opposes the fourth house of foundations. From the roots of a tree grow branches, and the tenth house represents the breadth of the branches of your life. The tenth house is the house of accomplishment, but more specifically what you bring into the world. I like to describe it as how our accomplishments will be seen by the world at large. Planets in the tenth house or close to the midheaven tend to become very noticeable parts of our character and color our reputation. Those planets and the midheaven's ruling planet can give hints about the nature of this achievement and how it is achieved. The midheaven is sometimes described as indicative of the qualities we aspire to embody. Overall, the tenth house and midheaven relate to the personal career. A good way of conceptualizing what "career" means in various contexts is to imagine how someone else would describe what you were doing or working on during a given time. The work done in the tenth house becomes the foundation for those that follow us. Traditionally, the tenth house also indicated our ability to attain and mingle with power.

The Eleventh House: Collective

The eleventh house opposes the fifth house of personal play and creativity, and it is about the collectives in our lives. This includes peers in school, attendees of the homeowner's association, people in a local scene, your Twitter followers, or even the concept of all of humanity itself. The eleventh house describes our relationship to groups of people identified by their common interests. It also describes the role we tend to play in the communities we find ourselves in, and planets there often describe the types of experiences that come to us via these communal settings. The eleventh is contrasted against the fifth as creative energy being spent in service of others, rather than upon self-oriented aspirations which might happen to include others. In its excess functionality, the emphasis on the collective can become so strong as to override self-interest, and in some cases even self-preservation. As the house following the tenth, it was traditionally also associated with hope and friendships with powerful people.

The Twelfth House: Release

If the sixth house represents the diligent maintenance and upkeep of material concerns to balance life's desires, the twelfth represents the breakdown and dissolution of that structure. The twelfth house describes experiences that don't fit into the structure of regular life: indescribable, ethereal, listless, wandering, lost. Metaphorically, the twelfth house is the stage of decay as all that has come before is; the final step before death becomes fertilizer, yielding yet more life. However, when thinking about this house it's important to resist the temptation to rush to the next house (the first again) by thinking of the beginnings that follow where we are—the end. This house is associated with the end of things and the liminal space they occupy. Unlike the sixth house, where we can use our talents at shaping and structuring the material world, the twelfth house often requires that we release and let go in order to ease, and sometimes heal during these finishing stages. More concretely, the twelfth house is associated with healing professions, psychic experiences, secrets, loss, wild animals, dreams, fantasies, and fears. The twelfth house is one of what the Hellenists called a "dark house", meaning that planets there have difficulty expressing themselves. When you have planets in dark houses, they can feel like parts of yourself that are harder to access, or more dormant. The ruling sign and planet often hints at the nature of how you can most easily access those twelfth house placements, which are most amenable to approaches that live within and explore the empty space of the twelfth house, rather than those that aim to structure and capture them.

Planets in Houses

Now that we've explored what the themes of the houses are, we can think about the planets' roles in them. We can describe them here in summary, but they mostly follow quite logically from the planets' fundamental meanings.

Sun

The house the Sun is in describes what the native ties their core sense of identity to. It shows the nature of the self-image and where creative energy is most effectively applied. The experiences of this house are often key to a vital sense of self.

Moon

The house the Moon is in describes what we need in order to feel secure. Experiences here are frequently tied up in our survival needs and primal fears, so when matters in these houses are in disarray we can feel frightened and regressive. This also shows us where we can spend extra time to nourish ourselves and feel more secure.

Mercury

The house Mercury is in describes where our intelligence is deployed and what we think about most. Communication and talking out loud helps us understand the dynamics of this house's themes. Mercury's house position can also sometimes show us the sorts of places we literally travel frequently by their mundane meanings.

Venus

The house Venus is in describes where we most freely experience pleasure, affection, joy, and happiness. Venus' house can describe what we value aesthetically or monetarily. It can also show where we tend to meet romantic interests or close friends.

Mars

The house Mars is in describes where we act most Mars-like, defending territory, exerting energy, initiating projects, and handling conflicts. Mars' house often describes the sorts of spaces we are most likely to conflict with others, but also where we are most willing to fight for what we believe in.

Jupiter

The house Jupiter is in describes where we can kindle faith, optimism, joy, and wisdom, as well as the activities can give a sense of personal growth and hope. This house can be a lens for seeing one's own potential to grow.

Saturn

The house Saturn is in describes where we experience themes of discipline, restriction, responsibility, duty, and limitation. This house often demands significant labor and work from us, but if we put that work in, it pays off handsomely.

Uranus

The house Uranus is in describes where we receive sudden inspiration, tend to innovate, and have a rebellious or unusual streak. This is where we express our inherent genius and how we can use it to help others.

Neptune

The house Neptune is in describes where we feel nebulous fears, have "delusional" fantasies, and experience the deepest yearnings of the soul to something beyond. We often experience a simultaneous aspiration and aversion with this house. We aspire to manifest the sublime reality Neptune's conveys, but at the same time avoid it due to the certain fear that the reality will never quite live up to the divine inspiration.

Pluto

The house Pluto is in describes where we have obsessions, compulsions, and control dynamics. This house is where we have difficulty letting things go, but also where we generate and devote a massive amount of energy. We tend to keep the matters of this house a secret, and there can be an irrational fear that we will be destroyed if we are exposed.

Chiron

The house Chiron is in describes where we experience the wounded healer dynamic. The concerns of the house often describe the fundamental nature of the wound we have suffered and cared for throughout life. At the same time, that experience in this house becomes a font of wisdom for us to help others.

The Nodes

The Nodes by house will pull our focus and attention to the two houses they occupy which will always oppose one another. The North Node points towards our personal fixations and urges for experience while the South Node points to our comfort zones, unconscious defaults, and defense mechanisms.

House Strength

One of the gifts Hellenistic astrology gives us is the doctrine of house strength. Ancient astrologers considered each of the houses to have its own character and purpose with their own inherent beneficence and maleficence, which influences how relatively well or poorly planets function within them.

- The broadly "good" houses, in order (most good to least good)[15]: 1, 10, 11, 5, 7, 4, 9, 3.
- The broadly "bad" houses, in order (least bad to most bad): 2, 8, 6, 12.

If you reflect on the meanings of each of these houses in turn, you can see how the ancients decided this order based on their opinion of the relative blessings bestowed by the domain of each good house, and the

---

15   Order from Chris Brennan's *Hellenistic Astrology: The Study of Fate and Fortune* (Amor Fati Publications, 2017).

burdens and undoings related to each bad house. However, in modern times, we also emphasize the dominance of free will and the fact that while planets may be overtly influenced by their house placement, these seemingly difficult placements can be honed into skills, experience, and deep wisdom resulting in huge reward.

It's also important to keep in mind as we discuss the rest of the house strength rules that this is only a sampling of some of the broadest Hellenistic house strength techniques—there are more which factor into the evaluation of planetary condition and can aid a planet in a weak house.

Angularity

A key concept from Hellenistic astrology is that of angularity, or closeness to the "angles". The angles (sometimes called "stakes") are the ascendant, descendant, midheaven, and imum coeli, which in the idealized whole sign natal chart are all at 90° angles to one another. The angles are said to be powerfully important points, and placements that are near them will be particularly influential in one's life. This is especially true when upon the ascendant or midheaven.

This idea of angularity also extends to the entire houses themselves: the first, fourth, seventh, and tenth houses are all considered angular. The houses that follow the angular houses are called succedent, and the houses that follow the succedent houses are called cadent. These classifications, broadly, describe the function and prominence of the planets in the house and the manner in which these planets express themselves

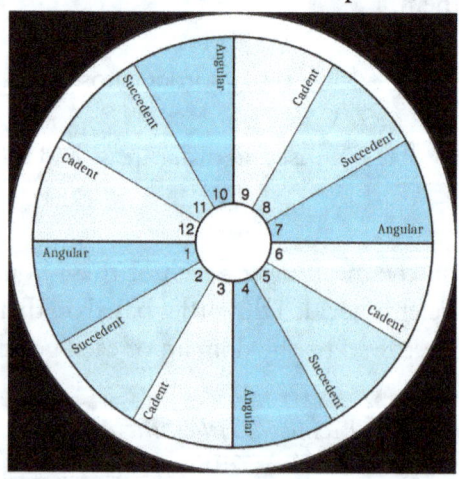

in life.

The general qualities of the house classifications are:

- Angular houses (1, 4, 7, 10)—passion, energy, force, beginning, starting
- Succedent houses (2, 5, 8, 11)—consolidation, forming, structuring, building, handling
- Cadent houses (3, 6, 9, 12)—connection, completion, contemplation, sharing, organizing, distributing

The easiest way to remember the angular/succedent/cadent classification is to remember the 4 points of the AC/MC/DC/IC (which the ancients would sometimes call "stakes") mark the beginnings of the angular houses if you are using Placidus, and that these are then followed in counter-clockwise order by the two succedent and cadent houses. Ancient astrologers sometimes refer to these houses as "falling away" from the initial burst of energy of the cardinal houses, so you can imagine the four stakes having the strongest burst on the 90° *angles* in the angular houses, then *successively*, the succedent houses, then finally *falling* (latin: *cadēns*) to the cadent houses.

Dark Houses

The fourth, eighth, and twelfth houses are sometimes called "dark houses" due to their association with topics that can bring misfortune and distraction such as money, possessions, taxes, inheritances, death, and loss. These houses are considered to obscure the planets within them, making their expression less effective and harder for the native to access. Psychologically, the dark houses generally tend to represent those things lurking beneath the surface of our psyches, and the planets within them are hidden from us due to their involvement in the themes of the house.

This can sometimes indicate suppression or projection of the functions of these planets in the personality, and that intentional work is needed to integrate their energy into the rest of the psyche. Planets in dark houses can be more easily accessed or exercised by expressing the energy of the planet ruling that house, or planets that make aspect to the planets in the dark houses. Enough work can eventually integrate these energies into the psyche, and these energies tied deeply into the subconscious become an asset rather than a burden.

Planetary Joys

The doctrine of planetary joys is a scheme that underlies many of the meanings of the houses, as well as foundational pieces of Hellenistic astrology itself.[16] Many of the houses' meanings are derived from the joy system, but the details are beyond our scope. However, we can list them and think about how their planetary nature relates to the houses they are assigned:

- Sun in 9th
- Moon in 3rd
- Jupiter in 11th
- Venus in 5th
- Mars in 6th
- Saturn in 12th
- Mercury in 1st

When a planet is in a house of its joy, it is considered to summon the best of its qualities, functioning particularly strongly.

House Interrelationships

Just as the aspects that exist between signs do a good job of describing key dynamics between those signs, so does the idea of aspects between the houses. For instance, consider these relationships:

- Six sets of two houses that oppose each other, suggesting their inherent tension and competing demands:

---

16   They are so foundational, in fact, that they present an entirely different pedagogy than the Astrological Alphabet by their associations. Advanced reading: see Chris Brennan's "The Planetary Joys and the Origins of the Significations of the Houses and Triplicities," hellenisticastrology.com.

- 1 (identity), 7 (other)
- 2 (possession), 8 (burden)
- 3 (environment), 9 (kingdom)
- 4 (foundation), 10 (work)
- 5 (play), 11 (collective)
- 6 (materiality), 12 (release)
- Four sets of three houses that trine each other, flowing harmoniously, logically leading into one another:
    - 1 (identity), 5 (play), 9 (kingdom)
    - 2 (possession), 6 (materiality), 10 (work)
    - 3 (environment), 7 (other), 11 (collective)
    - 4 (foundations), 8 (burdens), 12 (release)
- Three sets of four houses that square each other in turn, clashing dynamically and demanding integration:
    - 1 (identity), 4 (foundation), 7 (other), 10 (work)
    - 2 (possession), 5 (play), 8 (burden), 11 (collective)
    - 3 (environment), 6 (materiality), 9 (kingdom), 12 (release)
- Two sets of six houses that sextile each other, suggesting how they can connect to one another with a little applied effort:
    - 1 (identity), 3 (environment), 5 (play), 7 (other), 9 (kingdom), 11 (collective)
    - 2 (possession), 4 (foundation), 6 (materiality), 8 (burden), 10 (work), 12 (release)

While we could go on about the houses—and we have gone on—it's time to close on one last note and move on to Part 2.

On the Astrological Alphabet

You may learn online or from modern astrology books about the astrological alphabet which equates 12 letters and numbers with the signs, houses, and modern planets, like so:

1. A, Aries, Mars, First House
2. B, Taurus, Venus, Second House
3. C, Gemini, Mercury, Third House
4. . . .

As a mimetic aid the Astrological Alphabet is great, but when you conflate signs with planets with houses, you end up with meanings for the houses that are not supported by historical astrological texts. For instance, a very recent development that derives specifically from conflating Scorpio's highly sexual nature with the house whose number matches the sign, the 8th, is that the 8th house has to do with sex.[17]

It's important to note that the nature of signs is different from the nature of houses, and nuance is lost if you equate them directly. In the houses, signs don't express their personalities so much as their energetic *rhythms*. When I was first learning astrology I told someone that their 6th house being ruled by Aquarius suggests that they change their routines and health habits frequently or are constantly experimenting with it, due to Aquarius' modern association rebellion and change under eccentric Uranus, only to be told that I was wrong (rather bluntly, as they were a skeptic). He had a very fixed routine and health habits.

Aquarius is, after all, a *fixed* sign and energetically that is how it expresses itself in the nature of the house, which especially if we consider that taciturn and unrelenting Saturn is Aquarius' traditional ruler. Rather, Aquarius' house-nature is expressed by a combination of its myths, its mundane concerns, and the themes of the house itself. In combination with the 6th house, Aquarius there can suggest working amongst friends, in social groups, in a scientific or technologically sophisticated field, or that health is observed with modern technology like biometric tracking devices.

While Aquarius does express itself in a way that has been accurately perceived by thousands of modern astrologers, this is most typically in the context of a human personality expressing Aquarian energy in specific placements. When interpreting the houses, it is important to understand the sign's expression more along the lines of its archetypal nature. This may seem abstract at first, but the more you observe and

---

17   For extremely informative, educational, and entertaining reads on the problems with the Astrological Alphabet, the rationale behind the meanings associated with the houses, and a thorough exploration of why the 8th house is not associated with sex, see Patrick Watson's excellent articles "Why Aries ≠ The 1st House" and "RIP: The Little Death Of "La Petite Mort"® And Sex As An 8th House Topic."

learn about the signs, the more you will appreciate their layered expressions in different contexts.

Part Two: An Example Reading

If you've read this far, congratulations. Take a breather and settle in, because now we'll be doing an example reading.

No natal reading can really be done in isolation without the owner of the chart present to give us information. Ultimately, natal astrology exists to help people explore their own inner worlds and lives and should be done with the input of a client. Because of this, I almost always do live readings, whether over a video call or occasionally through a direct message chat. However, since you're reading my words on a page, I can only try my best to convey the act of synthesizing the many parts of a chart when you're doing a reading.

We'll use the chart from Part 1 for example delineation, but with whole sign house as that's what I use the most personally.

Example Chart, or EC, is actually a person, but I no longer remember who it is since I changed the chart name. That's preferable, as it keeps me from coloring the reading with my personal knowledge about this person. I will refer to EC's placements as if they are a client we are doing a reading for.

An Example Reading
Sun, Moon, Rising and Chart Ruler

First, examine the Sun, Moon, and Rising (the "Big Three" or SMR[18]). As you see what signs they are in and think about their meanings, consider each in turn.

The Sun is identity and vitality, so consider how that expresses itself by sign and house. Note any close aspects it takes, especially conjunctions. Look at what sign it's in, and think about the strength of the house as well as the house's themes. Briefly consider which if any planets are making those aspects. The nature of the planets making close aspect will involve themselves in the identity. Relate this to times you have felt

---

18   Credit to Chris Brennan for coining "SMR".

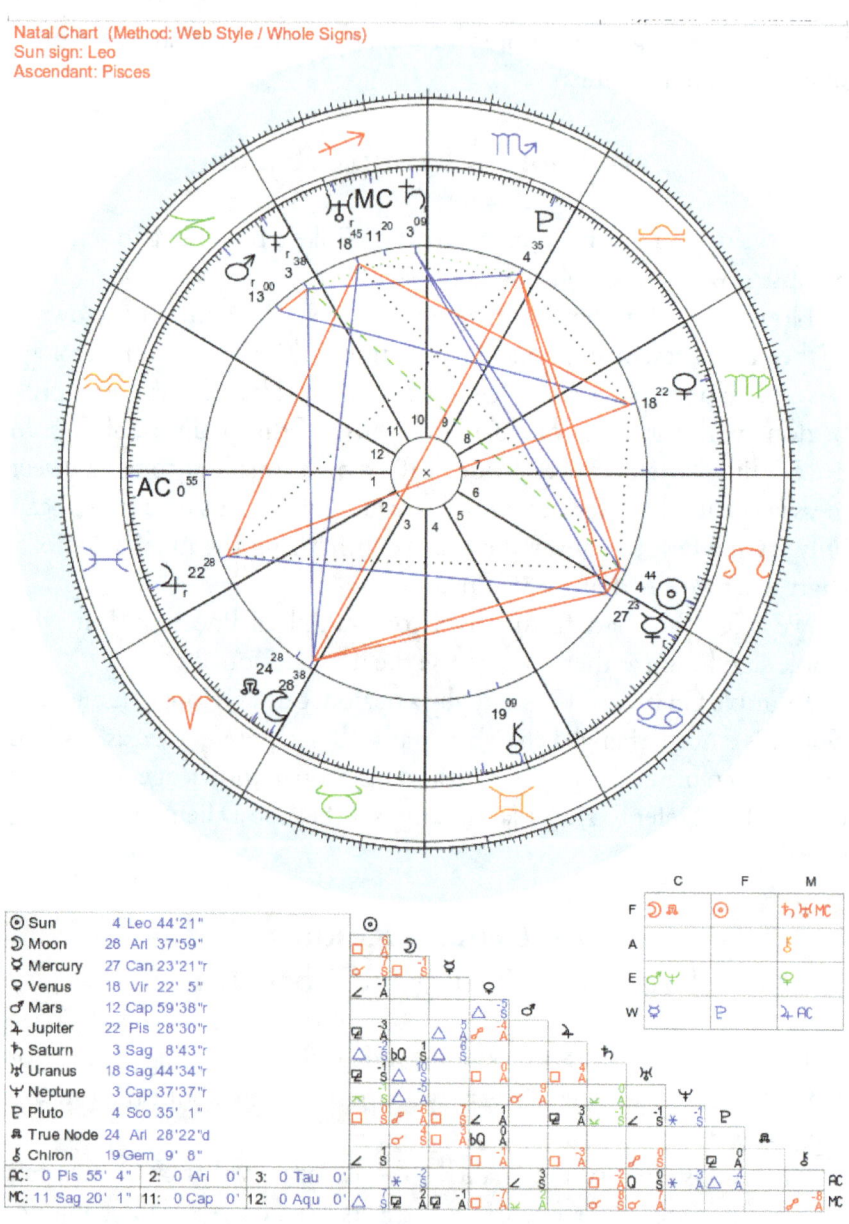

Natal Chart (Method: Web Style / Whole Signs)
Sun sign: Leo
Ascendant: Pisces

☉ Sun	4 Leo 44'21"
☽ Moon	28 Ari 37'59"
☿ Mercury	27 Can 23'21"r
♀ Venus	18 Vir 22' 5"
♂ Mars	12 Cap 59'38"r
♃ Jupiter	22 Pis 28'30"r
♄ Saturn	3 Sag 8'43"r
♅ Uranus	18 Sag 44'34"r
♆ Neptune	3 Cap 37'37"r
♇ Pluto	4 Sco 35' 1"
☊ True Node	24 Ari 28'22"d
⚷ Chiron	19 Gem 9' 8"
AC:	0 Pis 55' 4"	2: 0 Ari 0'	3: 0 Tau 0'
MC:	11 Sag 20' 1"	11: 0 Cap 0'	12: 0 Aqu 0'

proud of yourself, like you felt like you knew who you are, like you were on the right path, like you were in control of your destiny.

For instance, our example chart (EC) has their Sun in Leo, emphasizing a proud, playful, friendly, boastful, ambitious sense of self identity. However, being in the 6th house, the sense of self may be a little more muted, especially as it spends its time focused on sixth house themes of materiality, organization, restructuring, routine, and personal health habits; a Sun so involved in these activities does not have much time to focus on radiating selfhood, but will affirm itself through them. Pets may be particularly important to EC (6th house), especially cats (Leo, literally felines). Additionally, EC's Sun receives a very close square (07', that is, 0.12 of a degree) from Pluto in the 9th house, suggesting that themes of compulsion, obsessiveness, and desire for control figure strongly, giving the identity a Plutonian streak that wants to survive, and somehow a relationship to authority, institutional powers, or religion (9th house) has something to do with it. At the same time, the Sun receives a supporting trine from Saturn in the 10th house, which fortifies the personal vitality and sense of self. It is made sturdier, more responsible, and more patient. Since Saturn sends its trine to the Sun from the 10th house of career, self identity is also wrapped up into it. The Sun in this chart is very "active" and takes many other aspects, but we don't want to spend too much time dwelling on the other planets just yet.

Next, examine the Moon, similarly asking how its themes of emotional safety, comfort, nurturing, survival, and the overall temperament of the mind express themselves in its sign. Relate this to when you've reacted instinctively and emotionally, like when feeling moody, hungry, tired, cranky, caring, sympathetic, cozy—or even emotional extremes such as terror, rage, passion, joy.

EC's Moon is in the 2nd house in Aries which suggests that emotions are experienced very intensely, in a highly reactive and excitable way (Aries), and that having resources (2nd house) for survival and competition is important to feel safe. For bellicose Aries this can mean ownership of weapons, trophies, or even an athletic body. Being in the "bad" 2nd house may mean that EC's emotionality is somehow mishandled, which in the 2H I find manifests most often as increased insecurity and neediness until these resources are acquired. The Moon is actually involved in a T-square with Pluto and the Sun, which further intensifies the story of the Sun. The opposition to Pluto again suggests themes of obsession and control, and we can describe this as an internal dynamic of needing to control and transform one's own emotional nature, even if that means engaging in self-destructive habits and emotional patterns which leaks over into treatment of one's possessions since the Moon is in the 2nd house. However, the Moon's trine to Neptune in the 11th house suggests that aspiring to community oriented ideals is a fruitful endeavor for this person, especially when they are applied ambitiously and constructively (Capricorn).

Next, we look at the ascendant (AC).[19] Because the ascendant is in Pisces, my first thought is that EC is likely to have a receptive, open affect and be very sensitive to the moods and feelings of others. The AC, being an incredibly sensitive point, will also be modulated by close aspects it receives, and it does receive a sextile from Neptune, a square from Saturn, a trine from Pluto, and a sextile from the Moon. The most major aspects, the square and trine, will tend to make EC's presentation more business-like and reserved (square Saturn) while simultaneously having an alluring intensity and magnetism (trine Pluto). The AC will also be modulated by the presence of any planets in the first house. In this case the traditional ruler of Pisces, Jupiter, is there, making Jupiter's significations of a jovial, optimistic attitude and spiritual orientation even more prominent in the personality and expression. Finally, the close sextiles from the Moon and Neptune will add hints of a dreamy intuition (Neptune) as well as making the emotions easy to read, especially when stimulated (Moon). There is a LOT going on with EC's ascendant!

Finally, we need to look at the EC's chart ruler, or the planet that rules the sign of the Ascendant. Since the AC is in Pisces and Jupiter is the traditional ruler of Pisces, the chart ruler is Pisces, who we've already spotted. The chart ruler generally describes the fundamental nature of the native and a polarization toward certain modes of expression described by the planets. If we recall our polytheistic metaphor, the chart ruler is like the native's "patron god", and we can use this as a broad categorizational tool for describing the modalities and favored experiences that people pursue:

- Sun (Leo rising) — Solar people
- Moon (Cancer rising) — Lunar people
- Mercury (Gemini or Virgo rising) — Mercurial people

---

19   For my own interpretation I like to look at the ascendant first, because its placement dictates the house placement and thus relative strength of both the Sun and Moon. However, I usually describe the Sun to clients first because that's their typically their first contact with astrology.

- Venus (Taurus or Libra rising) — Venusian people
- Mars (Aries or Scorpio rising) — Martian people
- Jupiter (Sagittarius or Pisces rising) — Jovian people
- Saturn (Capricorn or Aquarius rising) — Saturnian people

Depending on the structure of the entire chart, it's possible that the chart ruler will not be as emphasized or another planet could be overwhelmingly emphasized, which can overtake the influence of the ruling planet in the native's subjective experience. However, the chart ruler will always be an important placement, especially by transit.

Whew! Let's now move on to Mercury, Venus, and Mars. We will get a little bit deeper into rulership schemes and the relationships between planets. Don't worry if it makes your head spin a little bit—take each concept one at a time and feel free to skim and double back later.

Mercury, Venus, Mars

These three planets show how we think and express (Mercury), how we love and value (Venus), and how we assert and achieve (Mars). Depending on these planets' relationship to the Sun, Moon and Ascendant (especially if ruling the ascendant) as well as their prominence in the chart they can be more or less emphasized in the personality and as a part of the individual's core experience.

Mercury

In EC's chart, Mercury is placed in the fifth house of Cancer. Mercury in Cancer tends to indicate that thoughts are intimately tied to the emotions. EC likely has good memory but personal feelings, emotions, and memories can interfere with intellectual objectivity. There may be an especially strong tendency to reflect on the past due to Cancer's concern with family, sentimentality, history, as well as the fact that Mercury is retrograde. Being in the 5th house it's likely that the mind is generative, creative, playful, and more extroverted than normal, and EC may have a particular love of intellectually-oriented (Mercury) games (5th house). The square that Mercury receives from the Moon in the second house indicates that emotionality is likely to interfere with EC's intellectual processes, especially when they are feeling stressed about needs and possessions related to survival. It can be difficult to express one's emotions clearly, because the relationship between between Moon (emotions) and Mercury (verbal/intellectual expression) is strained and discordant (square aspect).

There's an additional intricacy here: the Moon rules Cancer, and thus has a say in Mercury's ability to function. The Moon's condition thus becomes important for Mercury. Being in Aries, EC's emotional nature is likely to be bold, aggressive, and assertive, which will influnce Mercury's expression to be similar. This can grant EC a sharp wit and biting tongue. The fact that Mercury's ruler squares it can also be read something like, "Mercury in the Moon's home but the Moon is pissed about it", making Mercury's expression "stressed". The fact that Mercury also receives a sign opposition (sign-based aspect) adds more fuel to the fire, resulting in tension between EC's highly ambitious, persistent, disciplined approach (Capricorn) to problem solving (Mars) and their more emotional outward expression. Mars is especially powerful in Capricorn, due to its status of **exaltation** in that sign.[20] Thus, Mars likely "overpowers" or "overstimulates" Mercury, giving it a more blunt, matter of fact, no-nonsense edge. This, in tandem with Mercury being under the Moon's rulership and harsh aspect, can indicate that EC frequently speaks much more forcefully than they mean to, does not shy away from argumentation, and knows how to wield emotions as a weapon. This is not someone I want to get into a serious argument with!

Venus

Venus is in Virgo in the 7th house. In Virgo, Venus is in its **fall**, which is the opposite of exaltation, where the planet cannot perform its functions as effectively.[21] Venus in Virgo often makes the native very picky and particular (Virgo) about romantic partners, aesthetic experiences, and valuables (Venus), often rejecting romance due to its (sometimes

---

20   Every traditional planet is exalted in one sign.

21   Every traditional planet is also fallen in one sign, which is the sign opposing the sign in which it has exaltation. Thus, Venus' sign of exaltation is Pisces.

impossibly) high standards. This reflects Venus' fall in Virgo, since a hyper-picky Venus does not get to experience much of its entire point—love, sensuality, pleasure, and the richness of life. EC's Venus story gets more complicated when we note that Jupiter opposes Venus while both Uranus and Chiron square her, which actually forms a "grand cross" aspect pattern, which is two pairs of oppositions perpendicular to each other, resulting in four squares. These are very intense configurations, as each planet is involved in *three* dynamic aspects at once with every other planet in the grand cross. Generally we can understand the grand cross as a incessant circulation of dynamic energy between each planet which requires each placement's expression to be reorganized and reformed. Due to the constant dynamic energy coursing through its poles, a grand cross is often both a significant struggle but also a massive source of generative energy for the native. If they succeed in figuring out how to allow the inner dynamics represented by a grand cross flow more smoothly, this configuration becomes a powerful engine that can propel the native to even greater heights.

In examining Venus we can look at each placement of the grand cross in turn. Uranus, being closest in aspect, will be experienced the most strongly, and Uranus is the planet of sudden changes, excitement, genius, technology that helps humanity advance, and revolutionary impulses. In square to Venus from the 10th house we can say it's likely that EC's love nature (Venus) is prone to a constant and pressing need (square) for excitement (Uranus), but also that EC's professional life (10H) can be disruptive to their love life—both in exhilirating, exciting ways and unexpected, undesired ways. Uranus also makes Venus very demanding in general, requiring constant stimulation and excitement that most potential partners would not be able to keep up with.

Meanwhile, Chiron is squaring Venus second most closely. Chiron has to do with one's core wounds, and in the 4th house of foundations, Chiron likely signifies a complex relationship with the family and early life, particularly around the topics of speaking, knowledge, and information due to its placement in Gemini. Chiron's themes tend to be experienced in an extremely individual way[22] and attempting to delineate

---

22   As *Anna Karenina* begins: "All happy families are alike; each unhappy family is unhappy in its own way."

the specifics of EC's experience without their input and consent would likely be infringing as well as incorrect. What we can say is that it's very likely that these themes of core wounds, healing, and turning pain into sources of wisdom impact EC's love nature significantly, and are somehow related to the Uranian themes of sudden upheaval, concern for the collective (often over the individual and personal), and unreliability. It's also interesting to note that Chiron sacrificed his immortality for Prometheus, the figure most closely associated with Uranus, and in EC's chart they are in direct opposition, suggesting that their themes have come into conflict.

Finally, Jupiter, EC's chart ruler, opposes Venus. While no harsh aspect between the benefics (Venus and Jupiter) will ever be excessively negative in the way the malefics are frequently described, an opposition between Jupiter and Venus could be described as "an abundance challenge". Jupiter, being in his domicile in Pisces, is particularly strong, and likely to overpower Venus in her fall in Virgo. This may be experienced as a significant focus on EC's personal experience of self, as this is a core area for growth and sense of fulfillment that may be detrimental or excessive in the face of Venus' particular requirements in Virgo under pressure from both Uranus and Chiron.

You'll notice that as we delineate Venus, we are already beginning to delineate the other planets. This is unavoidable, especially when a placement is in tight aspect pattern with multiple others, as placements impact and color one another by their relationships.

Mars

Mars is in Capricorn in the 11th house. Mars in Capricorn usually shows a very strong work ethic and the ability to persevere tough conditions, and there is often be a bent towards traditional approaches to accomplishing tasks and doing things "the right way". In the 11th house this effort is strongly concerned with social groups, clubs, organizations, and helping people en masse. Mars' placement here indicates that EC's efforts are likely put toward groups of people, and that the default way in which EC goes about accomplishing tasks (Mars) will often involve many people building something (Capricorn) together (11th house).

Mars makes wide harmonious aspects to both Venus and Capricorn, suggesting that the themes the opposition these two planets represents can be resolved through Mars-like activity. For EC, this means applying dedicated energy and effort towards accomplishing goals with or for other people could be a fruitful way to express both Jupiter's powerful draw toward personal experience, identity, and meaning, as well as satisfy Venus' criteria by finding potential friends and romantic partners while working on these group projects. Mars does not make aspect to the other outer planets in EC's grand cross, Uranus and Chiron, suggesting that Mars' exertion is somewhat irrelevant to the themes of these planets in EC's experience.

EC's Mars is also copresent (in the same sign) with Neptune, which augments both the expression of Mars but also 11th house activities in general for EC. This could mean that Mars-like activity is often inspired by some sort of ideal vision or vague intuitions. In grounded and concrete Capricorn, Neptune's influence is likely utilized toward bringing these visions into manifest reality. Neptune is related to music, film, and the arts in general, so one example interpretation could be an interest in social dancing which combines the vigorous and physical energy of Mars in Capricorn, the group nature of the 11th house, and the inspired and artistic elements of Neptune.

Jupiter and Saturn

Jupiter and Saturn, the last two planets the ancients considered, were considered to be the major indicators of passages of history. They conjoin every 20 years, and do so in signs of the same element for 200 years at a time, marking the nature of that era.[23] These planets relate to forces and themes that connect us to the larger society and era we live within. In a natal chart, Jupiter shows where and how we tend to experience blessings, luck, growth, and our relationship to institutions of higher learning, law, and foreign cultures. Saturn shows where and how we tend to experience limitations and restrictions that demand hard work and responsibility, as well as our relationship to authority figures begin-

---

23   In late 2020, we marked a new epoch as Jupiter and Saturn made their first conjunction in the air sign Aquarius.

ning with our parents and evolving to governments, bureaucracy, and societal expectations.

Jupiter

In EC's chart, Jupiter is strongly placed in the first house, in its domicile in Pisces. This can indicate an overall sense of optimism about oneself, as the sense of personal identity is blessed by Jupiter's presence. Especially since EC's ascendant is also in Pisces, there's likely a tendency to an overall dreamy, intuitive sense of one's own possibility and luck and a particular draw toward sublimative, Piscean experiences such as art, religion, love, or perhaps even mind-altering substances and liquids.

However, Jupiter's participation in the powerful grand cross covered earlier is significant. These sources of joy can be opposed by an overly picky aesthetic taste (opposition to Venus in Virgo), occasionally disrupted in sudden and unexpected ways (square from Uranus), or tinged by experiences of old wounds and trauma (square from Chiron). However, as both benefics are involved in the grand cross, this is likely not experienced as harshly as if one or both of the malefics, Saturn and Mars, were involved in this configuration. Overall, EC likely experiences recognition and joy (Jupiter) through the expression of who they fundamentally are (1st house), especially when done sensitively and poetically (Pisces). Jupiter is also trine Mercury, suggesting that intellectual pursuits are particularly rewarding but also that they have the same (sometimes boastful) optimism that Jupiter provides.

Saturn

Saturn is very close to the highest point in EC's chart, the Midheaven, and already quite prominent just for being in the 10th house. For all of the dreamy and joyous elements of a Pisces Jupiter in EC's personal identity, Saturn shows a strong propensity for work and EC may be seen (midheaven, visibility) as an authority in their field. Whichever house Saturn is in, the native often experiences a powerful sense of obligation, duty, pressure, or responsibility related to that house's themes. In the 10th house, Saturn often drives one to work extraordinarily hard, often toward great personal accomplishment. Saturn's close trine to the Sun reiterates this theme, suggesting a very strong work ethic and general sense of responsibility and duty, as well as the opportunity to receive recognition (the Sun and 10th house) through that hard work. In Sagittarius, Saturn becomes concerned with matters of truth, higher learning, government, international affairs, and philosophy, and Saturn is often an indicator of the career of the native, especially when in a career-oriented house such as the 2nd, 6th, or 10th.

Uranus, Neptune, and Pluto

Being relatively recent discoveries, the outer planets Uranus, Neptune, and Pluto exist outside of the traditions of ancient astrology. Thematically, Jupiter and Saturn connect the native to society, culture, and history at large, and I treat the "outers" as connecting the native to forces and energies beyond what is recognized as ordinarily human. I find that they often override one's personal choice, presenting themselves as unavoidable energies that must be incorporated into the personality, rather than elements that come directly from oneself.

Uranus

Like Saturn, Uranus is also very prominent in EC's chart, being in the 10th house and so close to the midheaven. Because of this, Uranus' influence may be particularly noticeable to others and in EC's career: EC might be considered somehow revolutionary or eccentric in their approach to their work, career, and general reputation. We've discussed Uranus' influence on Venus and Jupiter, adding an element of disruption and discomfort (square) to both of these planets' functioning which demands novel and exciting (Uranus) modes of expressing these their themes. Uranus' close proximity to both of these placements also suggests that experiences ruled by Jupiter and Venus are prone to sudden changes in general throughout life. For Venus this can mean unexpected events in the realms of love and friendship, and for Jupiter it could mean sudden rewards and boons.

Neptune

Neptune tends to bring transcendent experiences, inexplicable intuition, and creative inspiration as well as evasive tendencies, irrational fears, and unreasonable expectations which cannot live up to reality. Its house position shows where the native tends to experience these the most. In the 11th house, Neptune likely colors EC's experience of the collective, public sphere with idealism and visions of what could possibly be built (Capricorn) together. At the same time, Neptune sometimes brings experiences of dissolution, either from the native themself or in the experience related to the house's themes. For instance, EC may sometimes retreat or avoid those same groups they're invested in, or at times the group may seem to evade or disappear from them. In a more general way, Neptune can bring feelings of confusion or lack of clarity around the topics of the house and sign it sits within.

Pluto

When Pluto is configured closely to personal planets it is often experienced very intensely. Pluto's darker themes are domination, control, obsession, paranoia, compulsion, secrecy, and sometimes violence. However, Pluto also has to do with deep transformation, accountability, ownership of self, and spiritual transcendence of its heaviest themes. In opposition to EC's Moon, Pluto can add a powerful need to hone, control, and transform the emotional self, and in the 2nd house, perhaps the body. In the 9th house, there may also be themes of control and power struggles related to academia, authority, or even occult and paranormal studies (Scorpio). Pluto also makes a very close square to EC's Sun, which can serve as an extremely powerful energy source as its intensity stimulates the Sun which represents one's vital energy. Along with this powerful energy can also come Pluto's negative aspects of paranoia, suspicion, hypervigilance, and the need to carefully control one's image, one of the Sun's concern (especially in Leo).

North Node, Midheaven, and Chiron

We'll touch briefly upon the North Node, Midheaven, and Chiron, as they are placements that are almost always important but highly contextual in a person's chart.

North Node

In my experience the North Node always has a significant story to tell in a natal chart, especially if it is closely aspecting a planet. In EC's chart it is conjunct the Moon in the 2nd house, suggesting that the dynamic the Moon represents for EC is a significant area of learning and development for EC. In Aries, the North Node emphasizes the need for the native to learn to fight for themselves, respecting their own needs and desires, and possibly even to learn to actively compete with or lead others. In the second house it also suggests the need to grapple with possessions in some way; combined with Aries this can be abstract possessions such as pride or courage, or physical trophies representing personal victories. Another interpretation could be the individual need to fight for one's own belongings; the south node as a counterbalance in Libra in the 8th house can suggest a tendency to overfocus on what other people have or need, or other people's problems.

Midheaven

The Midheaven is placed in the 10th house in Sagittarius. I tend to interpret the midheaven as the "style" of one's public recognition and accomplishments, so in Sagittarius it will tend to be bold, blunt, optimistic, direct, and honest—all Sagittarian themes. EC's capital-W Work may also involve mundane Sagittarian things such as philosophy, law, religion, international travel, diplomacy, etc. With the Midheaven almost exactly between Saturn and Uranus, EC's contributions likely also have to do with combining the traditional (Saturn) and the cutting edge (Uranus).[24]

---

24 This is a hint at another astrological technique called "midpoints", which are what they sound like: the middle point between two placements.

Chiron

We have already touched on Chiron in some detail while discussing his role in the grand cross formation. The themes for Chiron in EC's life likely involve family, the past, knowledge, information, ideas, speech, or perhaps even siblings (Gemini). Opposing Uranus it is likely that the nature of Chiron's wound is sudden or unusual, and may also involve love (Venus) or spirituality (Jupiter).

In Summary

We covered a massive amount of information in a short space. With all of this in mind, we can now tell a story about EC. This is someone who is optimistic, determined, who has experienced difficulty resolving the tension between their inner world and refined tastes and possible heartaches, but manages it all with a sense of discipline and duty. They have much to learn in the realm of fighting for their own stake in things and possibly managing a fiery temper and the tendency to lash out emotionally. Nonetheless, they are devoted to helping others, and they likely keep their commitments and promises.

As you have likely noticed, no placement in the chart lives in a vacuum. Each placement is colored by its house, sign, and its relationships to other placements by aspect and rulership. This is why descriptions of placements you find online or in astrology references which describe placements by house or sign often fall flat: they cannot possibly capture the highly contextual expression of a planet in an actual chart. These sorts of descriptions can certainly be useful as a baseline when learning, but you need to use your discernment to tease apart the core essence of each placement and how they relate to the other placements influencing them.

Midpoints are beyond the scope of this guide, but they add another rich and fascinating layer of complexity to the natal chart.

Closing Thoughts and Pointers

We have only done this reading for EC as an example in lieu of being able to go over your chart together. When it comes to reading your own chart, you have a bit of a challenge before you. Since all experiences are divided into various parts of the astrological system—signs, planets, aspects, houses, and more—we must make judgments as to what parts of our experience map onto what parts of our chart, at the same time we are learning about their various meanings. Astrology is also the first time many engage seriously with a system of self-knowledge, and confronting yourself can be disorienting in terms of figuring out what placements actually apply to you versus the natural tendency to want to see yourself (or NOT want to see yourself) in some placements. When I was first learning astrology, as I read more charts I began to realize just how vastly different other people were for me, and I developed a deep appreciation for how unique and deeply individual each person's experience can be. If you do this too, you will develop a refined sense of where the boundaries lie between archetypal significations, and will gain the ability to make increasingly precise interpretations of various placements. This is where your ability to hold the different components of your chart and reflect them against your own experience with honesty and discernment will shine through.

It's important to note that while astrological delineations as a broader collection of knowledge have been honed over time through repeated observation, every astrologer is an individual person who brings their own education, perspective, and experience to bear. When reading a chart "cold" like this, the best any astrologer can do is use the tools and wisdom at their disposal, but in a real reading setting the human being represented by the chart is needed to add their own experience, or at least affirm or adjust interpretations. While it can be very impressive to pull accurate interpretations out of thin air, ultimately a chart reading is for helping someone understand themselves, not to show off (though occasionally people are hoping for exactly that!).

This means it's important to keep flexibility in mind when learning astrology. Astrology is a dynamic system that results from the interplay between past, present, and future; astrologer and native; self and world. We will forever be iterating to the true essence of a human hinted at by the stars. Be wary of anyone who claims to have the ultimate truth, use scare tactics, or otherwise tell you that they have it all figured out. Do not be overly credulous. Think critically about what you read. I also recommend you ignore anything or anyone that tells you that something will or will not happen in your life as if it were a sure thing: do not give your fate away. Not to a book, or any author, no matter how much you grow to like or respect them. Never let someone else act as your brain, not even this guide—I have my own biases and slants, too.

And finally, never forget the person. The chart is just a map. And if you do choose to read for someone, treat their chart with kindness and dignity, because you hold a map of their life in your hands.

Approaches to Reading a Chart

In examining EC's chart we took a rather structured approach, working through the placements from the Sun and out. However, there are many ways to approach opening up a chart and find meaning and stories.

Here's a list of things you can try:

- Work through the Sun and out as we did
- Identify the chart ruler (planet ruling the sign of the ascendant)
- Examine the elemental composition of the chart to see compatibility between signs and general intrapersonal dynamics
- Look for hotspots in the chart—clusters of planets or heavily packed signs and houses
- Note the closest aspects
- Pick a planet and start from there, looking at its aspects, rulerships, function by house, and devise its story
- Identify interrelating themes among planets, houses, and signs
- Just gaze at the chart and see what arises in your intuition

You can start with one and go organically, or take a rigorous, structured line to reading through a chart. It's completely up to you, and I encourage you to experiment.

Where to go Next

If you've found reading your own chart to be an interesting experience and want to learn more, the best thing I can recommend is to pick up some good books and read more charts.

I can recommend the following books:

- *The Only Astrology Book You'll Ever Need* by Joanna Woolfolk — this is the first astrology book I ever read. While it overreaches in some places, it's an entertaining introduction with lots of colorful anecdotes and a great broad overview into the world of modern psychological astrology.
- *The Astrologer's Handbook* by Sakoian and Acker — more traditional and technical introduction to astrology along with an astrological dictionary, and their 3 related books on prediction, synastry, and patterns—better if you're looking for an astrology manual
- Stephen Arroyo's *Chart Interpretation Handbook* — useful reference guide at a high, process—oriented level which says plenty while avoiding being overly prescriptive
- *The Inner Sky* by Steven Forrest — I haven't personally read this one but if you're looking for an evolutionary/reincarnative astrology guide, Steven Forrest is excellent and this book comes highly recommended
- *Astrology, Psychology, and the Four Elements* by Stephen Arroyo — another Arroyo book at a somewhat higher level, this is a fantastic book for thinking about astrology in terms of the elements
- *Hellenistic Astrology* by Chris Brennan — an absolute tome of a book on the history and practice of ancient, Hellenistic astrology, but if you want to learn the roots of astrology you will find it here
- *Ancient Astrology Vol. I* by Demetra George — another take on the ancient astrology corpus, this book is more focused as a manual with less historical context than Brennan's book. Volume II is on the way soon!
- *Seven Stars Astrology* by Ant — technically a blog but practically a book (or an entire journal) in its depth and exploration of ancient astrology. Well worth your time once you have a grounding

in the basics, but SSA does also have a beginner's guide series you can explore

That should be plenty to get you started!

If you're interested in looking at the natal charts of public figures, I can highly recommend Astro-Databank and Astro-Seek.com. Astro-Databank has a massive collection of tagged and categorized natal charts of public figures, as well as a search engine tool for finding charts by specific criteria such as vocation, lifestyle, etc.

Finally, for a miscellany of astrology-related resources and content (amongst other weird things), you can check out my Obsidian homepage, a website hosted out of my personal notes.[25]

Thank You

That's everything. Well, everything that barely scratches the surface. We of course did not touch on the astrology of compatibility, family dynamics, finance, prediction, world events, and everything else that can be correlated and observed through the vast and powerful lens of astrology.

There are whole lifetimes of study that could be devoted to astrology, and I'm grateful I have had the opportunity to spend a solid chunk of mine on it. I'm also incredibly grateful to those who have supported me, tolerated me, and challenged me throughout my journey, including my personal friends and family, fellow astrologers, strangers who took a risk on purchasing readings from me, and my incredible Twitter friends and following, all of whom without I would not be where I am today.

I'd especially like to thank Alex Criddle for his ever patient support as I've nursed this writing into existence, and for giving me a reason to push it to its final form. And most especially, I'd like to thank you. If you read this guide, thank you so much for your time, interest, and investment. I promise that if you continue to approach astrology with an open mind, you will find that reality is far richer, and far more mysterious, than most would have you believe. It has indelibly changed my life for the better,

---

25 My Obsidian homepage can be found at publish.obsidian.md/sadalsvvd/

and if you have the temperament for it, it may be able to do the same for you.

Works Cited

Ant, *Seven Stars Astrology: Ancient Hellenistic and Persian Astrology in Practice*, sevenstarsastrology.com.

Arroyo, Stephen, *Astrology, Psychology, and the Four Elements: An Energy Approach to Astrology and Its Use in the Counseling Arts* (CRCS Publications, 1978).

————, *Chart Interpretation Handbook: Guidelines for Understanding the Essentials of the Birth Chart* (CRCS Publications, 2004).

Bernie Ashman, "What Do Planets in Intercepted Signs Mean?" January 8, 2018, llewellyn.com.

Brennan, Chris, "The Planetary Joys and the Origins of the Significations of the Houses and Triplicities," hellenisticastrology.com.

————, *Hellenistic Astrology: The Study of Fate and Fortune* (Amor Fati Publications, 2017).

Forrest, Stephen, *The Inner Sky: How to Make Wiser Choices for a More Fulfilling Life* (Seven Paws Press, reprint edition, 2012).

Garrison, Cal, "Intercepted Signs," November 13, 2019, mountaintimes. info.

George, Demetra, *Ancient Astrology in Theory and Practice: A Manual of Traditional Techniques, Volume I: Assessing Planetary Condition* (Rubedo Press, 2019).

Grasse, Ray, "Tectonic Triggers: The Hidden Power of Station Points (Part 1)," 2015, astro.com.

Green, Deva "Evolutionary Astrology: What the Moon's Nodes Mean in Your Chart," August 25, 2014, llewellyn.com.

Rudhyar, Dane, *The Astrological Houses: The Spectrum of Individual Experience* (Doubleday Paperbacks, 1972).

Sakoian, Frances and Louis S. Acker, *The Astrologer's Handbook* (Harper & Row, 1973).

Spiller, Jan, *Astrology for the Soul* (Bantam, 1997).

Sutton, Komilla, "Rahu Ketu: The Shadow Planets," komilla.com.

Whitaker, Anne, "The Moon's Nodes in Action," 2015, astro.com.
Woolfolk, Joanna Martine, *The Only Astrology Book You'll Ever Need* (Taylor Trade Publishing, 2012).

Bells and Spells:
Rosicrucianism and the Invocation of Planetary Spirits in Early Modern Germany

Hereward Tilton

Regarded as illicit by the major Christian confessions, the invocation of planetary spirits maintained a limited currency within a network of interrelated Paracelsian, Rosicrucian and Behmenist traditions in early modern Germany, primarily via a little-known Christian Cabalistic manuscript lineage I will address in the following paper. The value of these manuscripts within the economy of religious knowledge arose from their depiction of practical invocative techniques—fasting, prayer, entheogen use and quasi-Tantric ascetic practices—designed to cultivate altered states of consciousness. As post-Enlightenment historiographies of religion remain deeply informed by Protestant anti-enthusiasm, these techniques and their associated doctrines continue to be represented as a magical counter-category to both Christian faith and modern science; but for all their Neoplatonic and Jewish roots, they are more accurately described as marginalised forms of Christian religiosity. Within this suppressed form of Christianity the planetary intelligences constitute indispensable steps on an inner path to gnosis conceived as the reversal of an emanationist cosmogony. Despite the best efforts of Catholic, Lutheran and Calvinist authorities to abolish this alternative Christian worldview and way of life, the invocation of planetary spirits and the related theurgical animation of statues persisted among inheritors of the inspirationist tendency of the so-called Radical Reformation.

Today there is a growing recognition among scholars that 'magic' has always been the religion of an Other.[1] The identity of that magical Other has remained surprisingly constant within the broader history of Christian discourse on magic, as has Christian orthodoxy's hegemonic concern with the preservation of institutional power and a monopoly on the valid expression of religiosity.

As a polemical category, the term 'magic' first arose amongst the ancient Greeks in reference to practices originating among the Persian priests (*mágoi*); while *mageía* could be envisaged as an exotic but entirely legitimate *prisca theologia*, it also possessed the negative connotation of fraudulent wonder-working techniques lacking any sophisticated theological superstructure or higher philosophical intent.[2] Similar positive and pejorative characterisations of *magia* persisted in pagan Rome: both are depicted side-by-side in the *Apologia* of Apuleius, for example, while the conception of magic as a set of barbarous, charlatanic techniques qualitatively different to religion was most influentially advanced in the work of Pliny.[3]

By contrast, the Church Fathers employed the term in a purely negative sense against the gnostic-emanationist pagan competitors of the early Christian Church. Thus Augustine (354–430)—utilizing magic as a synonym for Neoplatonic and Hermetic theurgy—condemned the summoning of celestial intermediaries between humankind and higher divinity, declaring that anyone who has recourse to such 'demons' has strayed from 'divine religion'.[4] His words were aimed specifically at the

---

1   On magic and the demarcation of the boundaries of religion, see Randall Styers, *Making Magic: Religion, Magic and Science in the Modern World* (New York: Oxford University Press, 2004), pp. 96–116.

2   E.g. the positive connotation of Plato, *Alcibiades* 1.121e–122a, in Plato, *Alcibiades*, ed. Nicholas Denyer (Cambridge: Cambridge University Press, 2001), p. 60, and the negative connotation of Euripides, *Orestes* 1497, in Euripides, *Orestes*, ed. and trans. Robin Waterfield (Oxford: Oxford University Press, 2001), p. 89.

3   Apuleius, *Apologia*, pp. 25–26, in Apuleius, *Pro se de magia*, ed. Vincent Hunink (Leiden: Brill, 1997), pp. 86–90; Pliny, *Naturalis historia* 30.1–7, in Pliny, *Natural History libri XXVIII- XXXII*, ed. and trans. W. H. S. Jones (Cambridge, MA: Harvard University Press, 1963), pp. 279–283.

4   Augustine, *De civitate Dei* 8.24, 10.9, in Augustine, *The City of God*

statue-animating passages of the Hermetic *Asclepius,* which described the drawing down of celestial spirits into their artificial likenesses for divinatory purposes, and which was to inform subsequent Christian controversies regarding talismanic magic.[5] Such astrological divination not only contravened Augustine's teachings on free will, but also posed the threat of a surreptitious pagan influence within the Church, as the pagan gods were linked to the heavenly bodies as their rulers.[6] If these celestial beings existed at all, as rivals of the Church they could be nothing other than malevolent, and Augustine warned they must be distinguished clearly from the higher angels and other benevolent (Christian) powers of the supercelestial heavens.[7]

The defenders of nascent Christian orthodoxy also demonized gnostic emanationist rivals within the early Church's own ranks by blackening their names—e.g. Simon Magus, Marcus, Priscillian—with accusations of 'magic'.[8] The purpose of this polemic was not only to segregate the divine from the natural realms, but first and foremost to obstruct access to the divine via emanationist conceptions of nature, thus establishing the priests, rites and doctrines of the Church as the sole legitimate avenue to God.[9]

---

against the Pagans, Vol. 3, ed. and trans. David Wiesen (Cambridge, MA: Harvard University Press, 1968), pp. 116–129, p. 287.

5   *Asclepius* 24, 37, in Brian Copenhaver, trans., *Hermetica* (Cambridge: Cambridge University Press, 2000), pp. 81, 89–90.

6   Augustine himself had 'worshipped' these stellar and planetary rulers in his Manichaean years: *Confessiones* 3.6, 4.3, in Augustine, *Confessions,* Vol. 1, trans. William Watts (London: William Heinemann, 1912), pp. 114–121, pp. 153-157.

7   Augustine, *De civitate Dei* 10.26 (Augustine, *City of God,* pp. 369–370); in another place (*Ad Orosium contra Priscillianistas et Origenistas* 11.14) Augustine appeals to Sirach 3.22 ('what is hidden is not your concern') when considering the existence of planetary intelligences (Augustine, *Aurelii Augustini opera,* Vol. 15, No. 3 (Turnhout: Brepols, 1985), p. 177).

8   Acts 8.9-11; Irenaeus, *Adversus haereses* 1.15.6, 1.23.1, in Irenaeus, *Against the Heresies,* Vol. 1, No. 1, ed. and trans. Dominic Unger (New York: Newman Press, 1992), pp. 68, 81–82; Sulpicius Severus, *Historia sacra* 2.46, in Sulpicius Severus, *Historia sacra* (Leiden: Ex officinâ Elseviriorum, 1635), pp. 165–166.

9   This refusal of interaction with intermediary spirits is also evident

The close association of the polemic against magic with the marginalization of gnostic-emanationist religiosity persisted within medieval Christendom. Above all, it was the quest for sources of healing in the natural world that brought clerics and lay Christians alike into perilous proximity with marginalized texts and practices, particularly those of Hermetic provenance. Enduring problems for the Church hierarchies were posed by the twelfth- and thirteenth-century Christian reception of the Arabic *Picatrix*, which depicted the preparation of talismans in the context of a Neoplatonic natural philosophy coloured by Sabian-Hermetic star worship. As divine cosmogonic emanations, stellar and planetary spirits lend their occult powers to stones, rings or other objects engraved with their characters at the appropriate astrological moment. Usually worn as amulets, such talismans were employed for purposes of healing, fertility and the mitigation of various worldly travails.[10]

Responding to this increasingly popular practice, Thomas Aquinas (ca. 1225–1274) proscribed the use of *verba ignota* (unknown words) or talismanic characters.[11] For Thomas, all linguistic signs (words, characters, symbolic figures) are invocative (or 'addressative', to use Weill-Parot's neologism)—that is to say, they all address an autonomous intelligence to obtain its aid in performing the magical operation.[12]

---

among the Platonist Church Fathers; Origen, for example, anticipates Augustine when he declares 'all the heathen gods are demons' (*Contra Celsum* 7.69, cf. Psalms 96.5), and insists that 'the high priest' Christ is the only valid intercessor for prayer and supplication (*Contra Celsum* 5.4) (Origen, *Contra Celsum*, ed. and trans. Henry Chadwick (Cambridge: Cambridge University Press, 2003), pp. 266, 452).

10 *Picatrix* 1.5. in pseudo-Maǧrīṭī, *Picatrix: das Ziel des Weisen*, ed. and trans. Hellmut Ritter and Martin Plessner (London: Warburg Institute, 1962), pp. 24–34, 111–113.

11 Thomas Aquinas, *Summa theologiae* 2.2.96, articles 1, 4, in Thomas Aquinas, *Summa theologica*, Vol. 3, Part 2, Section 2, trans. the Fathers of the English Dominican Province (New York: Cosimo Classics, 2007), pp. 1602–1606.

12 Nicolas Weill-Parot, 'Astral Magic and Intellectual Changes (Twelfth-Fifteenth Centuries): "Astrological Images" and the Concept of "Addressative" Magic', in *The Metamorphosis of Magic from Late Antiquity to the Early Modern Period*, ed. Jan Bremmer and Jan Veenstra (Leuven: Peeters, 2002), pp. 167–188, p. 169. See in particular Thomas Aquinas, *Contra Gentiles* 3.105.10-

While Thomas' *Summa theologiae* states that textual amulets with Christian *verba divina* are a legitimate means of protection and healing, their efficacy derives from an understanding of the sense of those divine words rather than any power inhering in the form of their characters.[13] Thomas concedes the natural materials with which such amulets are created may indeed receive beneficial occult virtues from the heavenly bodies, but the use of talismanic characters resembles an act of prayer, and any such act directed beneath the divine (supercelestial) hierarchy is necessarily demonic.[14]

This segregation of the illicit invocation of celestial intelligences from the licit natural magical manipulation of occult sympathies and antipathies in nature went hand-in-hand with a 'dis-integration' of the cosmos and the disciplines used to investigate it, leading to the propagation of a form of the Scholastic 'double truth' (*duplex veritas*). Hence in his *De mineralibus* Albertus Magnus (1193–1280) praised not only the art of making talismans but also its founder, Hermes; through the engraving of images upon stones and metals one may lawfully receive occult virtues from their source in the divine *nous* via their intermediaries in the hierarchy of being, the stars and planets.[15] Yet in his theological writings Albertus makes the contradictory claim that 'the art of images is wicked', as it inclines to idolatry via the ascription of divinity to the stars them-

---

12, in Thomas Aquinas, *On the Truth of the Catholic Faith. Summa Contra Gentiles*, Vol. 3, ed. and trans. Vernon Bourke (New York: Image Books, 1956), p. 96.

13   Aquinas, *Summa theologiae* 2.2.96, article 4: 'Chrysostomus dicit . . . ubi est virtus Evangelii? In figuris litterarum, an in intellectu sensuum?', etc., in Thomas Aquinas, *Summa theologiae*, Vol. 3 (Ottawa: Impensis Studii Generalis O. Pr., 1942), p. 225; cf. Aquinas, *Summa theologica*, p. 1606.

14   Aquinas, *Summa theologiae* 2.2.96, articles 2, 4 (Aquinas, *Summa theologica*, pp. 1602–1606); note Thomas concedes planetary and stellar talismans may indeed produce their intended effects, but these are not natural physical effects, as they are achieved only indirectly via the intellectual natures (demons) they invoke; Aquinas, *Contra Gentiles* 3.104.7–12, 3.106.1–10 (Aquinas, *On the Truth of the Catholic Faith*, pp. 91–93, pp. 97–99).

15   Albertus Magnus, *De mineralibus* 2.3.3, in Albertus Magnus, *Book of Minerals*, trans. Dorothy Wyckoff (Oxford: Clarendon Press, 1967), pp. 134–137.

selves.[16] Techniques that may be licit in a natural philosophical context are illicit for any religious purpose: while occult virtues devolve from God, the stars are merely impersonal media in the natural process of the impression of forms (as are the talismanic images themselves, which will eventually become 'cold and dead' once the operation is finished).[17]

This disintegrative astrologizing of natural philosophy was developed further by Pietro d'Abano (1250/1257–1316) in his *Conciliator* (ca. 1310), in which he attempted to explain the perceived efficacy of talismanic magic within a non-invocative Aristotelian framework. Subsequent generations came to associate d'Abano with the invocative magic of the *Picatrix*, in part due to his medical experimentation with a Hermetic solar talisman.[18] However, d'Abano rejected the intervention of planetary intelligences as conceived in Hebrew and Arabic magical texts; rather, he ascribed the efficacy of talismans merely to an intransitive psychosomatic force of the imagination.[19] Notwithstanding his considerable post-mortem reputation as a student of 'damned magic',[20]

---

16   Albertus Magnus, *Super sententiarum* II 7.9: 'Sed imaginum ars ideo mala est, quia inclinans est ad idololatriam per numen quod creditur esse in stellis', in Albertus Magnus, *Opera omnia*, Vol. 27, ed. Stephan Borgnet (Paris: Ludovic Vivès, 1894), p. 158.

17   Albertus Magnus, *De mineralibus* 2.3.3 (Albertus Magnus, *Book of Minerals*, p. 137).

18   The operation in question was derived from two related Hermetic texts: see Nicolas Weill-Parot, 'Arnaud de Villeneuve et les relations possibles entre le sceau du lion et l'alchimie', *Arxiu de textos Catalans antics* 23/24 (2005), pp. 269–280, pp. 271–272). The amalgamated texts are to be found inserted within the Latin version of the *Picatrix*—a fact that gave rise to the suspicion (noted in later manuscript copies of the *Picatrix* itself) that the *Picatrix* had been d'Abano's source; David Pingree, ed., *Picatrix: The Latin Version of the Ghāyat Al-Ḥakīm* (London: Warburg Institute, 1986), pp. 82–85, 242.

19   Pietro d'Abano, *Conciliator differentiarum philosophorum et medicorum* (Mantua: Johann Wurster and Thomas Septemcastrensis, 1472), f. 290r (Diff. 156); cf. Vittoria Perrone Compagni, 'La differenza 156 del *Conciliator*: una rilettura', *Annali del Dipartimento di Filosofia* 15 (2009): pp. 65–107, pp. 88–89.

20   Brian Copenhaver, *Symphorien Champier and the Reception of the Occultist Tradition in Renaissance France* (The Hague: Mouton Publishers, 1978), p. 150.

d'Abano's persecution by the Inquisition was probably inspired by the deterministic implications of his rational naturalistic approach, and specifically by a doctrine set forth in the *Conciliator* associating the seven planetary rulers with astrologically determined historical epochs.[21] The hostility of the authorities towards both astrological determinism and his textual sources led d'Abano to disguise this doctrine's origin:[22] it was not derived from Averroes—as implied in the *Conciliator*—but rather from Eleazar of Worms' commentary on the *Sefer Yetzirah*.[23] As we shall see, Eleazar's angelic planetary rulers and epochs were to exert considerable influence on subsequent Christian practitioners of invocative astrological magic, chiefly via the works of d'Abano and Johannes Trithemius (1462–1516).

During the Renaissance Platonist revival, proponents of pagan theurgy sought to philosophically circumvent earlier medieval strictures against celestial invocations, creating cracks in the broader edifice of

---

21   D'Abano, *Conciliator*, f. 20r (*Diff.* 9): 'Nam prima quidem est Saturni cassiel [sic]. Secunda Iovis sackiel. Tertia Martis sammael. Quarta Solis micael. Quinta Veneris anael. Sexta Mercurii raphael. Septima vero Lune Gabriel.' D'Abano's brief allusion to his persecution follows at the end of *Diff.* 9 (f. 21r).

22   Witness, for example, Tempier's Parisian Condemnation of 1277, which threatens excommunication for the mere possession of invocative magical texts (*Chartularium universitatis parisiensis*, Vol. 1 (Paris: Delalain, 1889), p. 543), and which condemns a number of theses on astrological determinism and radical Aristotelian themes, leaving a naturalist such as d'Abano exposed to persecution on a number of grounds.

23   Eleazar ben Judah, פירוש ספר יצירה, London: British Library Add MS 27199, ff. 388v-470v (f. 438r); the same angels (קפציאל [Saturn], צדקיאל [Jupiter], סמאל [Mars], רפאל [Sun], ענאל [Venus], מיכאל [Mercury], גבריאל [Moon]) are given in Eleazar ben Judah's סודי רזיא, London: British Library Add MS 27199, ff. 1r-379v (f. 29r), a tract that was the chief source of the later grimoire *Sefer Raziel*. The Jewish provenance of the doctrine was well-known to d'Abano, as it also appears as an addendum to his translation of Abraham ibn Ezra's *Liber rationum: Abrahe Avenaris Iudei astrologi peritissimi in re iudicali Opera* (Venice: Petrus Liechtenstein, 1507), f. 43v. A similar list is to be found in Judah ben Barzillai's commentary (ca. 1200) on the *Sefer Yetzirah*, complete with the Babylonian planetary demons as attendant spirits, but there is no reference there to the 354-year epochs: Judah ben Barzillai, ספר יצירה פירוש (Berlin: M'kize Nirdamim, 1885), p. 247.

Christian orthodoxy that would contribute substantially to its widespread collapse in the course of the Reformation. Thus Marsilio Ficino (1433–1499) appealed to a work erroneously attributed to Thomas Aquinas (De fato) to claim that both the natural materials and the artificial graven images of a talisman are capable of drawing down occult virtues from the celestial realm—a notion in clear contravention of Thomas' genuine writings.[24] Indeed, the third book of Ficino's De vita ('On Obtaining Life from the Heavens') was essentially a commentary via Plotinus upon the theurgy of Asclepius—a text Thomas had specifically condemned.[25] Echoing the naturalism of d'Abano and Albertus, in De Vita Ficino emphasised that his astrological magic relied not upon the invocation of planetary and stellar intelligences, but rather upon the impersonal spiritus mundi mediating between the anima mundi and the sensible world.[26] Elsewhere, however, he effectively mounted a defence of Orpheus and the magi against St. Paul himself; in so doing, he revealed that his resurrection of the prisca theologia was indeed concerned with the invocation of numina (spirits), each of which constituted a rung on a great ladder between heaven and earth.[27]

There is less dissimulation evident in the work of the great magical Reformers, Paracelsus (1493–1541) and Agrippa (1486–1535), with

---

24   Brian Copenhaver, 'Scholastic Philosophy and Renaissance Magic in the De vita of Marsilio Ficino', Renaissance Quarterly 37, no. 4 (1984): pp. 523–554, pp. 532–534.

25   Thomas Aquinas, Contra Gentiles III 104.7–12.

26   Marsilio Ficino, De vita libri tres 3.25, in Marsilio Ficino, Three Books on Life: A Critical Edition and Translation, trans. and ed. Carol V. Kaske and John R. Clark (Tempe, AZ: Medieval and Renaissance Texts and Studies, 1998), pp. 37, 383. Cf. Plotinus, Enneads, 4.4.26, in Plotinus, Enneads IV.1-9, trans. A. H. Armstrong (Cambridge, MA: Harvard University Press, 1984), pp. 206–211; this spirit is the macrocosmic homologue of the fine material spiritus mediating between the soul and the body in the human individual; it transmits 'seminal reasons' (the Stoic logoi spermatikoi) which impress particular archetypal forms originating in the intellectual realm onto the world of matter: see Daniel Walker, Spiritual and Demonic Magic: From Ficino to Campanella (University Park, PA: Pennsylvania State University Press, 2003), pp. 112–113.

27   Ficino, In epistolas divi Pauli VIII; cited in Walker, Spiritual and Demonic Magic, pp. 48–51.

their 'overtly demonic, recklessly unorthodox magic'.[28] The Christian reception of Jewish Kabbalah and the Hekhalot literature by Pico, Reuchlin and their heirs contributed substantially to this 'reckless' tendency in late Renaissance magic, as did the emergence of various other inspirationist currents within the 'radical' wing of the Reformation, which took the newfound emphasis on individual religiosity, the priesthood of all believers, and direct, unmediated contact with the divine world to its furthest conclusion.[29] In this latter development lie the origins of magisterial Protestant and later Enlightenment polemics against 'enthusiasm', which were closely allied to the modern polemic against magic.[30]

As gnostic-emanationist religiosity stemming from the Hermetic and Kabbalistic traditions remained widely illicit in the early modern period, its practical invocative techniques often went unprinted, circulating instead in oral and manuscript form. The value of such manuscripts within the economy of religious knowledge was derived in part from the very strictures of Christian orthodoxy against their dissemination; in some cases, however, access to this knowledge was restricted because it was deemed by practitioners to be properly esoteric in character, i.e. unsuitable for the uninitiated.[31] Although such restricted knowledge is

---

28   Walker, *Spiritual and Demonic Magic*, p. 75.

29   On relevant figures such as the 'Platonic spiritualists' (e.g. Franck, Schwenkfeld, Weigel) see R. Emmet McLaughlin, 'Spiritualism: Schwenckfeld and Franck and their Early Modern Resonances', in *A Companion to Anabaptism and Spiritualism*, 1521-1700, ed. John D. Roth and James M. Stayer (Leiden: Brill, 2007), pp. 119–161; George Williams and Angel Mergal, eds., *Spiritual and Anabaptist Writers* (Louisville, KY: Westminster John Knox Press, 2006); and the classic study by George Williams, *The Radical Reformation* (Kirksville, MO: Sixteenth Century Journal Publishers, 1992).

30   The paradigmatic text in this regard is Johann Christoph Adelung, *Geschichte der menschlichen Narrheit*, 7 vols (Leipzig: Weygand, 1785–1789); cf. Monika Neugebauer-Wölk and Markus Meumann, 'Aufklärung—Esoterik —Moderne. Konzeptionelle Überlegungen zur Einführung', in *Aufklärung und Esoterik: Wege in die Moderne*, ed. Monika Neugebauer-Wölk, Renko Geffarth, and Markus Meumann (Berlin: Walter de Gruyter, 2013), pp. 1–36.

31   Although Richard Kieckhefer, *Magic in the Middle Ages* (Cambridge: Cambridge University Press, 1990), p. 140, uses the term 'occult' to characterise magical learning 'reserved for the few and concealed from the many', the

less visible to the contemporary historian, it would be unwise to accept Hanegraaff's claim that esotericism is 'an imaginative construct in the minds of intellectuals and the wider public', as we are studying marginalized European religious practices with historically and functionally related homologues in Levantine Jewish, Islamic and Indo-Tibetan contexts.[32]

The Rosicrucian tradition is a particularly important conduit for manuscript collections of invocative magical texts, the contents of which were constantly edited and interpreted anew by practitioners. On the whole these manuscripts deal with the induction of altered states of consciousness through prayer, music, chanting, fasting and the ingestion of alchemically produced entheogens—that is to say, psychoactive substances created in the laboratory that tend to elicit an experience of the divine.[33] The Rosicrucian manifestos of the early seventeenth century bear traces of these invocative practices, although they are indistinctly expressed. Indeed, the manifestos' vacillation on this subject is suggestive of two redactional layers within the texts, the first stemming from a Paracelsian inclined to invocative magic and the second from a disinclined Lutheran. This fact accords well with the theory of their joint authorship by Tobias Hess (1558–1614) and Johann Valentin Andreae (1586–1654).[34] The *Confessio fraternitatis* is the more heterodox of the

term 'esoteric' is far more exact and less ambiguous; notwithstanding its loose contemporary connotations in popular culture, I use the term here in accordance with its etymology, i.e. to refer to knowledge that is communicable to—or intelligible by—a privileged circle of initiates alone. Cf. William Eamon, *Science and the Secrets of Nature: Books of Secrets in Medieval and Early Modern Culture* (Princeton, NJ: Princeton University Press, 1994), p. 43.

32   Hereward Tilton, *Review of Wouter Hanegraaff, Esotericism and the Academy: Rejected Knowledge in Western Culture* (Cambridge: Cambridge University Press, 2012), *Journal of Religion in Europe* 6 (2013): pp. 491–493; Hanegraaff, *Esotericism and the Academy*, pp. 376–377.

33   On this subject see Hereward Tilton, 'Alchymia Archetypica: Theurgy, Inner Transformation and the Historiography of Alchemy', in *Transmutatio: La via ermetica alla felicità / The Hermetic Way to Happiness*, Quaderni di Studi Indo Mediterranei V (Alessandria: Edizioni dell'Orso, 2012), pp. 179–216, pp. 187-192.

34   The contribution of both Andreae and Hess to the manifestos has long since been established: see Martin Brecht, 'Johann Valentin Andreae.

two works, as it elaborates more fully on Paracelsian practices that are only implied or mentioned cursorily in the *Fama fraternitatis*. Hence in the earliest known manuscript copy of the *Fama fraternitatis* it is said that the legendary medieval scientist-monk Christian Rosenkreuz learnt his arts from the 'Elementarische Inwohner' (elementary inhabitants) of Fez, which are specifically contrasted with human beings.[35] The *Confessio fraternitatis* goes on to state that Christian Rosenkreuz gained his knowledge 'through the service of angels and spirits'; it also refers to *nectromantia*, or the art of knowing other people's secrets by controlling their familiar spirits, and to *necrocomia*, or the prophetic interpretation of heavenly signs through the evestrum or astral spirit.[36] And there is a specific reference in the *Confessio fraternitatis* to *Weltfürsten* or world rulers when it describes attracting spirits and 'entrancing the mighty sovereigns of the world' through a type of Orphic singing.[37]

Weg und Programm eines Reformers zwischen Reformation und Moderne', in *Theologen und Theologie an der Universität Tübingen*, ed. Martin Brecht (Tübingen: J. C. B. Mohr, 1977), pp. 270–343, pp. 285–290. A third party is also implicated in the authorship of the manifestos: see Carlos Gilly, 'Die Rosenkreuzer als europäisches Phänomen im 17. Jahrhundert und die verschlungenen Pfade der Forschung', in *Das Rosenkreuz als europäisches Phänomen des 17. Jahrhunderts. Akten zum 35. Wolfenbütteler Symposium*, ed. Carlos Gilly and Friedrich Niewöhner (Amsterdam: In de Pelikaan, 2001), pp. 19–56, pp. 28–32.

35 Pleun van der Kooij and Carlos Gilly, eds., *Fama fraternitatis: Das Urmanifest der Rosenkreuzer Bruderschaft* (Haarlem: Rozekruis Pers, 1998), pp. 11, 76, 104.

36 *Confessio fraternitatis oder Bekanntnuß der löblichen Bruderschafft deß hochgeehrten Rosen-Creutzes/ an die Gelehrten Europae geschrieben* (Frankfurt am Main: Johann Bringer, 1615), pp. 59–60; cf. Adam Haslmayr, *Antwort an die lobwürdige Brüderschafft der Theosophen von Rosencreutz* (Frankfurt am Main: Johann Bringer, 1615), pp. 97–98; Paracelsus, 'Astronomia magna: oder die ganze Philosophia Sagax der grossen vnd kleinen Welt', in *Paracelsus: Sämtliche Werke*, Vol. 12, ed. Karl Sudhoff (Munich: Oldenbourg, 1929), pp. 1–507, pp. 148–157.

37 'Die mächtige Fürsten der Welt': *Confessio fraternitatis*, p. 62. The nature of these 'sovereigns' is certainly ambiguous: the Latin edition of the *Confessio* gives 'the mightiest sovereigns of the terrestrial realm' (' . . . potentissimos imperii terreri [sic] principes . . . '), though the contrast with

Fig. 1. *Hieroglyphische Abbildung und Gegensatz der wahren einfaltigen und falschgenandten Brüder vom RosenCreutz.* Anonymous broadside, ca. 1625–1630. Wellcome Library, London.

Although the authors of the manifestos envisaged the integration of Biblical teaching with pagan philosophy and the abolition of the Scholastic *duplex veritas*—'it shall not be said, this is true according to philosophy, but false according to theology', as the *Fama fraternitatis* has it—their ambivalence vis-à-vis invocative astrological techniques reflects a broader ideological struggle within early Rosicrucianism.[38] This fact is succinctly illustrated in an anonymous and undated *Hieroglyphic Portrait and Contrast of the True, Simple Brother of the Rosy Cross and the Falsely So-called Brother* (*Hieroglyphische Abbildung und Gegensatz der wahren einfaltigen und falschgenandten Brüder vom RosenCreutz*, ca. 1625–1630) (Fig. 1). The false Rosicrucian depicted here is evidently

---

Pluto—the king of the underworld—suggests an allusion to angelic powers; *Confessio fraternitatis R. C. ad eruditos Europae* (Kassel: Wilhelm Wessel, 1615), f. H2r.

38   *Fama fraternitatis*, p. 99.

a Christian Cabalist, as he commands an angel with a wand and has Dee's hieroglyphic monad at his heart. A taloned foot betrays this diabolical impostor, whose gown is adorned with the names of Stoic philosophers—a reference to the pantheistic tendency of the Paracelsians to blur the distinction between the divine and natural realms.[39] To the left the sun is surrounded by the Zodiac and planetary signs, while an accompanying citation from the Book of Jeremiah implies that astrological magic leads back to the worship of the pagan gods.[40]

The persecution of ostensibly Rosicrucian groups in Hessen-Kassel, Hessen-Darmstadt and Württemberg during the early years of the Thirty Years War underlines the perceived threat to the social order posed by inspirationist Protestant currents—and specifically by those inspirationists inclined to invocative astrological practices. During his trial in 1619 the 'holy fool' Philipp Homagius was accused of distributing the late sixteenth-century Paracelsian grimoire *Arbatel* among a 'conspiratorial society' of Rosicrucians numbering over two hundred in Hessen-Kassel; he was subsequently sentenced to 'perpetual imprisonment' as an enthusiast, a pantheist and a threat to state security.[41]

The invocation of planetary spirits and rulers within seventeenth- and eighteenth century Rosicrucianism occurred in the context of an art the *Arbatel*—utilising Paracelsian terminology—terms 'Olympic magic'.[42] In the genuine work of Paracelsus, 'Olympic spirits' are hypostases of the stars, their astral operations and their governance of the world; according to the treatise *De causis morborum invisibilium* they are the key to the Cabalistic art, and constitute the invisible power behind the

---

39   Carlos Gilly, *Cimelia Rhodostaurotica Die Rosenkreuzer im Spiegel der zwischen 1610 und 1660 entstandenen Handschriften und Drucke. Ausstellung der Bibliotheca Philosophica Hermetica Amsterdam und der Herzog August Bibliothek Wolfenbüttel* (Amsterdam: In de Pelikaan, 1995), pp. 170–171.

40   Jer. 7.17-18: 'Do you not see what they are doing in the cities of Judah and in the streets of Jerusalem? The children gather wood, the fathers kindle fire, and the women knead dough, to make cakes for the queen of heaven; and they pour out drink offerings to other gods, to provoke me to anger.'

41   Karl Hochhuth, 'Mitteilungen aus der protestantischen Secten-Geschichte in der hessischen Kirche', *Zeitschrift für die historische Theologie* 32, no. 1 (1862): pp. 86–159, pp. 87–88, 128–129, 131.

42   *Arbatel de magia veterum* (Basel: Petrus Perna, 1575), p. 4.

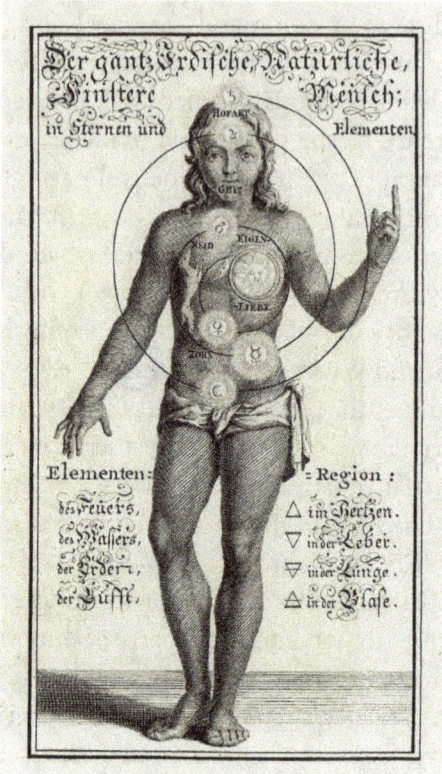

Fig. 2. The seven inner heavenly spheres, as depicted in Johann Georg Gichtel and Johann Georg Graber, *Eine kurtze Eröfnung und Anweisung der dreyen Principien und Welten im Menschen* (Leiden: [s.n.], 1696), figure IV.

visible stars in the heavens and the microcosmic stars within the human body.[43] Strangely, the *Arbatel* portrays the seven Olympic spirits as the visible stars themselves; they are 'governors of the cosmic machinery', and their duty is 'to determine fate and administer destiny, insofar as God permits it'.[44]

---

43   Paracelsus, 'De causis morborum invisibilium', in *Paracelsus: Sämtliche Werke*, Vol. 9 (Munich: Otto Wilhelm Barth, 1925), pp. 249–350, pp. 298–299.

44   Named with the faux-Hebrew and faux-Greek neologisms 'Aratron', 'Bethor', 'Phaleg', 'Och', 'Hagith', 'Ophiel' and 'Phul'. Their appointment to particular historical periods (*Arbatel*, pp. 23–25) is indirectly derivative of the aforementioned Kabbalistic tradition transmitted by d'Abano; however, the fact their names are given in 'Olympic speech'—i.e. an angelic *Ursprache*

While the magic of the *Arbatel*—in keeping with most grimoires—is primarily directed towards miraculous worldly ends such as the attainment of invisibility or purses pouring forth gold, among seventeenth-century networks self-identifying as 'Rosicrucian' we find invocative astrological practices employed (in accordance with Hermetic and Jewish Kabbalistic antecedents) for decidedly gnostic purposes. That higher religious intent—a spiral ascent through the heavenly spheres, conceived microcosmically as seven qualities of the human soul (Fig. 2)—has been preserved in the manuscript traces of a Behmenist-Rosicrucian circle that became known to posterity as the *Gold- und Rosenkreuz* (Gold and Rosy Cross).

The confluence of Behmenist and Rosicrucian currents dates to the earlier seventeenth century; an important intermediary was the Dutch engraver Michel le Blon (1587–1658), an associate of Erasmus Wolfart (fl. 1609),[45] Johann Arndt (1555–1621),[46] Paul Nagel (?–1624)[47] and Abraham von Franckenberg (1593–1652),[48] whose printed and manuscript works place invocative astrological magic within the framework of apocalyptic speculation on the seven angels of Revelations.[49] As a haven

uncoupled from a sacred language such as Hebrew—is reminiscent of Dee. *Arbatel*, p. 22.

45   Heinrich Khunrath's friend and editor.

46   The prominent proto-Pietist.

47   A follower of Böhme and early distributor of the Rosicrucian manifestos.

48   Publisher of Böhme and author of the first defence of the ancient Gnostics.

49   Revelations 1.20. In his printed response to the manifestos (*Antwort oder Sendtbrief/ an die von Gott erleuchte Bruderschafft vom Rosen Creutz* (Amsterdam: [s.n.], 1615), le Blon confesses his chief interest is the fraternity's 'theological magic', while his manuscript *Tractatus magicus de Astronomia supernaturali* (Dresden: Sächsische Landesbibliothek—Staats- und Universitätsbibliothek Dresden, MS App. 736) touches upon the relation of the planetary rulers to Revelations and is signed with a Rosicrucian motto (f. 66v). On the early confluence of Rosicrucian and Behmenist currents, see Theodor Harmsen, 'The Reception of Jacob Böhme and Böhmist Theosophy in the *Geheime Figuren der Rosenkreuzer*', in *Offenbarung und Episteme: Zur europäischen Wirkung Jakob Böhmes im 17. und 18. Jahrhundert*, ed. Wilhelm Kühlmann and Friedrich Vollhardt (Berlin: Walter de Gruyter, 2012), pp.

Figura Solis.   *Figura Lunæ.*

Figs. 3 and 4. Animated solar (left) and lunar (right) statues, from *Magia divina, oder gründ- und deutlicher Unterricht, von denen fürnehmsten Caballistischen Kunst-Stücken derer Alten Israeliten Welt-Weisen, und Ersten, auch noch einigen heutigen wahren Christen* ([s.l.]: L. v. H., 1745), pp. 58, 61.

of relative religious tolerance, Amsterdam formed the heart of this union of Behmenist and Rosicrucian doctrine and practice, which by the later seventeenth century had coalesced around Ulrich Pfeffer (?–1680) and the Angelic Brethren of Johann Georg Gichtel (1638–1710).[50]

The alchemico-Cabalistic grimoires of the order of the Gold and Rosy Cross stem from the circle of Pfeffer and Gichtel; although they list a great number of techniques for the invocation of planetary intelligences,

---

183–206, p. 195.

50   On Pfeffer, Gichtel and the origins of the Gold- und Rosenkreuz, see Hereward Tilton, 'The Urim and Thummim and the Origins of the Gold- und Rosenkreuz', in *Octagon: Die Suche nach Vollkommenheit im Spiegel einer religionswissenschaftlichen, philosophischen und im besonderen Masse esoterischen Bibliothek*, Vol. 2, ed. Hans Thomas Hakl (Gaggenau: H. Frietsch Verlag, 2016), pp. 4–70.

they rarely give any clear indication of their ultimate gnostic purpose (i.e., a *magia Metatrona* that had become the sole preserve of the order's highest grade of Magus).[51] The most important of the techniques in question deal with the summoning of celestial and supercelestial spirits via the animation of statues (Figs. 3 and 4) and the striking of bells.

Both classes of artefact—statues and bells—are manufactured from *electrum magicum*, an alloy of the seven alchemical metals that is uniquely receptive to planetary influences.[52] A pervasive material in European ritual magical practice, *electrum magicum* first enters the historical record in the sixteenth-century pseudo-Paracelsian *Archidoxis magica*. There the author claims to have met a necromancer in Spain who engraved certain names and talismanic characters upon the interior of an electrum bell, which when rung would summon the corresponding intelligence; in this way the Olympic spirits exercise an influence upon the star (*astrum*) or 'invisible human' lying hidden in the mind and thoughts of the visible human being.[53]

Elaborating upon the practices referred to in the *Archidoxis magica* and the *Arbatel*, the texts of the order of the Gold and Rosy Cross effectively describe the *binding* of lower planetary spirits via the invocation of their commanding angels from the supercelestial realm.[54] Hence two

---

51　Tilton, 'Urim and Thummim', pp. 46–54. The principal tracts in this regard are 'Jehova Jeschua Metatron, das ist, Magia Dei alba Jesu unsers Heylandes und Gnadenthrons', in *Septimus sapientiae: Liber verus ac genuinus* (Munich: Bayerische Staatsbibliothek, MS Kiesewetteriana 1e), pp. 399–421; 'Magia Metattrona [sic], das ist, die gute Heilige Geistkunst der cabalistischen weissen Magiae', *Septimus sapientiae*, pp. 422–425; 'Dei Magia, oder Magia divina, seu Praxis Cabulae albae et naturalis Theophrasti Paracelsi', *Septimus sapientiae*, pp. 426–556; 'Jesus spricht: In meines Vaters Hause sind viel Wohnungen', *Septimus sapientiae*, pp. 560–587; and *Das Buch mit sieben Siegeln* (Yale: Beinecke Rare Book and Manuscript Library, Mellon MS 110).
52　On the production of *electrum magicum* see Hereward Tilton, 'Of Electrum and the Armour of Achilles: Myth and Magic in a Manuscript of Heinrich Khunrath (1560-1605)', *Aries* 6, no. 2 (2006): pp. 117–157, p. 119 n.7, pp. 128–131.
53　Pseudo-Paracelsus, *Archidoxis magica*, in *Paracelsus: Sämtliche Werke*, Vol. 14, ed. Karl Sudhoff (Munich: Oldenbourg, 1933), pp. 437–498, p. 488.
54　The centrality of Paracelsian Olympic magic to the order's practice is evident in 'Liber Theophrasti de septem stellis', *Septimus sapientiae*, pp. 182–

Fig. 5 (left) and **Fig. 6 (right)**. Electrum magicum bells from *De magia divina oder Caballistischer Geheimnüsse* (London: Wellcome Library, MS 4808), pp. 223–263 (pp. 246, 248).

types of magical electrum bell are described in the order's *De magia divina*: one for the summoning of 'the seven princes of the planets' (which are given the names of the Olympic spirits from the *Arbatel*), the other for summoning their angelic superiors.[55] The former 'bell of the lesser angel' (Fig. 5) is cast with Latinised Hebrew names of God: on the

---

342, pp. 227– 228: '... der erste und oberste Fürst über die 7. Himmel ... wenn er in seiner eigenen vom HERRN empfangenen Kraft in diesem Mysterio Magno, von einem magnetischen Lichte eines wahren Kindes GOTTES beweget wird, der thut alsdenn mehr, denn alle äußerliche sichtbare Sterne am Firmamente, so sich also in descendente erzeigen'; cf. *Liber de septem stellis dr. Philippi Theophrasti Paracelsi ab Hohenheim eigener hand abgeschrieben zu Saltzburg anno 1570* (Leipzig: Universitätsbibliothek Leipzig, Cod. mag. 39), f. 2r, where we find the same pseudo-Paracelsian tract without the order's Behmenist accretions.

55 *De magia divina oder Caballistischer Geheimnüsse* (London: Wellcome Library, MS 4808), pp. 223–263, pp. 244–248. A third *electrum magicum* bell utilizing the characters of the moon and Aquarius to summon subterranean spirits is described in a version of the order's *Thesaurus thesaurorum* entitled γνῶθι σεαυτόν *seu noscete ipsum* (Munich: Bayerische Staatsbibliothek, MS Kiesewetteriana 1d), p. 291.

exterior, 'Saday' and 'Tetragrammaton', together with the planet and constellation of the operator's birth; on the interior, 'Elohim'; and on the clapper, 'Adonay'.

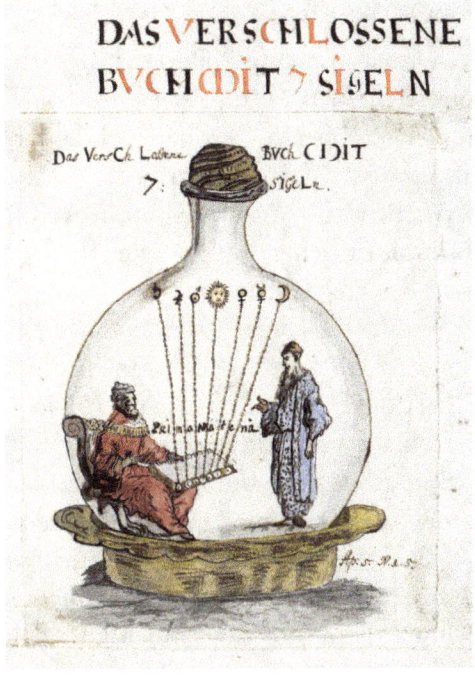

Following ritual purification and prayer, the name of the planetary spirit to be summoned is written within the bell; a coloured ink matching the spirit's planetary provenance is used, and this ink is also laid out with paper and quill to receive the angel's answers (presumably a form of automatic writing is alluded to here).

The 'bell of the greater angel' (Fig. 6) is cast with 'Jesus', 'Tetragrammaton' and 'Adonay' upon the ex-

Fig. 7. The closed book with seven seals, from Das Buch mit sieben Siegeln (Yale: Beinecke Rare Book and Manuscript Library, Mellon MS 110), f. 8r.

terior, together with the names of 'the seven angels' (Oriphiel, Sachiel, Samuel, Michael, Aniel, Raphael and Gabriel). These are the *Angeli planetarum* of Trithemius and d'Abano,[56] although the order's texts describe them variously as archangels and thrones, and also associate them with Böhme's seven source spirits.[57] Likewise, the order's gnostic journey through the seven microcosmic celestial spheres corresponds to the opening of the seven seals, with all its apocalyptic repercussions (Fig.

---

56   Hence the distinctive corruption of קפציאל as 'Oriphiel' via Trithemius' 'Oriffiel' and d'Abano's 'Caffiel'; cf. n.27, 29 supra and Trithemius, *Steganographia, hoc est, Ars per occultam scripturam animi sui voluntatem absentibus aperiendi certa* (Frankfurt am Main: Johannes Berner, 1606), p. 162.

57   'Liber Theophrasti de septem stellis', *Septimus sapientiae*, pp. 221–22.

7).[58]

One curious instruction is of particular interest: 'a grain's weight of astral tincture' together with 'something fragrant' is to be placed under the operator's tongue while the bell of the lesser angel is struck and the invocation performed.[59] This detail is suggestive of the use of an alchemically produced entheogen; the operation is in any case an example of alchemically assisted theurgy, a category of magical practice I have described elsewhere.[60]

While the order's (mechanically) animated statues seem to be inspired—in part, at least—by Agrippa's citation of Ficino's various reflections on the *Asclepius*, the *electrum magicum* bells belong to an artefactual tradition that can be traced to the alchemico-Cabalist Heinrich Khunrath (1560–1605) via Ulrich Pfeffer.[61] Earlier incarnations of the order's bells are depicted in an emblem of Khunrath's *Amphitheatrum sapientiae aeternae* and a ritual magical tableau associated with Khunrath;[62] what is more, an *electrum magicum* planetary bell owned by Khunrath's protector Emperor Rudolph II is still in existence today (Fig. 8).[63]

It is an intriguing fact that early seventeenth-century Rosicrucians were implicated in invocative magical practices closely related to those

---

58   'Liber Theophrasti de septem stellis', *Septimus sapientiae*, 283 ff.

59   *De magia divina*, Wellcome Library, p. 246.

60   Tilton, '*Alchymia Archetypica*', pp. 187–192.

61   Agrippa, *De occulta philosophia* 1.39 (Heinrich Cornelius Agrippa von Nettesheim, *De occulta philosophia libri tres* (Venice: Curtius Navò, 1551), ff. 24v–25r); Ficino, *De vita* 3.20, in Ficino, *Three Books on Life*, pp. 348–355; *Picatrix* 3.5, pseudo-Maǧrīṭī, *Picatrix: das Ziel des Weisen*, pp. 193–197; *Asclepius* 24, 37 (Copenhaver, *Hermetica*, pp. 81, pp. 89–90); Tilton, 'Urim and Thummim', pp. 44–46, 51.

62   *Tabulae theosophiae Cabbalisticae* (London: British Library, Sloane MS 181), ff. 1v-2r; cf. the work of the tableau's discoverer, Peter Forshaw, '"Behold, the dreamer cometh": Hyperphysical Magic and Deific Visions in an Early Modern Theosophical Lab-Oratory', in *Conversations with Angels: Essays towards a History of Spiritual Communication*, ed. Joad Raymond (Houndmills: Palgrave Macmillan, 2011), pp. 175–200, pp. 184–186.

63   On Rudolph's *electrum magicum* planetary bell, see Beket Bukovinská and Ivo Purš, 'Die Tischglocke Rudolfs II.: Über ihren Urheber und ihre Bedeutung', *Studia Rudolphina* 10 (2010), pp. 89–104.

Fig. 8. A replica of a spirit-summoning bell of Rudolph II, ca. 1600; the original is to be found at the Kunsthistorisches Museum, Vienna, KK 5969 (artist: Hans de Bull; dimensions: 7.8 x 6.3 cm; materials: the seven alchemical metals, gilded). Depicted on the bell's exterior are the seven planetary spirits, their characters and their constellations; around the bell interior and clapper are indecipherable spiralling strings of Greek and Hebrew *verba ignota*.

current among the eighteenth-century inheritors of the Rosicrucian mantle—yet the earlier circles were the bane of established religious and social hierarchies, while the Gold and Rosy Cross in its late quasi-Masonic phase became their staunch defender. Indeed, Prussia's Friedrich Wilhelm II himself became one of the seven *Magi* at the order's apex in April 1783 after consulting an *electrum magicum* 'Urim and Thummim', the order's most important ritual magical artefact.[64] The response to his subsequent ascent to the Prussian throne from a prominent Enlightened scientist is telling:

> Well may Europe lament the death of the great king [Frederick the Great]! For the glimmer of the Enlightenment and freedom of thought we had vainly cherished while his great example prevailed is extinguished. Now let us bow before the Magus Magorum and seek among the true sages – for whom the Philosophers' Stone is a mere trifle – the Urim and Thummim that grants a glimpse into the realm of the spirits. For we have another great paragon who encourages us to do just this, and who consigns that abominable freedom

---

64   See the letter from Johann Christoph von Woellner to Johann Rudolf von Bischoffwerder (Berlin: Geheime Staatsarchiv Preußischer Kulturbesitz, BPH Rep. 48 - König Friedrich Wilhelm II, Nr. 8, Bd. 1), f. 20r (22 April 1783).

of thought to the abyss. All hail to an epoch in which
Protestant Inquisitions, too, will be advancing the happiness
of humanity![65]

Although Frances Yates portrayed the early Rosicrucian phenomenon as a proto-Enlightenment, by the dawn of modernity proper the
inspirationist tendencies within Rosicrucianism constituted a reaction
to the advance of mechanistic science and Enlightenment philosophy,
which had discarded the ambiguous esoteric discourse of alchemy and
rejected divine inspiration as a legitimate path to scientific knowledge. As
the anti-enthusiast polemic moved from a Reformation to an Enlightenment context, inspired knowledge evolved from the status of diabolical
heresy to mere trickery: thus the divinatory art of animating statues of
the planetary rulers detailed in the *Magia divina* was portrayed by the
arch-enemies of the Gold and Rosy Cross, the Illuminati, as the epitome
of religious manipulation of the masses.[66] In turn the inspired sciences
of astrology and alchemy gave way to disciplines with no place for either
heavenly influences or the investigation of poorly-understood psychosomatic phenomena, and the social response to the excluded modes of

---

65   Brigitte Leuschner, ed., *Georg Forsters Werke*, Vol. 14 (Berlin:
Akademie Verlag, 1978), p. 557: 'Den Tod des großen Königs mag Europa nur
beweinen! denn nunmehr ist der Schimmer von Aufklärung und Denkfreyheit
wohl auf immer dahin, womit man sich einmal schmeichelte, solange seyn
großes Beyspiel den Ton angab. Jetzt wollen wir uns vor dem Magus Magorum
beugen und das Urim und Thummim, welches den Blick ins Reich der Geister
öfnet, bey den wahren Weisen suchen, denen der lapis eine Kleinigkeit ist;
denn wir haben ja ein anderes großes Beyspiel, welches uns dazu aufmuntert,
und die abscheuliche Denkfreyheit in den Abgrund verdammt. Heil den
Zeiten, wo auch protestantische Inquisitionsgerichte das Glück der Menscheit
befördern werden!'
66   Frances Yates, *The Rosicrucian Enlightenment* (New York: Routledge,
1972); Anon., *Der Rosenkreuzer in seiner Blösse* (Amsterdam: [s.n.], 1781),
pp. 38–40; cf. Lucian, *Alexander* 26, in *Lucian*, Vol. 4, trans. A. M. Harmon
(Cambridge, MA: Harvard University Press, 1961), p. 211; Hippolytus,
Refutatio 4.28, in Hippolytus, *The Refutation of all Heresies*, trans. J. H.
McMahon (Edinburgh: T&T Clark, 1868), pp. 93–97. For the Enlightenment
reception of this ancient rhetorical topos, see Fontenelle's *Histoire des Oracles*
(The Hague: Gosse et Neaulme, 1728).

thought and practice shifted from prohibition to mere ridicule—a state of affairs that continues until the present day.

WORKS CITED

Adelung, Johann Christoph, *Geschichte der menschlichen Narrheit*, 7 vols (Leipzig: Weygand, 1785–1789).

Anon., *Der Rosenkreuzer in seiner Blösse* (Amsterdam: [s.n.], 1781).

Apuleius, *Pro se de magia*, ed. Vincent Hunink (Leiden: Brill, 1997).

Aquinas, Thomas, *On the Truth of the Catholic Faith. Summa Contra Gentiles*, Vol. 3, ed. and trans. Vernon Bourke (New York: Image Books, 1956).

———, *Summa theologiae*, Vol. 3 (Ottawa: Impensis Studii Generalis O. Pr., 1942).

———, *Summa theologica*, Vol. 3, Part 2, Section 2, trans. the Fathers of the English Dominican Province (New York: Cosimo Classics, 2007).

Augustine, *Aurelii Augustini opera*, Vol. 15, No. 3 (Turnhout: Brepols, 1985).

———, *Confessions*, Vol. 1, trans. William Watts (London: William Heinemann, 1912).

———, *The City of God against the Pagans*, Vol. 3, ed. and trans. David Wiesen (Cambridge, MA: Harvard University Press, 1968).

Barzillai, Judah ben, פירוש ספר יצירה (Berlin: M'kize Nirdamim, 1885).

Brecht, Martin, 'Johann Valentin Andreae. Weg und Programm eines Reformers zwischen Reformation und Moderne', in *Theologen und Theologie an der Universität Tübingen*, ed. Martin Brecht (Tübingen: J. C. B. Mohr, 1977), pp. 270–343.

Bukovinská, Beket and Ivo Purš, 'Die Tischglocke Rudolfs II.: Über ihren Urheber und ihre Bedeutung', *Studia Rudolphina* 10 (2010): pp. 89–104.

Chartularium universitatis parisiensis, Vol. 1 (Paris: Delalain, 1889).

Confessio fraternitatis oder Bekanntnuß der löblichen Bruderschafft deß hochgeehrten Rosen-Creutzes/ an die Gelehrten Europae geschrieben (Frankfurt am Main: Johann Bringer, 1615).

Confessio fraternitatis R. C. ad eruditos Europae (Kassel: Wilhelm Wessel, 1615).

Copenhaver, Brian, 'Scholastic Philosophy and Renaissance Magic in the *De vita* of Marsilio Ficino', *Renaissance Quarterly* 37, no. 4 (1984): pp. 523–554.

———, *Symphorien Champier and the Reception of the Occultist Tradition in Renaissance France* (The Hague: Mouton Publishers, 1978).

d'Abano, Pietro, *Conciliator differentiarum philosophorum et medicorum* (Mantua: Johann Wurster and Thomas Septemcastrensis, 1472).

Das Buch mit sieben Siegeln (Yale: Beinecke Rare Book and Manuscript Library, Mellon MS 110).

De magia divina oder Caballistischer Geheimnüsse (London: Wellcome Library, MS 4808), pp. 223–263.

Septimus sapientiae: Liber verus ac genuinus, (Munich: Bayerische Staatsbibliothek, MS kiesewetteriana 1e).

Eamon, William, *Science and the Secrets of Nature: Books of Secrets in Medieval and Early Modern Culture* (Princeton, NJ: Princeton University Press, 1994).

Euripides, *Orestes*, ed. and trans. Robin Waterfield (Oxford: Oxford University Press, 2001).

Ficino, Marsilio, *Three Books on Life: A Critical Edition and Translation*, trans. and ed. Carol V. Kaske and John R. Clark (Tempe, AZ: Medieval and Renaissance Texts and Studies, 1998).

Fontenelle, Bernard Le Bovier de, *Histoire des Oracles* (The Hague: Gosse et Neaulme, 1728).

Forshaw, Peter, '"Behold, the dreamer cometh": Hyperphysical Magic and Deific Visions in an Early Modern Theosophical Lab-Oratory', in *Conversations with Angels: Essays towards a History of Spiritual Communication*, ed. Joad Raymond (Houndmills: Palgrave Macmillan, 2011), pp. 175–200.

Gilly, Carlos, *Cimelia Rhodostaurotica. Die Rosenkreuzer im Spiegel der zwischen 1610 und 1660 entstandenen Handschriften und Drucke. Ausstellung der Bibliotheca Philosophica Hermetica Amsterdam und der Herzog August Bibliothek Wolfenbüttel* (Amsterdam: In de Pelikaan, 1995).

————, 'Die Rosenkreuzer als europäisches Phänomen im 17.
Jahrhundert und die verschlungenen Pfade der Forschung', in
*Das Rosenkreuz als europäisches Phänomen des 17. Jahrhunderts.
Akten zum 35. Wolfenbütteler Symposium*, ed. Carlos Gilly and
Friedrich Niewöhner (Amsterdam: In de Pelikaan, 2001), pp.
19–56.

Hanegraaff, Wouter, *Esotericism and the Academy: Rejected Knowledge
in Western Culture* (Cambridge: Cambridge University Press,
2012).

Harmsen, Theodor, 'The Reception of Jacob Böhme and Böhmist
Theosophy in the *Geheime Figuren der Rosenkreuzer*', in
*Offenbarung und Episteme: Zur europäischen Wirkung Jakob
Böhmes im 17. und 18. Jahrhundert*, ed. Wilhelm Kühlmann
and Friedrich Vollhardt (Berlin: Walter de Gruyter, 2012), pp.
183– 206.

Haslmayr, Adam, *Antwort an die lobwürdige Brüderschafft der
Theosophen von Rosencreutz* (Frankfurt am Main: Johann
Bringer, 1615).

Hermetica, trans. Brian Copenhaver (Cambridge: Cambridge University
Press, 2000).

Hippolytus, *The Refutation of all Heresies*, trans. J. H. McMahon
(Edinburgh: T&T Clark, 1868).

Hochhuth, Karl, 'Mitteilungen aus der protestantischen Secten-
Geschichte in der hessischen Kirche', *Zeitschrift für die
historische Theologie* 32, no. 1 (1862): pp. 86–159.

ibn Ezra, Abraham, *Liber rationum: Abrahe Avenaris Iudei astrologi
peritissimi in re iudicali Opera*, trans. Pietro d'Abano (Venice:
Petrus Liechtenstein, 1507).

Irenaeus, *Against the Heresies*, Vol. 1, No. 1, ed. and trans. Dominic
Unger (New York: Newman Press, 1992).

Kieckhefer, Richard, *Magic in the Middle Ages* (Cambridge: Cambridge
University Press, 1990)

Leuschner, Brigitte. ed., *Georg Forsters Werke*, Vol. 14 (Berlin: Akademie
Verlag, 1978).

*Liber de septem stellis dr. Philippi Theophrasti Paracelsi ab Hohenheim
eigener hand abgeschrieben zu Saltzburg anno 1570* (Leipzig:
Universitätsbibliothek Leipzig, Cod. mag. 39).

Lucian, *Alexander the False Prophet* 26, in *Lucian*, Vol. 4, trans. A. M. Harmon (Cambridge, MA: Harvard University Press, 1961), pp. 173-254.

Magnus, Albertus, *Book of Minerals*, trans. Dorothy Wyckoff (Oxford: Clarendon Press, 1967).

——, *Opera omnia*, Vol. 27, ed. Stephan Borgnet (Paris: Ludovic Vivès, 1894).

McLaughlin, R. Emmet, 'Spiritualism: Schwenckfeld and Franck and their Early Modern Resonances', in *A Companion to Anabaptism and Spiritualism*, 1521-1700, ed. John D. Roth and James M. Stayer (Leiden: Brill, 2007), pp. 119–161.

Neugebauer-Wölk, Monika, and Markus Meumann, 'Aufklärung - Esoterik - Moderne. Konzeptionelle Überlegungen zur Einführung', in *Aufklärung und Esoterik: Wege in die Moderne*, ed. Monika Neugebauer-Wölk, Renko Geffarth, and Markus Meumann (Berlin: Walter de Gruyter, 2013), pp. 1–36.

Origen, *Contra Celsum*, ed. and trans. Henry Chadwick (Cambridge: Cambridge University Press, 2003).

Paracelsus, 'Astronomia magna: oder die ganze Philosophia Sagax der grossen vnd kleinen Welt', in *Paracelsus: Sämtliche Werke*, Vol. 12, ed. Karl Sudhoff (Munich: Oldenbourg, 1929), pp. 1–507.

——, 'De causis morborum invisibilium', in *Paracelsus: Sämtliche Werke*, Vol. 9, ed. Karl Sudhoff (Munich: Otto Wilhelm Barth, 1925), pp. 249–350.

Pingree, David, ed., *Picatrix: The Latin Version of the Ghāyat Al-Ḥakīm* (London: Warburg Institute, 1986).

Plato, *Alcibiades*, ed. Nicholas Denyer (Cambridge: Cambridge University Press, 2001).

Pliny, *Natural History libri XXVIII- XXXII*, ed. and trans. W. H. S. Jones (Cambridge, MA: Harvard University Press, 1963).

Plotinus, *Enneads* IV.1-9, trans. A. H. Armstrong (Cambridge, MA: Harvard University Press, 1984)

pseudo-Maǧrīṭī, *Picatrix: das Ziel des Weisen*, ed. and trans. Hellmut Ritter and Martin Plessner (London: Warburg Institute, 1962).

Pseudo-Paracelsus, *Archidoxis magica*, in *Paracelsus: Sämtliche Werke*, Vol. 14, ed. Karl Sudhoff (Munich: Oldenbourg, 1933), pp. 437–498.

Severus, Sulpicius, *Historia sacra* (Leiden: Ex officinâ Elseviriorum, 1635).

Styers, Randall, *Making Magic: Religion, Magic and Science in the Modern World* (New York: Oxford University Press, 2004).

Tabulae theosophiae Cabbalisticae (London: British Library, Sloane MS 181).

Tilton, Hereward, 'Alchymia Archetypica: Theurgy, Inner Transformation and the Historiography of Alchemy', in *Transmutatio: La via ermetica alla felicità / The Hermetic Way to Happiness,* Quaderni di Studi Indo Mediterranei V (Alessandria: Edizioni dell'Orso, 2012), pp. 179–216.

———, 'Of Electrum and the Armour of Achilles: Myth and Magic in a Manuscript of Heinrich Khunrath (1560-1605)', *Aries* 6, no. 2 (2006): pp. 117–157.

———, 'The Urim and Thummim and the Origins of the Gold- und Rosenkreuz', in *Octagon: Die Suche nach Vollkommenheit im Spiegel einer religionswissenschaftlichen, philosophischen und im besonderen Masse esoterischen Bibliothek,* Vol. 2, ed. Hans Thomas Hakl (Gaggenau: H. Frietsch Verlag, 2016), pp. 4–70.

———, *Review of Wouter Hanegraaff, Esotericism and the Academy: Rejected Knowledge in Western Culture* (Cambridge: Cambridge University Press, 2012), *Journal of Religion in Europe* 6 (2013): pp. 491–493.

Van der Kooij, Pleun, and Carlos Gilly, eds., *Fama fraternitatis: Das Urmanifest der Rosenkreuzer Bruderschaft* (Haarlem: Rozekruis Pers, 1998).

Walker, Daniel, *Spiritual and Demonic Magic: From Ficino to Campanella* (University Park, PA: Pennsylvania State University Press, 2003).

Weill-Parot, Nicolas, 'Arnaud de Villeneuve et les relations possibles entre le sceau du lion et l'alchimie', *Arxiu de textos Catalans antics* 23/24 (2005), pp. 269–280.

Weill-Parot, Nicolas, 'Astral Magic and Intellectual Changes (Twelfth-Fifteenth Centuries): "Astrological Images" and the Concept of "Addressative" Magic', in *The Metamorphosis of Magic from Late Antiquity to the Early Modern Period,* ed. Jan Bremmer and Jan Veenstra (Leuven: Peeters, 2002).

Williams, George and Angel Mergal, eds., *Spiritual and Anabaptist Writers* (Louisville, KY: Westminster John Knox Press, 2006).

Williams, George, *The Radical Reformation* (Kirksville, MO: Sixteenth Century Journal Publishers, 1992).

Woellner, Johann Christoph, Correspondence with Johann Rudolf von Bischoffwerder (Berlin: Geheime Staatsarchiv Preußischer Kulturbesitz, BPH Rep. 48 - König Friedrich Wilhelm II, Nr. 8, Bd. 1), f. 20r (22 April 1783).

Yates, Frances, *The Rosicrucian Enlightenment* (New York: Routledge, 1972).

Cannabis in Jewish Magic and Alchemy

Chris Bennett

The potential role of cannabis in the origins of the Jewish religion, is something I have proposed for close to 30 years, expanding on the work of the Polish Jewish etymologist and anthropologist Sula Benet's work identifying the Hebrew 'kaneh bosm' with cannabis'. When understood in the context if the Biblical narrative, these references clearly indicate magical, or at least shamanic use of cannabis. The recent archeological evidence of cannabis resins found to have been burnt on an altar in 8th century BCE Jerusalem, take these references beyond the realm of pure speculation, and are rewriting our understanding of the techniques of religious worship in the ancient world.

In Exodus 30:23 Moses is commanded to make a holy oil that contained cannabis under the name kaneh bosm and is advised to both anoint his body with it and burn it on the altar of incense. The resulting pillar of smoke that arose before Moses in the 'Tent of the Meeting', is referred to as the 'Shekinah' and is identified as the physical evidence of the Lord's presence. None of the other Hebrews in the Exodus account either see or hear the Lord, they only know that Moses is talking to the Lord when the smoke is pouring forth from the Tent of the Meeting. It is hard not to see all the classical elements of shamanism at play in this description of Moses' encounter with God, and like Zoroaster, Moses can be seen as a ecstatic shamanic figure who used cannabis as a means of seeking celestial advice. Such techniques of invocation certainly occur in later magic.

The Magician Moses scryed his messages from the Lord in an act of Biblical capnomancy, and this was a traditional use of cannabis in magical rituals that has been carried on in occult circles into modern times. As Ernest Bosc De Veze, who also wrote a Treatise on Hashish, noted in *Petite Encyclopedie Synthetique des Sciences Occultes*, in reference to "capnomancy. . . for divination . . . the smoke obtained from psychic plants such as verbena, hashish or Indian hemp . . . [are]used."[1] In cases like this, not only was there the psychoactive effects of the smoke used, but the smoke provided the partially material basis in which the invoked entity or vision might be viewed. "The magician. . . burned aromatic substances and anointed his/her body with perfumed ointments. The whole set-up for an epiphany was there: now all that was necessary was for the deity to appear."[2]

As Prof. Georg Luck has noted: "The idea that Moses himself and the priests who succeeded him relied on 'chemical aids' in order to touch with the Lord must be disturbing or repugnant to many. It seems to degrade religion—any religion—when one associates it with shamanic practices "[3] Luck experienced these reactions himself, when his decades of research into magic rites in the ancient world, drew him to such a hypothesis. "As I was doing research on psychoactive substances used in magic and religion and magic in antiquity, I happened to come across chapter 30 in the Book of Exodus where Moses prescribes the composition of sacred incense and anointing oil. It occurred to me, judging from the ingredients, that . . . [these]substances might act as 'entheogens,' the

1   Frater A. T. A. (The Theoretical and practical treatise of Hashish), which become 'The Treaty of Hashish—and other Psychic Substances' by Ernest Bos De Veze, Annotated, Reviewed, and Expanded Into English, (2018).

2   William M. Brashear, *Magica Varia* (Fondation Egyptologique reine Elisabeth, 1991).

3   Georg Luck, "Psychoactive Substances in Religion and Magic," *Arcana Mundi: Magic and the Occult in the Greek and Roman Worlds, A Collection of Ancient Texts*, 2nd ed. (Baltimore, Md.: Johns Hopkins University Press, 2006).

incense more powerful than the oil."[4]

> [T]he smoke itself was the epiphany. The smoke was inhaled
> by the magician and his client, and the vision came in trance.
> The smell of psychoactive substances . . . acts on the human
> brain in a very quick, very predictable way.
> [T]he inhalation of the sacred incense could create a powerful
> vision of the deity in the priest. Other factors were probably
> involved too, the smell of the holy oil with which the priest,
> the altar, and other sacred objects within the temple were
> anointed, the golden surface of the altar that reflected the
> shine of lamps . . . The shiny surfaces, reflecting the sacral
> lamps nearby, could help induce trance in the priest as he was
> breathing smoke.[5]

We see this same technique with cannabis resins, in the later 12th-century *Picatrix*, where cannabis resin are used to invoke the 'servant of the moon' in a pillar of smoke that was fueled by a combination that included over a pound of cannabis resin mixed with stag's blood and other ingredients.

Just as Moses received his answers in a billowing cloud of cannabis resin infused smoke, we can see from a reference in Isaiah, that when the cannabis was lacking, the scryed answers were more difficult to bring forth! the Lord complains he has been shortchanged his offering of cannabis. When the prophet seeks advice, the Lord complains: "Thou hast bought me no sweet [smelling] cane (kaneh) with money, neither hast thou filled me with the fat of thy sacrifices: but thou hast made me to serve with thy sins, thou hast wearied me with thine iniquities."

Other textual evidence from Isaiah, gives clear indications that at times the Lord's hunger for his favourite smoke was being appeased by the use of a shamanic incense inside the precincts of the temple, in elaborate shamanic ceremonies:

> And the posts of the door moved at the voice of him that
> cried, and the temple was filled with smoke.
> Then said I, "Woe is me, for I am undone; because I am a

---

4   Ibid.
5   Ibid.

man of unclean lips, and I dwell in the midst of a people of
unclean lips; for mine eyes have seen the King, the Lord of
hosts."
Then flew one of the seraphims unto me, having a live coal
in his hand, which he had taken with the tongs from off the
altar, And he laid it upon my mouth and said, "Lo, this hath
touched thy lips; and thine iniquity is taken away, and thy sin
purged." (Isaiah 6:4-7)

Besides these indications of topical and inhaled use of cannabis,
others have suggested that the Important Biblical and Apocrypha figure
Ezra, consumed a cannabis infused wine. Ezra was a key figure of the
Jewish monotheistic reformation after the Persians had returned them
to their homeland. Interestingly, at least two researchers, living more
than a century apart and from different parts of the world, have conclud-
ed that Ezra received his inspiration for this act, from the same source
of inspiration as his Zoroastrian overlords did: a cannabis infused wine!
Here is Ezra's own account of this. Ezra told the people not to seek him
for forty days, and he left for the desert, taking with him five people who
were to act as his scribes:

> The next day, behold a voice cried to me saying. Esdras open
> thy mouth, and drink what I give you thee to drink! Then
> opened I my mouth, and behold, he reached me a full cup,
> which is full as it were with water, but the color of it was like
> fire. I took it, and drank: and when I had drunk of it, my
> heart uttered understanding, and wisdom grew in my breast,
> for my spirit strengthened and my memory; and my mouth
> was opened and shut no more: and they sat forty days, and
> they wrote in the day, and at night they ate bread. As for me,
> I spake by the day, and I held not my tongue by the night. In
> forty days they wrote two hundred and four books (2 Esdras
> 14:38-44).

As George W. Brown recorded of this more than a century ago:

> A voice bid him open his mouth, he—*the voice*, of course—
> reached Esdras a full cup. It would be interesting to know
> whose voice it was which possessed such unnatural powers; yet

we apprehend the reader is much more anxious to know the
contents of the cup ... which possessed such wondrous ability,
probably the same possessed by the 'fruit of the tree' which
grew 'in the midst of the garden,' the eating of which opened
the eyes of our first parents, and enabled them to see 'as Gods
knowing good and evil.' We think we can furnish this desired
information, to do which we are compelled to anticipate
some facts existing among Zoroastrian worshippers; many
centuries before the date religionists ascribe to Abraham, and
which was practiced in Persia, Assyria and Babylonia at the
very time Ezra was writing Jewish history under the influence
of the 'fiery cup.'
Among other duties required on occasional sacrifices of
animals to Ahura-Mazda, additional to prayers, praises,
thanksgiving, and the recitation of hymns, was the
performance ... of a curious ceremony known as that of the
Haoma or Homa. This consisted of the extraction of the
juice of the Homa plant by the priests during the recitation
of prayers, the formal presentation of the liquid extracted to
the sacrificial fire ... the consumption of a small portion of
it by one of the officiating ministers, and the division of the
remainder among the worshippers.
What was the Haoma or Homa, the production of the
moon-plant, growing in those regions of Asia to far north
for the successful growing of the grape, and yet yielding such
intoxicating properties? It is known in the medical books as
Apocynum Cannabinum, and belongs to the Indian Hemp
family, *Cannabis Indica* being an official preparation from it.
It is now known in India as *bhang*, and is popularly known
with us as hashish, the stimulating and intoxicating effects of
which are well known to physicians.[6]

I have discussed the case for cannabis as haoma at length in another
article. More than a century after Brown, Vicente Dobroruka also noted
a comparison between the Persian technique of shamanic ecstasy and
that of Ezra in his essay "Preparation for Visions in Second Temple Jewish Apocalyptic Literature": "Similar drinks appear in Persian literature
...Vishtapa has an experience quite equivalent in the *Dinkard* ... where

---

6   George W. Brown, *Researches in Oriental History,* (1890).

mention is made to a mixture of wine (or haoma) and hemp with henbane . . . The *Book of Artay Viraz* also mentions visions obtained from wine mixed with hemp, and for the preparations of the seer."[7] I have discussed these Zoroastrian accounts elsewhere.

Dobroruka revisited this theme in more detail a later article, and again draws direct comparisons between Ezra's cup of fire, and the mang mixed infused beverages of the Zoroastrian psychonauts.[8] Interestingly, Rabbi Immanuel Löw, referred to a later Jewish recipe (Sabb. 14. 3 ed. Urbach, 9th-11th century) that called for wine to be mixed with ground up saffron, Arabic gum and hasisat surur, "I know 'surur' solely as a alias for the resin the Cannabis sativa."[9]

Low made no comment on the word "hasisat" which is very reminiscent of the name for cannabis resins in the medieval Arabic world "hasis" (hashish), and the term is generally thought to have been derived at in that period. However, the 19th century scholar John Kitto also put forth two different potential Hebrew word candidates for the origins of the term "hashish" in *A Cyclopaedia of Biblical Literature*. Kitto pointed to the Hebrew terms Shesh, which originates in reference to some sort of "fibre plant", and the possibly related word, *Eshishah* (E-shesh-ah?) which holds a wide variety of somewhat contradictory translations such as "flagon" "sweet cakes", "syrup", and "unguent." This last reference is interesting in relation to what we have already seen in regard to the cannabis infused Holy Oil, which was basically an unguent. According to Kitto, this Eshishah was mixed with wine. "Hebrew *eshishah* . . . is by others called *hashish* . . . this substance, in course of time, was converted into a medium of intoxication by means of drugs."[10] With the cognate pronunciation similarities found between the Hebrew *Shesh* and *Eshishah* one can only speculate on the possibility of two ancient Hebrew references to one plant that held both fibrous and intoxicating proper-

---

7   Vicente Dobroruka, "Preparation for Visions in Second Temple Jewish Apocalyptic Literature," *Phoinix* 8 no. 1 (2002): 372-391.

8   Vicente Dobroruka, "Chemically induced visions in the Fourth Book of Ezra in light of comparative Persian material," *Jewish Studies Quarterly* 13 (1) (2006): 1-26.

9   Immanuel Low, *Die Flora der Juden*, (1967).

10   John Kitto, *A Cyclopaedia of Biblical Literature*, (1845).

ties. It seems likely that what is referred to is hashish resin, with the addition of the word *"surur"* indicating the possibility of hashish oil, (which the Arabs prepared by boiling the tops of the plant and collecting the drops of oil that formed on top of the water). A very potent preparation. "The palm wine of the East . . . is made intoxicating . . . by an admixture of stupefying ingredients, of which there was an abundance . . . Such a practice seems to have existed amongst the ancient Jews."[11]

Talmudic reference indicates this use as well: "The one on his way to execution was given a piece of incense in a cup of wine, to help him fall asleep" (Sanh. 43a). Such preparations were used by the ancient Jews, for ritual intoxication, and for easing pain. A Reverend E. A Lawrence, in an essay on "The wine of the Bible" in a 19th-century edition of the *Princeton Review* noted that:

> It appears to have been an ancient custom to give medicated or drugged wine to criminals condemned to death, to blunt their senses, and so lessen the pains of execution. To this custom there is supposed to be an allusion, Prov. xxxi. 6, 'Give strong drink unto him that is ready to perish,' . . .To the same custom some suppose there is a reference in Amos 8, where the 'wine of the condemned' is spoken of . . . The wicked here described, in addition to other evil practices, imposed unjust fines upon the innocent, and spent the money thus unjustly obtained upon wine, which they quaffed in the house of their gods.
> Mixed wine is often spoken of in Scripture. This was of different kinds . . . sometimes, by lovers of strong drink, with spices of various kinds, to give it a richer flavor and greater potency (Is. v. 22; Ps. lxxv. 8). The 'royal wine,' literally wine of the kingdom . . . Esther i. 7), denotes most probably the best wine, such as the king of Persia himself was accustomed to drink.[12]

Thus, this infused wine, not only had pain numbing qualities, but was also "quaffed in the house of their gods" giving clear indication it was

---

11   Ibid.

12   Reverend E. A. Lawrence, "Wine of the Bible," *Princeton Review* 43 (1871).

sought after for entheogenic effects as well. That it is compared to the wines of the Kind of persia, also brings us back to the cannabis infused wines of the Zoroastrian period, such as that taken by King Vishtaspa. In reference to "unguents" such as the Holy oil, placing "incense" into wine, we are reminded of the cannabis infused incenses and anointing oils referred to earlier, indicating these substances may have come to have been placed directly into wine. In regards to myrrhed wine, it is worth noting that Dr. David Hillman, who holds combined degrees in Classics and Bacteriology, has suggested that ancient myrrh was often doctored with cannabis resins "The [ancient] Arabs . . . will take the rub, basically the hashish . . . they adulterate it with myrrh, so you end up with these combinations of plants that actually end up together . . . myrrh and cannabis, you see them associated often."[13]

In *The A to Z of Prophets in Islam and Judaism*, Scott B. Noegel and Brannon M. Wheeler wrote:

> The use of drugs, especially alcohol . . . as a means of inducing or enhancing the prophetic experience is attested periodically throughout the ancient Near East, and is probably related to the mantic's role as an herbalist and medical practitioner . . . Evidence for opium use has been found throughout the ancient Near East, especially in Cyprus, thought its connection to Cypriot cults has been questioned. The practice of inhaling intoxicating substances like cannabis and incense also appears . . . Texts from Mari demonstrate that at least some prophets partook in excessive wine drinking as a means of accessing the divine. Ugartic tablets also detail the events of the marzeah feast, a repast in which . . . dead kings were summoned to wine and dine with the living.[14]

Like Amos' condemnation of those who quaffed such mixtures in the House of the gods, Isaiah condemned those who seek oracles from the dead through inebriation (Isaiah 28:7-22).

13   Interview with David Hillman, "Smoke of the Oracles," (2014).

14   Brannon M. Wheeler and Scott B. Noegel, *The A to Z of Prophets in Islam and Judaism*, (Scarecrow Press, 2010).

And these also stagger from wine
and reel from beer:
Priests and prophets stagger from beer
and are befuddled with wine;
they reel from beer,
they stagger when seeing visions,
they stumble when rendering decisions.
All the tables are covered with vomit
and there is not a spot without filth.
You boast, "We have entered into a covenant with death,
with the realm of the dead we have made an agreement.
When an overwhelming scourge sweeps by,
it cannot touch us,
for we have made a lie our refuge
and falsehood[b]our hiding place."

These references show, even though in a negative light, that such cultic practices were both known and taking place in the region. Indeed, the use of infused wines for ecstatic purposes seems to have been so prevalent that at times there was an overlap between the worship of Yahweh and the Greek God of Intoxication, Dionysus, as I have noted elsewhere.

Cannabis in Later Jewish Magic

Rabbi Aryeh Kaplan has noted of early Kabbalistic schools who used magic and other means of communion for mystic exploration, that "some practices include the use of 'grasses,' which were possibly psychedelic drugs."[15] Kaplan's *The Living Torah* includes cannabis as a possible candidate for the Hebrew kaneh bosem, "due to cognate pronunciation."[16] The Kabbalistic text the Zohar records:

There is no grass or herb that grows in which G-d's wisdom is not greatly manifested and which cannot exert great influence in heaven" and "If men but knew the wisdom of all the Holy One, blessed be He, has planted in the earth, and the power of all that is to be found in the world, they would proclaim

---

15   Aryeh Kaplan, *Meditation and Kabbalah*, (Weiser Books, 1989).
16   Aryeh Kaplan, *The Living Torah*, (Moznaim Publishers, 1981).

the power of their L-rd in His great wisdom. (Zohar 2,80B)

Prof. Benny Shannon, who has speculated about ancient jewish use of psychoactive substances, felt somewhat vindicated when he was directed by the works of the medieval Kabbalist and scholar Rabbi Jacob Ben Asher (*Rabbeinu Be'cha'yei ben Asher*). "Rabbeinu Be'cha'yei writes that the purest of foods were created at the very beginning of Creation in order to allow for the attainment of higher knowledge. He explicitly relates this to the biblical tree of knowledge, and comments further that such higher knowledge can also be gained through the use of drugs and medicines available at his time. In addition, he notes that the Manna had such qualities as well."[17] Clearly cannabis and its various preparations, along with opium and other psychoactives, were well known for its mystical properties at Ben Asher's time.

In his *De Occulta Philosophia* (1651) Agrippa refers to how "Rabbi Israel made certain cakes, writ upon with certain divine and angelicall names, and so consecrated, which they that did eat with faith, hope, and charitie [charity], did presently break forth with a spirit of prophecie [prophecy]." We read in the same place that "Rabbi Johena the son of Jochahad, did after that manner enlighten a certain rude countryman, called Eleazar, being altogether illiterate, that being compassed about with a sudden brightness, did unexpectedly preach such high mysteries of the Law to an assembly of wise men, that he did even astonish all that were neer him." A description that indicates more than sigils on cakes in use, although the ingredients of said cakes are not included.

Like the Zoroastrian royalty and priesthood, as well as the Levites, there are indications that early Kabbalists enjoyed the use of the herb but prevented its consumption by the common people. In the *P'sachim*, "Rav Yehudah says it is good to eat . . . the essence of hemp seed in Babylonian broth; but it is not lawful to mention this in the presence of an illiterate man, because he might derive a benefit from the knowledge not meant for him." (*Nedarim*, fol. 49, col. 1). Other sources have noted a Kabbalistic comparison to the effects of cannabis with divine perception, noting an "intriguing reference to cannabis in the context

17   Benny Shannon, "Biblical Entheogens: A Speculative Hypothesis," *Time and Mind* 1 (2008): 51-74.

of a fleeting knowledge of God: *Zohar Hadash, Bereshit,* 16a (*Midrash ha-Ne'elam*)."[18]

This brings us into the era of Merkavah Mysticism, (100-1000 AD), which is centred on the sort of visionary experience of Ezekiel, who as we saw earlier, came to his experience through eating a "scroll". Modern magician Aaron Leitch believes Merkavah Mysticism held a strong influence over the later western magical tradition. "The Merkavah's use of ritual drugs, its focus upon talismans and seals, the summoning forth of Angelic gatekeepers, and the gaining of mystical visions are elements that run throughout the grimoiric spells."[19]

That cannabis might have played a role in such forms of Jewish mysticism, is indicated by references to it well into the late medieval period. Another interesting reference can be found with Rabbi Berel Wein, who has written and lectured extensively on Jewish history, has connected the use of hashish with the Kabbalistic inspired Jewish messianic movement of the 17th century. Wein refers to the Morrocan Jew, Joseph ben Zur, who was popularly identified with the prophesied messianic figure Messiah ben Joseph, a claim that was propped up by Rabbi Elisha Ashkenazi and thousands of Jews in Morocco, Algeria and Tunisia believed this and followed Joseph ben Zur as a result. According to Wein:

> Joseph ben Zur was probably mentally unstable. At the very least, though, he was guilty of a very prevalent habit in the Middle East: smoking hashish. Now, smoking hashish in the 17th century was not seen in the same negative light as the modern world views it. Nevertheless, Joseph ben Zur was both slightly touched and usually high, which together is a lethal combination. He claimed he saw a vision when an angel came to him and said that he was the Messiah ben Joseph.[20]

This scenario of scrying under the influence of cannabis, fits with both the suggestion of cannabis in the Kabbalistic writing referred too, as well as the confirmed use of cannabis for scrying in the Kabbalistic

---

18   Daniel Chanan Matt, *Zohar: The Book of Enlightenment,* (Paulist Press, 1983).

19   Aaron Leitch, *Secrets of the Magickal Grimoires,* (Llewellyn, 2005).

20   Rabbi Berel Wein, "False Messianic Fervor and Fever," (2013).

inspired *Sepher Raziel: Liber Salomonis*, which was composed in this same time period.

In regard to Solomonic magic, and the role of the Kabbalah, there may have been some survival of the ancient cannabis use among later Jewish Kabbalists and Alchemists. The Kabbalah is a system of mysticism considered by many to be the secret teachings of the Jews, and which holds a number of parallels with the Jewish and Christian Gnostic sects of the 1st-4th century AD, as well as with the sort of astral magic contained in the *Ghayat AlHakim* and the *Picatrix*, which also survives in Hebrew translations, some taken directly from the original Arabic.

In reference to what we have stated about ancient and medieval use of topical preparations of cannabis and other drugs for magical and religious purposes, one of the most interesting references occurs in the 16th century Grimoire, *Sepher Raziel: Liber Salomonis*, where it is used for seeing spirits and devils in a magic mirror. Often "referred to as "Sepher Raziel", and also known as "Liber Salomonis", this grimoire has 7 known surviving versions in manuscript form. It should be noted that *Sepher Raziel* is also referred to under its library catalog names, Sloane MS 3846 and Sloane MS 3826, were particularly looked at for this study, and these catalog names are used to distinguish it from a variety of similarly named grimoires. *Sepher Raziel: Liber Salomonis* was transcribed in 1564, by a William Parry of London at the bequest of one John Gwyne. It is seen as a "Christian product, though one which borrowed from Jewish, Arabic, and Græco-Roman scholastic and folk sources."[21]

Solomon has often been associated with magic, and this is particularly true of medieval European magical traditions where grimoires like the 14-15th-century *Clavicula Salomonis*, "The Key of Solomon" and the 17th-century *Clavicula Salomonis Regis*, "The Lesser Key of Solomon" both of which represents a typical example of Renaissance magic.

However, Solomon's reputation for magic, goes back much further than this. *The Testament of Solomon*, thought to date from sometime between the 1st and 3rd century AD, is one of the oldest magical texts concerning the ancient Jewish king. This text is pseudepigraphic catalog of demons summoned by King Solomon, and how they can be countered by invoking angels and other magical techniques. *The Testament*

21   Don Karr, *Liber Salomonis: Cephar Razie*, (2016).

of Solomon refers to a story where the magician-king forces a demon to spin hemp! "So I commanded her to spin the hemp for the ropes used in the building of the house of God; and accordingly, when I had sealed and bound her, she was so overcome and brought to naught as to stand night and day spinning the hemp" (*The Testament of Solomon*, 100-300 AD). In this regard, it should be noted that it was claimed by the etymologist Sula Benet that Solomon's Song of Songs' 4:14 made reference to cannabis along with other 'incense trees'.

Sepher Raziel: Liber Salomonis was written in the Solomonic tradition, which also brought us the still popular *The Keys of Solomon*, and both texts, which come from the same period, have been attributed to the ancient Hebrew King, in an attempt to give them more authority. Even in the ancient world, Solomon was highly regarded for his knowledge of magic. In his excellent overview of the subject, *Secrets of the Magical Grimoires*, Aaron Leitch identifies a number of potent fumigations, and recipes that contained a variety of psychoactive plants. He noted are passages from *The Key of Solomon* that give instructions for a "Magic Carpet" that is "proper for interrogation." As *The Key of Solomon* (14th-15th century) describes: "Taking thy carpet, thou shalt cover they head and body therewith" and then hovering over a bowl of burning incense. Through this method "thou shalt hear distinctly the answer which though shalt have sought." Although the ingredients for the incense fumigated in *The Key of Solomon* are not clear, the recipes of the *Sepher Raziel: Liber Salomonis* are clearer.

As the *Sepher Raziel* records "I Salomon put such a knowledge & such a distinction, & explanation in this booke to evry man that readeth or studieth it, that he know whereof he was and from whence he came."

Most sixteenth-century manuscripts of magic remain unedited and unpublished, perhaps because the majority of them . . . are dominated by liturgical conjuration. This is a style of magic that has attracted less academic attention than Solomonic magic and Renaissance theurgy, perhaps because it is perceived as a hangover of the medieval period. However, liturgical demon conjuring is every bit as typical of early modern magic. Copiers of Solomonic magical texts like the *Sepher Raziel* sought to return to purified form of conjuration drawn from Kabbalistic Jewish traditions supposedly passed down from Solomon himself, at a time when Renaissance humanists were interested in recovering the Kabbalistic tradition.[22]

As the occult writer A. E Waite explained of *Sepher Raziel*: "It is an English translation of a Latin original . . . and purports to have been sent to Solomon by a prince of Babylon, who was greater and more worshipful than all men of his time . . . The Latin title of the the treatise is said to be *Angelus Magnus Secreti Creatoris*; it was the first book after Adam, was written in the language of Chaldea and afterwards translated into Hebrew."[23] (There are no known surviving copies of the Latin original refried too.) Stephen Skinner, in a recently published translation of *Sepher Raziel* suggests the roots "were probably a Hebrew original, filtered through a Latin intermediary, to the present Middle English version."[24]

Julia Cresswell, who has written extensively on British myth and magic, suggests "that although the manuscript may be sixteenth century, some of the language is rather old-fashioned for that date, except perhaps for an old person writing in the early sixteenth century. I would guess that the text is a reworking if an earlier one, pushing the origin of the material back into the Middle Ages."[25] Occult writer Damon Lycourinos, agrees with this, suggesting *Sepher Raziel* is "derived from thirteenth century Latin sources."[26]

The text itself tells us, that prior to this, it had been passed down through the hands of figures like Adam and Solomon, and it reveals the ultimate author as the Angel Raziel. A number of other medieval magical texts, claim this authorship as well, and this seems to have been away as describing a document that was in part scryed or channelled. "The most explicit transmission of Jewish magical material into the Christian Latin tradition of magic was the translation of works associated with the

---

22   Paul Foreman, *The Cambridge Book of Magic*, (Francis Young, 2015).

23   Arthur Edward Waite, *The Book of Ceremonial Magic*, (1911).

24   Don Karr and Stephen Skinner, *Sepher Raziel: Liber Salomonis*, (Golden Hoard, 2017).

25   Julia Cresswell, *The Watkins Dictionary of Angels*, (Watkins Publishing, 2006), 9.

26   Damon Zacharias Lycourinos, *Occult Traditions*, (Manticore Press, 2012).

name—Raziel an angel present in Jewish angelology and Arabic astrological texts who was said to have revealed a book of secrets to Adam."
The name Raziel itself means 'secrets of God', and this is a fitting title
for the Promethium transmitter of secrets that the figure represents in
the magical tradition.

The Judeo-Christian mystic origins are obvious, as *Sepher Raziel,
Liber Salomonis*, is clearly reminiscent of the planetary accession-based
magic of Gnosticism, Merkavah and the Kabbalah.

> The text is divided into seven sections, covering different
> topics including the use of astrology, incense, timings, purity,
> and the seven heavens and their angels. As can be seen from
> the sevenfold emphasis, this is another essentially planetary
> grimoire.[27]

The area of interest in relation to this study, lays in the second book,
which details the virtues of stones, herbs and beasts. Plants play an important role in the magic of Sepher Raziel, Liber Salomonis. For as the
grimoire explains, it was by Adam and Eve's sin of eating the forbidden
fruit that they were expelled from Eden and the company of God. The
Angel Raziel, feeling empathy for lost humanity, in a sense played the
role of Prometheus, and shares the secret knowledge of plants so that the
descendants of the first couple, might be restored to their former place
of Glory. As the Grimoire records of this:

> Know thou that in herbs is vertue of the most that may be .
> . . Know thou that among herbs there be some with which
> thou may do good & euill. As to heale & make sicke. And so
> understand thou in these that shall be said furthermore. And
> Adam said by a tree came wretchednes into the world that is
> by the tree I sinned in it. And Raziel said, An herbe shall be
> thy life. And Salomon said, A tree shall be & shall wexe of
> which the leaues shall not fall. And it shall be medicyne of
> men. (*Sepher Raziel*)

Apparently cannabis was held in high regard in the search for knowledge. In the *Sepher Raziel*, cannabis is combined with artemisia, also

---

27   Ibid.

known as wormwood, an ingredient in the famous 19th-century liqueur of the poets. Wormwood contains thujone, a psychoactive chemical, that attaches itself to the same receptor sites. in the brain that THC, the active chemical of cannabis, does. As the *Sepher Raziel* instructs of the use of these combined plants for magical invocation:

> The third herbe is Canabus [cannabis]& it is long in shafte & clothes be made of it. The vertue of the Juse [juice]of it is to anoynt thee with it & with the juse of arthemesy & ordyne thee before a mirrour of stele [steel]& clepe thou spiritts & thou shallt see them & thou shalt haue might of binding & of loosing deuills [devils]& other things.

There are two act of magic taking being combined here, *katapharmakeuo* which means "to dose (or anoint) with drugs" and *katoptromanteria*, "divination by means of mirrors".[28]

In regard to katoptromanteria, also referred to as captromany it has long been known that trance states "could be induced by gazing at polished or shiny surfaces illuminated by lamps, through a kind of self-hypnosis."[29] "Mirrors . . . [have]long been part of shamanic paraphernalia. As a receptacle of for souls, the mirror often served as a means for entering the trance state."[30] This of course is the magic "mirror, mirror on the wall" that survives in fairy tales. "All ancient civilizations had such things (crystals, pools of water or ink, silver or glass mirrors) and the magical literature abounds in directions for their manufacture and use."[31]

One may get some idea of the influence of the *Sepher Raziel*'s method of drug induced mirror scrying on magic, by looking at the contemporary accounts of Dr. John Dee and Edward Kelly. When we consider the role of the cannabis anointing oil at the time of Moses to invoke the 'spirit of the Lord' to the recipe for a cannabis ointment to scry visions

---

28 Definition from Luck's *Vocabula Magica*.

29 Ibid.

30 Gloria Flaherty, *Shamanism and the Eighteenth Century*, (Princeton University Press, 1992).

31 John Patrick Deveney, *Paschal Beverly Randolph: A Nineteenth-Century Black American Spiritualist, Rosicrucian, and Sex Magician*, (State University of New York Press, 1996).

of spirits in the mirror, one can only wonder if this was some sort of continuous tradition among the more esoterically minded Jews.

Solomon's "legend figures into late traditions of Freemasons. Rumours which suggest the wise king left secret books of magic seem never to have died—nor have slumbered—since ancient times."[32] And indeed, as I have noted a number of well-known Freemasons were in possession of *Sepher Raziel*.

Another important figure in the rituals of Freemasonry, is a character named Hiram Abiff, said to be the architect and builder of Solomon's Temple. Also known as the Widow's son, Hiram Abiff is the central character of an allegory presented to all candidates during the third degree in Freemasonry. In the mythology of the story Abiff is murdered by three ruffians, who want him to reveal the secret signs and passwords of the higher degrees of masonry, which were used in receiving payment for work on the temple. Some of the central initiations of Masonry, are death and rebirth ceremonies based on this particular story.

Interestingly, the first public retelling of this mythos, had the tale tied up with the occult use of hashish, as well as the first Western reference to its use in the Bible. The French poet, Gérard De Nerval (1808–1855), included what has been suggested as the first published account of the Masonic story of Hiram Abiff. As the authors of *The Temple and the Lodge* noted of this:

> Nerval not only recited the basic narrative. He also divulged— for the first time, to our knowledge—a skein of eerie mystical traditions associated in Freemasonry with Hiram's background and pedigree. What is particularly curious is that Nerval makes no mention of Freemasonry whatsoever. Pretending that his narrative is a species of regional folktale, never known in the West before, he claims to have heard it orally recited by a Persian raconteur, in a Constantinople coffee-house.[33]

---

32   Karr and Skinner, *Sepher Raziel*.

33   Michael Baigent and Richard Leigh, *The Temple and the Lodge: The Strange and Fascinating History of the Knights Templar and the Freemasons*, (Little Brown & Co., 1989).

In the story there is an account of an asylum being paid a visit by the great Arab alchemist Ebn-Sina (Avicenna), and he is overheard saying "The word hachichot appears in the Song of Songs, and the inebriating properties of this mixture."[34] The narration breaks on that point, but it is worth noting that Nerval's account is the first known written reference which refers openly to cannabis in the Bible that I am aware of, and interestingly it also ties it with a noted alchemist.

Cannabis in Jewish Alchemy

The use of cannabis infused wines goes back to ancient times in the Mid-East. References from the 3-4th century alchemist, Zosimos to cannabis infused wines, who was heavily influenced by Jewish sources in his writing on alchemy, as well as the saffron and cannabis resin combination used in wine referred to by Rabbi Immanuel Low in the 9th century (Sabb. 14. 3 ed. Urbach) indicate Jewish use in this context. This use continued into the medieval period and such infusions of cannabis and other substances were used in *Quintessences* and other forms by Jewish alchemists and mystics.

In regard to alchemy, there may have been some cross pollination between medieval Jews and Arabs. The 11th-century Byzantine Jewish Doctor, Simeon Sethus wrote "the dried leaf, when drunk, as meal, or rather [as dried meal for a drink] produces a hospitable drunkenness and lack of sensation by the eater. For it is crushed or kneaded among the Arabs for wine, and it inebriates." As Rabbi Aryeh Kaplan, has noted, a number of medieval Kabbalists, refer to a technique of philosophical meditation, that included drinking a cup of "strong wine of Avicenna", that induced a trance in order to aid the adept in pondering difficult philosophical questions.[35] Unfortunately no recipe for this remains, but the medieval Islamic alchemist and physician, Avicenna, refers in his works to the effects of hashish, opium and datura extracts, and he was familiar with the infusion of these drugs into wine. Moreover, it has long

---

34   Gerard de Nerval, *Journey to The Orient*, Trans. by Norman Glass, (New York University Press, 1972).

35   Nachman of Breslov, *Rabbi Nachman's Stories*, Trans. by Aryeh Kaplan, (Breslov Research Institute, 1985).

been suggested that cannabis infused wines were used by the Ismai'li with whom Avicenna has long been associated. Simeon Sethus, an 11th century Byzantine Jewish doctor wrote of cannabis as follows: "Arabs will squeeze [the oils?] into wine to intoxicate."[36] Charles Dickens annual 19th weekly journal, *All the Year Round*, noted such combinations, in use well into the 19th century by Jews and Moslems alike. "Pure wine, however, is not for the topers of Ispahan and Teheran, the Jewish and Armenian dealers ministering to that fondness for narcotics which tend so greatly to enervate the East, by mixing myrrh, incense, and the juice of the Indian hemp with the finest growths."[37]

In this regard, some references to alchemical recipes that call for cannabis and other psychoactive plants to be infused into wine or other more potent alcoholic preparations, come to mind. In an earlier article I discussed references from the 4th century alchemist Zosimos, to cannabis and darnel infused in wines or beers for magical purposes, and Zosimos himself was said to have gathered much of his own knowledge from a female Alchemist known as "Mary the Jewess" (*Mary Hebraea*). "The first nonfictious alchemists of the Western world, lived . . . in Hellensitic Egypt. And the earliest among them was Maria . . . the Jewess, for whom are chief source was Zosimos."[38]

Mary the Jewess is credited with the invention of several kinds of chemical apparatus and is considered to be the first true alchemist of the Western world. Her works are often referred to by later alchemists. Carl jung, who studied both alchemy and Gnosticism, believed her work "may go back to very early times and thus to Gnostic societies."[39] Plants seem to have been involved in her alchemical processes as well. "Maria the Jewess was said to have identified the philosophers's stone with a mysterious 'white herb of the mountain.'"[40]

In *Better Living Through Alchemy*, Lynn Osburn, who has been

---

36   Christian Gottfried Gruner, *De Zythorum Confectione Fragmentum*, (1814).

37   Charles Dickens, *All the Year Round*, (Chapman & Hall, 1859-1895).

38   Raphael Patai, *The Jewish Alchemists: A History and Source Book*, (Princeton University Press, 1994).

39   Carl Jung, *Psychology and Alchemy, Collected Works of C. G. Jung*, (Princeton University Press, 1968).

40   Ibid.

researching alchemical texts for decades, and who has written about quintessences, suggests that Mary the Jewess may have also made a veiled reference to cannabis, (Osburn seems to have been unaware of the direct references to cannabis is the surviving writings attributed to Zosimos):

> Unfortunately, the alchemical writings of Maria Prophetissa are incomplete, surviving only in fragments copied by later writers. In one treatise ascribed to her—Practica Mariae Prophetissae in artem alchemicam . . . she discusses *matrimonium alchymicum* (alchemical wedding) with the philosopher Aros. From it comes the oft repeated alchemical dictum "Marry gum with gum in true marriage." C. G. Jung, wrote concerning the nature of that alchemical gum, "Originally it was 'gum arabic', and it is used here as a secret name for the transforming substance, on account of its adhesive quality. Thus, Kunrath declares that the 'red' gum is the 'resin of the wise'—a synonym for the transforming substance." Had Jung been an initiate of alchemy he would have known that gum arabic was itself a pseudonym for the true transforming substance—the red resin of the wise—a gum gathered from the resinous flower clusters of female Cannabis sativa plants. That highly fragrant reddish resin has been produced in India since time immemorial and carried to the west by Arab traders.[41]

Zosimos testified that the "true teachings about the Great Art" were to be found in "the writings and books of the Jews." "Azulai speaks of the philosopher's stone in his Midbar Kedemot, and calls it esev ('weed') as it was also called by the alchemists (and as it is called in other kabbalistic writings as well as in Hebrew manuscripts dealing with alchemy)."[42] The Hebrew term 'esev' "weed", has in modern times been used to designate cannabis and its products, however it is not clear how far back this association can be dated. Although, as 'hashish', meaning 'herb' goes back to the early islamic period, that such an association may have been used in medieval times with 'esev' deserves at least some consideration.

---

41   Lynne Osborne, *Better Living Through Alchemy Vol. I: Origins of Alchemy,* (2019).

42   *Encyclopedia Judaica,* (2008).

As a result of this Jewish influence, numbers of Old Testament figures, such as Moses, Isaiah, Ezra, and most notably Isaiah, were deemed medieval practitioneers of alchemy, by later medieval and renaissance alchemists. "Several of the biblical prophets were considered adepts in alchemy. The prophet Elijah was often referred to by Christian alchemists, several of whose work carry the name Elijah in their title. In some of these treatises Jewish influence is evident."[43]

Elijah, in this respect, is an interesting choice, for in the Islamic world Elijah, has been identified with the Green one, Khidr, seen as the patron saint of cannabis. And in that respect, it is important to note of the Jewish and Gnostic influences, all of this came to European alchemists after it had been filtered by Islamic ones.

The techniques of preparation of disease fighting, life preserving elixirs was the core of alchemy for many medieval and renaissance alchemists, and this again was an adaption from middle eastern influences that came into Europe following the Crusades. In references to figures such as "Lully, Paracelsus, Jerome Cardan, etc." Albert G. Mackey in his *Encyclopedia of Freemasonry*, wrote that these figures were not "occultists . . . They had been physicians and chemists; the 'alchemy' they studied was chemistry, and they studied it for medical uses (along with botany, etc.)." Interestingly, as discussed in *Liber 420*, all three of the figures mentioned by name have associations with cannabis elixirs, Cardano and Paracelsus both left recipes for cannabis preparations, and cannabis appears in a number of Llullian texts.

> These attempts to assuage human physical suffering were manifested in the utilization of the sacred narcotic herbs; the extraction of the sedative qualities of mandragora and Indian hemp; the concoctions of the alchemist; the magical powers of alleviating pain by a resignation transcending even the powers of potentates or priests.[44]

---

43   Patai, *The Jewish Alchemists*.

44   William John Gies, *Horace Wells, Dentist; Father of Surgical Anesthesia: Proceedings of Centenary Commemorations of Well's Discovery in 1844 and Lists of Wells Memorabilia, Including Bibliographies, Memorials and Testimonials*, (Case Lockwood and Brainard, 1948).

These preparations came under various names such as arcanums, tinctures, and quintessences (fifth essence), and all were equated with having the same sort of life preserving effects and qualities as the Philosopher's stone by their adherents. From the very beginning "quintessence became linked to the Arab elixir—a substance that could prolong life."

> The elixir holds a similar position in the alchemical tradition to the philosopher's stone; indeed, the two are sometimes interchangeable. Zoismos . . . wrote an encyclopedia of alchemy, the Cheirokmeta, in which he mentioned a potent alchemical preparation called the Xerion, a word derived from the Greek for "dry." It seems to allude to a dry powder, but in its Arabic form of al-iksir it became later identified as a miraculous potion.[45]

It is in the branch of alchemy known as Spagyrics from Ancient Greek σπάω spao "I collect" and ἀγείρω ageiro "I extract", a name thought to have been coined by the European alchemist Paracelsus. And refers to extraction processes involving fermentation, distillation, tincturing, as well as extraction of essential oils with vapours and extraction of mineral elements from the ash of plants through calcination.

Tincturing, was one of the major arts of alchemy, since the time of Zosimos, and this included tinctures of plants, animals, stones and metals. One of Zosimos' own surviving works, the Final Quittance, is devoted to this art. and he discusses the "differences between 'opportune tinctures', which are astrologic and daimonic in origin, and 'natural tinctures', which are grounded in a more empirical methodology and technique."[46] Comments which reveal the combination of magic and science at work in alchemy.

It was in his excellent essay and accompanying translation, *An Unknown Hebrew Medical Alchemist: A Medeival Treatise on the Qunita Essentia* that the respected scholar of Jewish history, Raphael Patai, first discussed a number of alchemical texts devoted to the Quintessence,

---

45 Philip Ball, *The Devil's Doctor: Paracelsus and the World of Renaissance Magic and Science*, (Farrar, Straus and Giroux, 2006).

46 Kyle A. Fraser, "Zosimos of Panopolis and the Book of Enoch: Alchemy as Forbidden Knowledge" *Aries* 4 (2004).

and particularly identifies preparations containing cannabis, opium and other psychoactive plants. Patai returned to this topic in his pivotal work *The Jewish Alchemists*. He noted that "among the many Latin writings published by Ramon Lull there are several that deal with the fabulous quinta essentia. the purest of essences, which was supposed to rejuvenate the old and cure all kinds of diseases including mental aberrations."

Of such texts, Patai's work was directed at a Hebrew alchemical text devoted to the Quintessence, attributed to an anonymous author who claimed it was a copy of a text written by "a great sage whose name is Raimon", a name believed to have been used in hopes of of associating it with the works of Ramon Llull. This centuries old text, written in Hebrew, appeared in a medieval manuscript alongside selections from the works of Avicenna. It was likely a copy of an even earlier lost Latin manuscript that did not survive and may have been destroyed in the Church's 14th century purge of such documents.

The 14th-15th century Hebrew manuscript opens with the words "And now I shall copy for you a great secret of the fifth essence, which is called in their language [Spanish] qinta esensia . . . It was written by a great sage whose name Raimon." Raphael Patai notes that as "for the identity of the author, all that can be said was that he was a Jewish physician whom lived in Spain in the fourteenth or fifteenth century, and knew, in addition to Hebrew, Latin, Spanish, Arabic, Persian, Turkish and Sanskrit." Like the English *The Book of Quintessence*, with which it holds some strong comparisons, the author "influenced by the alchemical teachings of his time in which the quinta essentia occupied a prominent place. He repeats again and again that the admixture of the quinta essentia will increase the effectiveness of drugs." As the Hebrew text records:

> If you want to prepare a potion for a disease . . . place those drugs which are appropriate for that potion into our Fifth Essence, and it will become like the potion, and it will be more effective, one part of it to a hundred. And likewise . . . the fragrant drugs, and thus all things of this kind, and thus all the cordial drugs must be pounded to utter thinness, until one cannot feel it by palpitation.

The author of the 14th-century Hebrew text goes onto give a variety of medicinal plants to be infused into the Fifth Essence and prescribes them for various ailments and conditions. Preparations of poppy, belladonna were also noted, via an infusion of 'popillion ointment', prepared opium, wolfsbane, henbane, monkshood, mandrake, and a variety of plants under foreign names which are not always clearly identifiable, as well as a preparation of "Pills . . . from India" so it is clear exotic imported ingredients were also in use. As the author of the tractate author states of such plants and preparations "apply these things to our heaven [quintessence]." Patai notes of this in *The Jewish Alchemists*, where he also discusses this Hebrew alchemical text, "It should be noted that his instructions throughout the lists of his medicaments is to add them to 'our heaven, that is, the fifth essence, whereby the original medicinal property and effectiveness of the substances in question will be maximized." It is clear, that the term 'heaven' was used in reference to this ethanol like preparation, the quintessence, that could absorb the 'essence' or 'soul' of the plant, and leave the material body behind, as with the concept of the human soul leaving the mortal body and ascending to Heaven. Patai suggests that:

> Like Lull, he considers that the quinta essentia can cure almost anything, from melancholy, to pestilential fever, and from poisoning to demoniac possession . . . it can rejuvenate old men, renew the spirit of life, and endow women with beauty. Yet despite these clearly alchemical features, one gains the impression that the author relies more on the curative powers of the drugs themselves than on the quinta essentia added to them. Nowhere does he recommend the application of the quinta essentia by itself; he always suggests its use as an agent intensifying or augmenting the curative powers of drugs.

I think Patai has it incorrect of his understanding of what has taken place. The *quinta essentia* was not "added" to the plants, the alchemical view was that the essence of the plant itself was extracted into the elixir, and the potion became the *Quintessence* of the plant or plants used. The anonymous author of the Hebrew treatise also refers to a mixture used both internally and topically that includes "chaff of hemp" for the treatment of "dropsy" and "Persian fire" which is thought to have been a form of venereal disease, and a variety of other ailments. Noting that the mixture is "also utterly effective against the illness of cancer if it is imbibed with sabar [aloe]." According to the anonymous Hebrew author of this 14th century tractate on the quintessence: "This medicine was invented by a great sage, and many old diseases came upon him, and he saw this in a dream, and made it, and was cured, and he put it in writing so as to help many people. And it helps internal [diseases]by drinking and external [diseases]by way of a plaster chaff of qanavos (hemp). And we have tried this medicine many times, and all those who take the above mentioned mixture will be saved form leprosy and perselia [palsy?], and from bad diseases which have no [other]cure." Miraculous cures reminiscent of the tales of the Holy Grail.

In this respect, it should be remembered that even things like curing maladies, was considered miraculous, and the maladies themselves, as in ancient times, were often considered demonic in nature. As Raymond de Tarrega, recorded in *De secrets naturae sive quinta essentia*:

> The demons are attached to human bodies because of bad dispositions and corrupt humour, or because of melancholic infection which generates evil, black, and horrible images in fantasy, and disturbs the intellect, for the demons habitually take on such forms, and generally dwell in obscure and solitary places. When by virtue of the fifth essence [*quintessence*] and other things this humor, which is the reason they enter such a body, is expelled from it, then at the same time also the demons vanish at once altogether with the humor.
> And because of this there exists a revelation of how the sensate medicines have the effect of expelling demons from any body. Use, therefore that aforementioned medicine, and you will cure any demoniac.

This act of herbal healing is compared by de Tarrega to "Solomon's act of necromancy, with which demons were forced to perform good works; or with evil virtue of words, stones, and plants. It is therefore clear how the demons are subject to the action of senate things." Thus, to cure someone of disease, was equal to, control over demons, and even an exorcism, and herein may have laid the issues the Church had with the alchemists who were preparing the quintessence and writing about its various manifestations from different plant preparations. Indeed, the threat of persecution by the Church, was the force behind the need to keep their inner lives secretive was a reality shared by Jews, Alchemists, and Magicians alike, so little wonder these avenues at times crossed paths.

WORKS CITED

Baigent, Michael and Richard Leigh, *The Temple and the Lodge: The Strange and Fascinating History of the Knights Templar and the Freemasons*, (Little Brown & Co., 1989).

Ball, Philip, *The Devil's Doctor: Paracelsus and the World of Renaissance Magic and Science*, (Farrar, Straus and Giroux, 2006).

Brashear, William M., *Magica Varia* (Fondation Egyptologique reine Elisabeth, 1991).

Brown, George W., *Researches in Oriental History*, (1890).

Cresswell, Julia, *The Watkins Dictionary of Angels*, (Watkins Publishing, 2006).

de Nerval, Gerard, *Journey to The Orient*, Trans. by Norman Glass, (New York University Press, 1972).

Deveney, John Patrick, *Paschal Beverly Randolph: A Nineteenth-Century Black American Spiritualist, Rosicrucian, and Sex Magician*, (State University of New York Press, 1996).

Dickens, Charles, *All the Year Round*, (Chapman & Hall, 1859-1895).

Dobroruka, Vicente, "Chemically induced visions in the Fourth Book of Ezra in light of comparative Persian material," *Jewish Studies Quarterly* 13 (1) (2006): 1-26.

———, "Preparation for Visions in Second Temple Jewish Apocalyptic Literature," *Phoinix* 8(1) (2002): 372-391.

Encyclopedia Judaica, (2008).

Flaherty, Gloria, *Shamanism and the Eighteenth Century*, (Princeton University Press, 1992).

Foreman, Paul, *The Cambridge Book of Magic*, (Francis Young, 2015).

Fraser, Kyle A. "Zosimos of Panopolis and the Book of Enoch: Alchemy as Forbidden Knowledge" *Aries* 4 (2004).

Frater A. T. A., (The Theoretical and practical treatise of Hashish), which became 'The Treaty of Hashish—and other Psychic Substances' by Ernest Bos De Veze, Annotated, Reviewed, and Expanded Into English, (2018).

Gies, William John, *Horace Wells, Dentist; Father of Surgical Anesthesia: Proceedings of Centenary Commemorations of Well's Discovery in 1844 and Lists of Wells Memorabilia, Including Bibliographies, Memorials and Testimonials*, (Case Lockwood and Brainard, 1948).

Gruner, Christian Gottfried, *De Zythorum Confectione Fragmentum*, (1814).

Hillman, David, Interview "Smoke of the Oracles," (2014).

Jung, Carl, *Psychology and Alchemy, Collected Works of C. G. Jung* (Princeton University Press, 1968).

Kaplan, Aryeh, *Meditation and Kabbalah*, (Weiser Books, 1989).

———, *The Living Torah*, (Moznaim Publishers, 1981).

Karr, Don and Stephen Skinner, *Sepher Raziel: Liber Salomonis*, (Golden Hoard, 2017).

Karr, Don, *Liber Salomonis: Cephar Razie*, (2016).

Kitto, John, *A Cyclopaedia of Biblical Literature*, (1845).

Lawrence, Reverend E. A., "Wine of the Bible," *Princeton Review* 43 (1871).

Leitch, Aaron, *Secrets of the Magickal Grimoires*, (Llewellyn, 2005).

Low, Immanuel, *Die Flora der Juden*, (1967).

Luck, Georg, "Psychoactive Substances in Religion and Magic," *Arcana Mundi: Magic and the Occult in the Greek and Roman Worlds, A Collection of Ancient Texts*, 2nd ed. (Baltimore, Md.: Johns Hopkins University Press, 2006).

Lycourinos, Damon Zacharias, *Occult Traditions*, (Manticore Press, 2012).

Matt, Daniel Chanan, *Zohar: The Book of Enlightenment*, (Paulist Press, 1983).

Nachman of Breslov, *Rabbi Nachman's Stories*, Trans. by Aryeh Kaplan, (Breslov Research Institute, 1985).

Osborne, Lynne, *Better Living Through Alchemy Vol. I: Origins of Alchemy*, (2019).

Patai, Raphael, *The Jewish Alchemists: A History and Source Book*,

(Princeton University Press, 1994).

Shannon, Benny, "Biblical Entheogens: A Speculative Hypothesis," *Time and Mind* 1 (2008): 51-74.

Waite, Arthur Edward, *The Book of Ceremonial Magic*, (1911).

Wein, Rabbi Berel, "False Messianic Fervor and Fever," (2013).

Wheeler, Brannon M. and Scott B. Noegel, *The A to Z of Prophets in Islam and Judaism*, (Scarecrow Press, 2010).

Rudolf Steiner and the Astrological Architecture of Early Mormonism

Christian Swenson

The Salt Lake Temple stands like a medieval fortress in the heart of an American city. It does so awkwardly, of course: its monochrome granite spires and crenellations straddle romanesque and gothic architecture. It therefore stands between worlds, and it does so in more than one way. It is both the believer's portal to heaven and a reminder to the modern viewer of the premodern past it announces. Clasped hands and constellations speckle its exterior. Its interior—invisible though it is—nevertheless stands out all the more to the curious tourist. The bleached, palatial monument interrupts the streamlined capitalism of the buildings surrounding it. It announces another world. Or maybe more than one, as the planets, moons, suns, and stars lining its outside walls may suggest.

The Architect Truman Angell described the constellations that appear on the building's west center tower as "in alto relievo [high relief], Ursa Major (commonly called in this country the Dipper) with the Pointers ranging with the North Star."[1] Near the ground on each of its fifty buttresses, circular "earthstones" meet you, originally designed to show the planet from as many different angles. Above them a viewer will see "moonstones": carvings that depict various phases of the lunar cycle "in its different phases."[2] Still higher, a tourist can crane her neck to notice, logically, "sunstones": circles surrounded by spikes of light that depict "the full face of the Sun." This ascent from stars through moon to sun recalls Paul's understanding of resurrected bodies in his first epistle to the Corinthians.[3] The sunstones also recall the "vision"

of cosmic realms as depicted in section 76 of the Latter-day Saint or "Mormon" Doctrine and Covenants.[4]

The stones that complete this sequence near the top of the pilaster do so less logically. Or they would have done so, since their planned designs were never implemented. In architect Truman Angell's blueprints, on the side wall buttresses, earth stands below moon, moon stands below sun, and sun stands below

---

1   Truman Angell, "The Salt Lake City Temple" *Millennial Star* vol. 36 no. 18 (1874): 273-275.

2   Ibid.

3   1 Cor. 15:41.

4   D&C 76:70-71, 81.

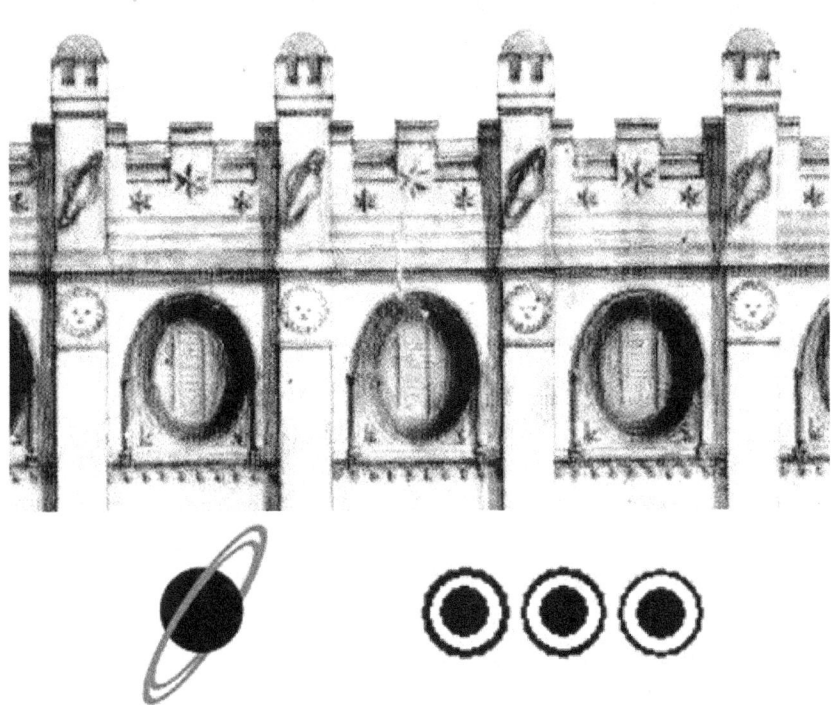

Saturn. The plans below depict his phalanx of ringed planets to orbit the topmost frieze. Moreover, at the level Saturn was meant to stand on the buttresses, the towers were meant to display "clouds and descending rays of light."

This design for these "Saturnstones," which was never implemented, was replaced by a frieze of circles within circles. Sources differ on what to call these revised figures, but if they are Saturnstones, they are minimalist ones.

These designs frustrate easy interpretations. While the Latter-day Saint canon is characteristically focused on the heavens, at least explicitly, Saturn is absent in the religion's revelation and liturgy. And yet here the planet stands (or *would* have stood) in the most prominent position on the temple's southern facade.

It gets stranger, however. The fourfold progression from earth through moon and sun to Saturn also shows up, albeit in reverse, in Rudolf Steiner's esoteric worldview. Rudolf Steiner was an Austrian esotericist, philosopher, social, educational, and agricultural reformer. He called the worldview he founded "Anthroposophy". Drawing on

Theosophy, but supplementing it with his own "spiritual scientific research," Steiner would posit a reincarnating earth, an earth whose existence went through "four planetary incarnations": its Saturn, Sun, Moon, and Earth phases. These names describe the earth's past and not the solar system's present, but Steiner chose the names to resonate and align with astronomical language.[5] Steiner first made these observations in his 1909 work *Outline of Esoteric Science*, long after Joseph Smith was dead and more than thirty years after Truman Angell planned his astronomical symbolism, and so plagiarism from east to west is not at play here. Steiner also clearly could not have plagiarized the plans for an American religious building that were never implemented. A search on the Rudolf Steiner Archive for the word "Mormon" only gives one result: Steiner in a 1913 lecture satirically reading the table of contents from the text *Sects of Perdition. A Warning for Protestant Christians.* "Mormons—4 pages." Theosophy was half a page.[6] Steiner shows no awareness of Latter-day Saint ritual or theology. Its architecture–half the world away–would have been unknown to him. And yet the bizarre coincidence remains.

I posit that this bizarre parallel between Mormonism and Anthroposophy can be explained through what Steiner and Smith had in common: astrology and astronomy. In other words, the worldviews of all three of them are characterized by the use of astrological concepts in the milieu of a world that prefers astronomical ones. Both blend the two. If later Latter-day Saints ended up frowning on astrology,[7] its founder certainly didn't: Joseph Smith was an enthusiastic and lifelong devotee of the astrological worldview. That worldview is just as insistent, if more explicitly so, in Rudolf Steiner's immense output of books and lectures. In this essay, I will make clear that astrology is central to the spiritual science of Rudolf Steiner, to the life and language of Joseph Smith, and

5   Rudolf Steiner, *Outline of Esoteric Science* (Anthroposophic Press, 1997): 125-128.

6   Rudolf Steiner, Truths and Errors of Spiritual Research, February 16, 1913.

7   On May 6, 1865, for instance, Brigham Young said that "astrology . . . leads [its practitioners] into thousands of illusions . . . astrology and mesmerism do lead them astray." *Discourses of Brigham Young*, compiled by John A. Widtsoe (Deseret Book Company, 1954), 75.

to the texts inherited from him by Truman Angell.

I will also point out that—in specific—Saturn characterizes the cosmologies and cosmogonies of both Anthroposophy and Mormonism. Saturn is the outermost planet visible to the naked eye and therefore guards the threshold between the visible and the invisible. It symbolizes beginnings, endings, cycles, limits, and time. Both Mormonism and Anthroposophy teach about a planet at the dawn of time that initiates time. Mormons call it "Kolob," and Anthoposophists call it "Old Saturn." I suggest that the doctrine of these ancient planets reflects the anxiety brought about by the Kant-Lapalce nebular hypothesis. It claims that the sun and our solar system were originally a whirling stellar cloud or "nebula," and it was commonly taught in classrooms and lecture halls throughout the nineteenth century. Kolob and Saturn—which ontologically and temporally precede the sun—reflect worldviews where the nebular darkness before the creation of the sun is a way of describing God brooding over the primordial chaos. They both integrate the traditional and secular worlds. Moreover, Truman Angell would have been very aware of the Kant-Laplace theory, since Latter-day Saint apostle Orson Pratt lectured extensively on it in 1852.

If we wanted to show that Steiner was aware of astrology, we would find it easy. He referenced it explicitly and often. Perhaps the most notable thing he ever said about astrology is the following meditation:

> The Stars once spoke to man
> It is World Destiny that they are silent now.
> To become aware of this Silence
> Can become Pain for Earthly humanity.
> But in the deepening Silence
> There grows and ripens what the
> Human Being speaks to the stars.
> To become aware of this Speaking
> Can become Strength for Spirit Humanity.

Steiner, who saw modernity as a necessary loss of atavistic, instinctive clairvoyance meant to prepare us for a future, conscious participation with the higher worlds, saw the stars as a portal to higher worlds and the study of the stars as a way to connect with those higher worlds. While he asserted that most modern astrology was nonsense,[8] he nevertheless claimed that the stars expressed a wisdom that we would do well to notice.

For him, the Zodiac functioned as a map for how unity and multiplicity expressed themselves in each other. He asserts that any truth can only be adequately grasped from no less than twelve separate standpoints or perspectives[9] and that the unity of the physical self is fractured into twelve in higher worlds.[10] He posits twelve senses[11] and twelve archetypal philosophical worldviews.[12] He names twelve consonants[13] and links them with twelve corresponding movements in a kind of dance called Eurythmy.[14] He identifies the biblical covenant with Abraham in Genesis of seed "which in their ordering are arranged as the number of stars in the heavens" with the twelvefold arrangement of the Zodiac.[15] He even gave meditations for the "mood" of each astrological sign[16] and designed mandala-esque "planetary seals" for each of the seven planets.[17] In each case, the Zodiac (which he accurately defines as the "animal circle"[18]) gives a model for a unity that avoids the pitfalls of uniformity. A

---

8   In one lecture Steiner ridicules, for instance, "the modern astrologers who outdo materialism with their methods, simply adding ignorant superstition to materialistic ignorance." Rudolf Steiner's Words before the Eurythmy Presentation of the "Twelve Moods" in Dornach, August 29, 1915.

9   Theoretically, an infinite number of points of view is possible, but actually, twelve are sufficient. Rudolf Steiner, The Gosepl of St. Matthew: Lecture VII, September 7, 1910.

10   Rudolf Steiner, Occult Reading and Occult Hearing: Lecture II, December 4, 1914.

11   Rudolf Steiner, Toward Imagination: Lecture III: The Twelve Human Senses, June 20, 1916.

12   Rudolf Steiner, Human and Cosmic Thought: Lecture III, January 22, 1916.

13   Rudolf Steiner, Occult Reading and Occult Hearing: Lecture IV, October 6, 1914.

14   Rudolf Steiner, Words before "Twelve Moods".

15   Rudolf Steiner, The Ego: Lecture II, December 7, 1909.

16   Rudolf Steiner, Twelve Moods.

17   https://anthroposophy.eu/Planetary_seals

18   Rudolf Steiner, Speech and Song, December 2, 1922.; "Zodiac" *Online Etymology Dictionary*, www.etymonline.com.

Joseph Smith's Jupter Talisman

circle of twelve perspectives linked by incremental metamorphosis along the circumference and resonance along the diameter offered, for him, "the task of acting as peacemaker among the various world-outlooks."[19] Moreover at least some of these schemata involved a sevenfold corollary to the planets (seven vowels[20] corresponding to seven eurythmy movements and seven musical tones,[21] seven world-outlook-moods,[22] seven human life-processes[23]).

Joseph Smith was also astrologically literate. Though he never publicly taught astrology as such, there is evidence that he believed in it explicitly. Perhaps the most glaring proof of this fact is the "Jupiter Talisman," a stone amulet with astrological symbols, that was apparently on his body when he died. This amulet uses formulae from the 1801 text *The Magus* by Francis Barret, a book with instructions on ritual magic with constant reference to astrology. That text also informed a series of magical parchments the Smith family owned—each of which is littered with occult and magical symbols.[24] Smith was born under both Jupiter

---

19   Steiner, Human and Cosmic Thought: Lecture III.

20   Steiner, Occult Reading and Occult Hearing: Lecture IV.

21   Rudolf Steiner, Eurythmy as Visible Singing: Lecture III, February 21, 1924.

22   Steiner, Human and Cosmic Thought: Lecture III.

23   Rudolf Steiner, The Riddle of Humanity: Lecture VIII, August 13, 1916.

24   These include the "Holiness to the Lord Parchment," the "Jehovah, Jehovah, Jehovah Parchment," and the "St. Peter Bind Them Parchment." See D. Michael Quinn, *Early Mormonism and the Magic Worldview* (Signature

The Smith family's "Holiness to the Lord" parchment.

and Saturn, and at least one scholar has claimed that his affinity with these planets influenced his revelatory career.[25]

More implicitly, Smith's biography demonstrates a consistent fascination with heavenly bodies and their meaning. For instance, the earliest account of his "First Vision" describes celestial bodies in sympathy with nature and—as Steiner taught in the above meditation—a chorus of voices preaching and testifying of God:

For I looked upon the sun, the glorious luminary of the earth, and also the moon, rolling in their majesty through the heavens, and also the stars shining in their courses, and the earth also upon which I stood, . . . My heart exclaimed, "All, all these bear testimony and bespeak an omnipotent and omnipresent power, a being who maketh laws and decreeth and bindeth all things in their bounds, who filleth eternity, who was and is and will be from all eternity to eternity." And I considered all these things and that that being seeketh such to worship him as worship him in spirit and in truth.[26]

The "testimony" of the heavens, the way they (together with the earth) "bespeak" Deity, repeats the basic intuition of astrology: the stars speak. Astron-logia.[27] Earlier in the account, Smith talked about "dif-

---

Books, 1987): 111-115.

25   Quinn, *Early Mormonism and the Magic Worldview*, 72.

26   "History, circa Summer 1832," p. 2, The Joseph Smith Papers, https://www.josephsmithpapers.org/paper-summary/history-circa-summer-1832/2.

27   "Astrology," *Online Etymology Dictionary*.

ferent denominations" that "did not adorn their profession with a holy walk and a godly conversation."[28] While the stars and planets—in their differences—"bear testimony" of God, the preachers and professors of religion—in their differences—condemn each other. Astrology promises (even if it fails to deliver) a solution to sectarianism.

Continual references to heavenly bodies and their cycles returns through his life. According to the account canonized by the modern Church of Jesus Christ of Latter-Day Saints, the Angel Moroni announced Smith's task as translator of the Book of Mormon on the fall equinox in 1824, and he instructed Smith to return to a specific spot every day on or near the fall equinox until 1827.[29] A design on the golden plates themselves—according to three separate accounts—include a stylized sun surrounded by twenty-four miniature moon phases combined with stars.[30] Another revelation canonized by the LDS church as the seventy-sixth chapter of the Doctrine and Covenants, called the "Vision," speaks of the glories of the sun, moon, and stars as ways of referring to the glories of various levels of heaven.[31]

Even Smith's 1844 platform for the United States Presidency uses astrological imagery. He asserts that the "aspirations and expectations of a virtuous people" as embodied in the United States Constitution ought to be held with "as much sanctity, as the prayers of the saints are treated in heaven, that love, confidence and union, like the sun, moon and stars should bear witness."[32]

These descriptions are striking, but they are certainly not exhaustive.

---

28   "History, circa Summer 1832," p. 2, The Joseph Smith Papers.

29   Joseph Smith–History 1:53. https://www.churchofjesuschrist.org/study/scriptures/pgp/js-h/1?lang=eng.

30   Charles Anthon to William E. Vibbert, August 12, 1844.; Turner, *History of the Pioneer Settlement*, in Dan Vogel *Early Mormon Documents* (Signature Books, 2000): 3:52.; Francis Gladden Bishop, *An Address to the Sons and Daughters of Zion, Scattered Abroad, Through All the Earth* (1851): 48.

For a discussion of these three accounts see Don Bradley, *The Lost 116 Pages* (Greg Kofford Books, 2019): 20-26.

31   D&C 76: 70-98.

32   "General Smith's Views of the Powers and Policy of the Government of the United States, circa 26 January–7 February 1844," p. 4, The Joseph Smith Papers.

The most impressive revelations given by Joseph Smith in relation to astrology, however, are an 1832 revelation currently canonized as the 88th section of the Doctrine and Covenants, known as "The Olive Leaf," and the Book of Abraham. The former speaks of Deity as the "light of truth" and insists that this light is what sustains and shines from all heavenly bodies (sun, moon, stars) and earthly bodies. It describes them as follows:

> And their courses are fixed, even the courses of the heavens and the earth, which comprehend the earth and all the planets. And they give light to each other in their times and in their seasons, in their minutes, in their hours, in their days, in their weeks, in their months, in their years—all these are one year with God, but not with man. The earth rolls upon her wings, and the sun giveth his light by day, and the moon giveth her light by night, and the stars also give their light, as they roll upon their wings in their glory, in the midst of the power of God.[33]

This language—times, seasons, sun, moon, stars, rolling, comprehending, light, days, weeks, months, and years—is very astrological. It speaks to orbit and rhythmical progression: a body is defined by its orbit. According to the 1828 Webster's dictionary, to "comprehend" meant "to understand" or "to conceive" only by extension. Its primary meaning implies an orbital logic: "to contain, to include, to comprise."[34]

The revelation also includes a parable where God describes himself as "a man having a field" with twelve laborers, one with striking astrological resonances:

> Behold, I will liken these kingdoms unto a man having a field, and he sent forth his servants into the field to dig in the field. And he said unto the first: Go ye and labor in the

---

33   D&C 88:43-45.

34   Noah Webster, *American Dictionary of the English Language*, 1828. Webster's 1828 dictionary was contemporary with Joseph Smith and the early Mormon church and provides the closest example of what they understood the words to mean.

field, and in the first hour I will come unto you, and ye shall behold the joy of my countenance. And he said unto the second: Go ye also into the field, and in the second hour I will visit you with the joy of my countenance. And also unto the third, saying: I will visit you; And unto the fourth, and so on unto the twelfth. And the lord of the field went unto the first in the first hour, and tarried with him all that hour, and he was made glad with the light of the countenance of his lord. And then he withdrew from the first that he might visit the second also, and the third, and the fourth, and so on unto the twelfth. And thus they all received the light of the countenance of their lord, every man in his hour, and in his time, and in his season— Beginning at the first, and so on unto the last, and from the last unto the first, and from the first unto the last; Every man in his own order, until his hour was finished, even according as his lord had commanded him, that his lord might be glorified in him, and he in his lord, that they all might be glorified.[35]

The progress of "The Lord of the Field" from one servant to another, the movement "hour by hour" of "the light of the countenance of his Lord" in a cycle of twelve, resonates and aligns with the basic movement of the sun through the Zodiac or the astrological houses. The sun "withdraws" from one sign or house, "tarries with it for an hour" "until its hour is finished," and then progresses to another so that they can each "receive the light of its countenance." This revelation, which had just referenced the reciprocal shining and glorification of sun, moon, and stars, openly invites astrological readings of the parable it contains. It is also worth noting, on this point, that the "sunstones" on the Nauvoo temple depicted the face or "countenance" of the sun.

The most important text for present purposes, however, is the Book of Abraham—a canonized text purportedly translated from a set of Egyptian papyri, one that focuses on the stars. It is controversial and often lampooned. However, it is not science-fiction Christianity. Because it depicts an order or heavenly orbits arranged hierarchically from above to below, the model is geocentric. As such, it is not astronomy. It is astrology.

---

35   D&C 88:51-60.

It retells the events in and around Genesis 12 from the pen of the main character. It narrates Abraham's[36] encounter with Deity as he is liberated from his role as a sacrificial victim. In a way that mirrors Steiner's language of the "Egypto-Chaldean Epoch" of history, it describes both Chaldeans and Egyptians.[37] Through "the Urim and Thummim," Abraham receives a revelation from God on the structure of the cosmos, a revelation that God shows him before his descent into Egypt.[38] It describes a cosmology of hierarchical bodies, light, and time. Each body has a "set time" and "times of reckoning."[39] The words stars, planets, lights, facts, and things are used almost synonymously. The planets both govern and are governed: they transmit light and order through radiation. The light of a body's radiation corresponds to the length of that body's revolution. As such, a slower or longer orbit means a greater light.

God places his hands on Abraham's eyes, and Abraham watches as these celestial bodies multiply. God connects this multiplication with the multiplication of Abraham's seed.[40] Upon receiving this vision, Abraham learns the stars and planets' names: Kokob for star, Olea for moon, Shinehah for sun. Kolob is a star, is one of the "Kokaubeam," and Abraham learns that it is closest to God.[41] Abraham learns that the hierarchies of gods, stars, and intelligences (a word for the human spirit) all correspond to each other: that he himself is a kind of fallen star, a being from a starry world that is destined to return upward, a god with amnesia.[42] This intuition is somewhat Platonic and resonates overwhelmingly with Steiner's Anthroposophy. He etymologically connects the astral body–the third of four human bodies together with

---

36   The text does not reflect that, at this point in the Genesis narrative, Abraham's name was still Abram.

37   The text opens with "in the land of the Chaldeans" (1:1) and describes within a page how Abraham was to be sacrificed to the "god of the king of Egypt" (1:6).

38   Abraham 3:15.

39   Abraham 3:6.

40   Abraham 3:15.

41   Abraham 3:12-16.

42   Abraham 3:23.

physical body, etheric body, and "I"—with the stars.[43] As he describes it, the human being as an astral being from the starry world is a starry being. A more striking connection of the Book of Abraham to astrology is that both claim that the planets (Venus, Mars, Saturn, etc.) are gods and have the names of gods.

Joseph Smith and Rudolf Steiner's worldviews were both animated by astrological assumptions. Both saw human beings and human relationships in terms of the heavens, the stars, and the planets. If we were to look for a common orientation to Saturn in their respective worldviews, we would find it. Steiner and Smith both saw a planet—somehow prior to or ontologically higher than the sun–at the beginning of time. Both saw this planet as the ultimate marker of time. Steiner writes that time only began on Old Saturn,[44] and the Book of Abraham observes that Kolob is the planet whose revolution—like Saturn's—is outermost and longest in terms of time and length.[45] Steiner associated the Saturn phase with the primeval chaos in the opening verses of Genesis,[46] and Smith as-

---

43   No wonder that an ancient science, instinctively clairvoyant, describes this third member of our human organism as the "astral" or "starry" body, seeing that it is of like nature with that which reveals itself to us in the stars. Rudolf Steiner, The Festivals and Their Meaning III: Ascension and Pentecost, June 4, 1924.

44   It will be especially difficult for the present-day consciousness to accept the statement that with the *Saturn* state of heat what is called "time" first makes its appearance, for the preceding states are not at all temporal. They belong to the region that in spiritual science may be called "duration." Rudolf Steiner, An Outline of Occult Science IV: The Evolution of the Cosmos and Man.

45   Abraham 3:9: And thus there shall be the reckoning of the time of one planet above another, until thou come nigh unto Kolob, which Kolob is after the reckoning of the Lord's time; which Kolob is set nigh unto the throne of God, to govern all those planets which belong to the same order as that upon which thou standest.

46   It was something the same with the Elohim, when they said to themselves: "Let us now reflect upon what arises in our souls when we recall what took place during the ancient Saturn, Sun and Moon evolutions. Let us see how it looks in recollection." What it looked like is expressed in the phrase tohu wabohu; it could be expressed by a picture such as I have given you, as streams radiating from a centre outwards into space and back again, in such

serts in his "translation" of one of the Book of Abraham facsimiles that the sun "borrow[s] its light from Kolob through the medium of Kae-e-vanrash, which is the Grand Key." At the time the Book of Abraham was transcribed, "medium" meant that through which bodies move[47] and therefore would have meant something like the cosmic medium which the sun emerged as referenced in contemporary physics. Both figures, then, saw an impossibly old planetary body as the primordial origin of the Earth, preceding the Sun.

Saturn is the outermost visible planet and therefore the threshold between the visible and invisible worlds. It governs limits, rhythm, authority, and time. Saturnalia marked the end of the Roman year, and in many countries, Saturday marks the end of the week. The Roman God Saturn presided over humanity's golden age. As a Titan who overthrew his father and was overthrown by his son, he is the archetype of the revolutionary. The famous phrase by Jacques Mallet du Pan, "Like Saturn, the revolution devours its own children," would have had Saturn and his own revolution in mind. The word "revolution" itself—when used politically—was coined in reference to planetary revolutions.[48]

Saturn, then, meant something like time itself, or the border between time and timelessness. Like Saturnalia marked the end of the old year and the beginning of a new year, and like Saturday tends to mark the end of one week and the beginning of a new week, Saturn seems to preside over beginnings and endings. Beginnings are, in this sense, a continual phenomenon, something that keeps happening. The beginning can return, and indeed, it must. Time in this sense was and is cyclical, and astrology is a way to keep track of the circular nature of time. In this sense, astrology is a characteristic image of the pre-scientific world, a world where time was not measured linearly but conceived in terms of days, seasons, and years. The earthly was conformed to the heavenly.

---

a way that the elements are interwoven in this streaming of forces. Thus the Elohim could say to themselves: "At the stage to which you have so far brought things this is what they look like. This is how they are resumed." Rudolf Steiner, Genesis: Lecture II, August 18, 1910.

47   "Medium", Webster, *American Dictionary of the English Language.*; John Durham Peters, *The Marvelous Clouds: Toward a Philosophy of Elemental Media* (University of Chicago Press, 2015): 2.

48   "Revolution", *Online Etymology Dictionary.*

Because crops depended on it, humanity depended on it. The transition between astrology and astronomy is, in many ways, also the transition between quality and quantity. Though they were originally interchangeable, the first person to make the distinction between astrology (the speech of the stars) and astronomy (naming the stars) was the Iranian scholar Al-Biruni,[49] a figure of the Islamic golden age who also introduced the division of the hour into sixty minutes.[50] Astronomy, like the clock,[51] focuses on isolated objects and less on relationships, more on things and less on meanings.[52] It names and does not listen to the stars. It has all the myopia of someone who focuses so much on the typeface of a book that she forgets to read it.

The above passages from Steiner and Smith demonstrate that–for them–the speech of the stars was all-important. Modernity is–in many ways–the gradual silencing of nature in general and of the stars in specific. Steiner and Smiths' cosmologies cry out for the soul of the world, and more specifically, for the soul of the starry world. As such, their worldviews speak for the stars when they insist on seeing the cosmos as ultimately human and the human as ultimately cosmic or stellar. Astrology *is* this union of the human and cosmic worlds.

And Saturn—in particular—is significant for any attempt to re-en-

---

49   Shlomo Pines, "The Semantic Distinction between the Terms Astronomy and Astrology according to al-Biruni", *Isis* 55 (3) (September 1964): 343–349.

50   Muḥammad ibn Aḥmad Bīrūnī, *The Chronology of Ancient Nations: An English Version of the Arabic Text of the Athâr-ul-Bâkiya of Albîrûnî, Or "Vestiges of the Past"*, Translated and Edited by C. Edward Sachau (1879): 147–149.

51   The clock, notably, is both an image of the zodiac and a representation of the sun's movement.

52   G. I. Gurdjieff seems to be referencing this fact when, in his massive, difficult, allegorical tome *Beelzebub's Tales to His Grandson*, he has Beelzebub remark "At that period on the Earth the beings occupied with such observations and studies were called 'astrologers.' But later, when that psychic disease of your favorites called 'wiseacring' was finally fixed in them, and these specialists 'shriveled and shrank,' becoming 'specialists' only in giving names to remote cosmic concentrations, they came to be called 'astronomers'". See chapter 23 "The fourth personal sojourn of Beelzebub on the planet Earth" in G. I. Gurdjieff, *Beelzebub's Tales to His Grandson* (Harcourt, 1950).

chant the world. Saturn presides over endings and beginnings, and Mormonism in particular is focused on endings and beginnings. The language of "restoration" speaks to the recreation of a world that had dissolved and unraveled, the beginning again of a world that had ended. In one of the last sermons Smith ever gave, he asserts that we need "to go back to the beginning . . . in order to understand and be fully acquainted with the mind, purposes, and decrees of the Great Elohim . . . It is necessary for us to have an understanding of God himself in the beginning." He says that "if we start right, it is easy for us to go right all the time; but if we start wrong, we may go wrong, and it be a hard matter to get right."[53]

To accomplish this task, Smith actually goes "back to the beginning" of the Bible, to the word "Beginning" or *Berosheit*.[54] *Berosheit bara elohim*, traditionally translated as "In the beginning God created . . . ," Smith reads differently. He asserts that *Berosheit* is best understood in terms of *rosh*, "the head," where "the head," is best understood as He who initiates creation, who "heads" it, what Smith then calls "the head God." He translates the opening verses of Genesis, then, as "The Head God brought forth the Gods in the grand council." "In the Beginning" becomes something like the Beginning as a proper noun for a person, a name. Elohim becomes not God but the gods. Since it's not an event but a person, the "Beginning" seems to be a role or a tite. It refers to whatever or whoever organizes chaos, that which begins the world anew. It implies that the Beginning refers to many people and occurs at many times. These claims suggest a somewhat circular view of history: that it can and must repeat, that human beings are the agents for organizing a world that tends to fall into disorder. Human beings, then, would be agents for restoration, recreation, and resurrection.

In this sense, the Beginning describes what Saturn is for classical astrology: a rhythmic beginning and ending. Saturn is the drumbeat of reality, a twenty-nine year thrum that keeps reality in check, the end of the visible and the beginning of the invisible, the end of time and the beginning of timelessness, and vice versa. Steiner's Old Saturn is a threshold

---

53   Joseph Smith, "The King Follet Sermon," *History of The Church of Jesus Christ of Latter-day Saints* (Deseret Book Company, 1950): 6:303.

54   The Hebrew word for the book of Genesis is *Berosheit*.

like this at the beginning of cosmic evolution, and he claims that every phase of reality since—Old Sun, Old Moon, and the present incarnation of the earth—begins with a recapitulation of the Saturn phase.[55] The beings who had their human phase on Saturn, interestingly, are called the Spirits of Personality, the Archai, or the *Beginnings,* who Steiner at least sometimes uses as synonyms of the Zeitgeist or the "spirit of the time." Steiner and Smith, then, clearly both see history as a cycle of dissolutions and recreations, a rhythm of chaos and order, where a primeval, timeless planet stands at a beginning that happens many times.

In addition to these astrological parallels, there is also a connection between the Saturnstones and Steiner's *Outline of Esoteric Science* in terms of the Kant-Laplace nebular hypothesis. The word "nebula" or "nebule," which originally just meant a cloud or mist, was already in astronomical use in 1828.[56] In fact, it was coined in its astronomical sense in 1734 by none other than Emanuel Swedenborg—seer, Christian mystic, and an arguable influence on early Mormonism—in his book *Prodromus Principiorum Rerum Naturalium* or *On the Principles of Natural Things.*[57] In his book, Swedenborg argues that the planets had once been part of the sun and the solar system itself once resembled the luminous, cloud-like patches astronomers could discern through their telescopes. This hypothesis was elaborated by the philosopher Immanuel Kant and the mathematician Pierre-Simon Laplace, and a specific version of it became known throughout the nineteenth century as the "Kant-Laplace theory." Rudolf Steiner opposed the theory, and so did the early Mormon apostle, mathematician, and astronomer Orson Pratt, whose lectures on the subject would likely have been attended by Truman Angell, the architect of the Salt Lake Temple.

---

55   For instance, "Man attains this higher state of consciousness in the course of Sun evolution through the fact that the etheric or life-body is now incorporated in him. But this cannot take place until the Saturn conditions have been recapitulated." Rudolf Steiner, "Man and the Evolution of the World" in Occult Science - An Outline, or "The physical life of man passes in recapitulation through the stages of Saturn evolution, but under altogether changed conditions."

56   "Nebule" in Webster, *An American Dictionary.*

57   Michael Mark Woolfson, "Solar System – its origin and evolution". *Quarterly Journal of the Royal Astronomical Society* 34 (1993): 1–20.

Pratt critiqued the Kant-Laplace system on mathematical grounds. In his 1852 series of lectures, he asserts that "The ring theory of La Place and others, to account for the origin of planets and satellites, cannot be sustained. Its impossibility can be mathematically demonstrated."[58] Pratt was a well-known astronomer who was noted for his mathematical skill independent of his religious associations.[59] In these lectures—given to large audiences—he took the congregation on a tour of the solar system, its genesis, and its structure. Though he opens the series with religious language and returns to religious concerns sporadically, the language in it is far more mathematical than devotional. It requires the attention you pay to a physics course. It is quantitatively intense. His critique of the Kant-Laplace theory is not a critique of the nebular theory as such but instead one of mathematical details.

Steiner, however, critiqued the Kant-Laplace theory because it was mechanical in a self-defeating way. He often used it as a bogeyman to ridicule the abstract, decontextualized attitude of modern science. Teachers, he said, who put a drop of oil in a glass of water, pierce it with a pin, and make it rotate to create a "miniature planetary system" are "creating a grave error of thought" because they "have forgotten one thing that ordinarily it might be well to forget occasionally and this is themselves. They forget that they themselves have brought the whole thing into formation."[60] The system implies an outside mover but looks only inside at the closed system. He repeated this analogy in many recorded lectures.[61]

As such, Steiner's critique of the theory is a critique of how it makes the world abstract and depersonified at the theory's own expense. "Had this fact [that the teacher brought the whole experiment into motion]

---

58   Orson Pratt, *Wonders Of The Universe: Or A Compilation Of The Astronomical Writings Of Orson Pratt*, Compiled by Nels B. Lundwall (1937): 170.

59   Pratt, *Wonders of the Universe*, 2-3.

60   Rudolf Steiner, *Anthroposophy in Everyday Life* (Steiner Books, 1995): 6.

61   See, for instance, Rudolf Steiner, The Child's Changing Consciousness and Waldorf Education, April 15, 1923 and Rudolf Steiner, Health and Illness, Volume I: Concerning the Soul Life in the Breathing Process, December 23, 1922.

been observed and applied logically to the cosmic system, then they would have been using complete healthy thinking."[62] Steiner's goal was to integrate the scientific and the spiritual, the cosmic and the human, and for him, the Kant-Laplace theory represents a failure of science because it fails to take the spirit, the human, into account. His critique is not, therefore, about the claim that the sun had not always existed, which Steiner also taught explicitly.

Moreover, despite Pratt's mathematicism, and despite the fact that he does not connect it to the Kant-Laplace theory as such, he shares Steiner's emphasis on the human in the world described by science. He saw science—and astronomy in particular—as an almost personal encounter with the god who framed the stars. In the opening of the first lecture, for instance, he asserts that astronomy unveils divine power, wisdom, and goodness:

> [astronomy] is that science which lifts the veil of obscurity . . . which, above all others, is calculated to give us the most profound, sublime, and exalted views, of the power, wisdom, and goodness of that Being who formed those magnificent systems from the eternal elements, and devised laws, calculated to maintain their stability, through all their complicated and infinite variety of movements, for indefinite ages to come.[63]

He refers to "nature's Author"[64] and the desire to unlock the heavenly archives."[65] Both Pratt and Steiner see cosmic law as an evidence of cosmic intelligence. Pratt, like Steiner, sees the fact that science can extract wisdom from nature as evidence that wisdom was implanted into it by a wise or intelligent being.[66]

The Kant-Laplace nebular theory threatens a theocentric view of re-

---

62   Steiner, *Anthroposophy in Everyday Life*, 6.

63   Pratt, *Wonders of the Universe*, 1.

64   Ibid., 2.

65   Ibid.

66   Thus, when a man thinks about things he only re-thinks what is already in them. See Rudolf Steiner, Practical Training In Thought, January 18, 1909.

ality like this. The nebular theory asserts that the sun had an origin, that the light of the world was originally darkness, and implies that light both literal and figurative arose mechanically without purpose or intelligence. The common spiritual insight between Steiner's Anthroposophy and Mormonism as generated by Smith and elaborated by Pratt is to see this nebular reality in terms of the first few verses of Genesis. Though the nebular hypothesis sets the sun adrift in cosmic time like Copernicus set the earth adrift in cosmic space, the Bible, too, asserts that darkness preceded light. God was there when it was dark. Perhaps the nebula, then, was this darkness. Perhaps the darkness was sacred. This insight connects theory with tradition and science with the spirit.

Moreover, the Book of Abraham—in one of at least two separate and different versions Joseph Smith gave of the Genesis creation account—boldly claims that "they, that is the Gods, *organized* and formed the heavens and the earth."[67] Creation is then neither from nothing nor from God: the divine contribution is the form, the intelligence, or the meaning imposed on a pre-existent formless chaos. Perhaps a cosmic hand, then, did set the drops of cosmic oil in motion. This reading of Genesis—with all its deeps and darks and hovering winds—is one that stays close to the imagery of the text and aligns surprisingly well with the nebular theory. It suggests as true both that God existed at the beginning and that the light did not. It suggests a divine darkness, a world that, like Steiner's Old Saturn, was more heat than light. Moreover, the nebula would have looked like Saturn. For Swedenborg, Kant, and Laplace, that light was preceded by a formless, swirling cloud whose periphery had not yet withdrawn into a solid central mass. It existed in both the center and the border: a center with an orbiting periphery. As such, reflection of the Book of Genesis in the context of Pratt's lectures about solar origins would naturally lead to saturnine images. Alongside the Saturnstones, remember, were carvings of clouds (the literal meaning of "nebula").

Truman Angell was neither an astronomer nor an astrologer. However, he likely heard Pratt speak about astronomy and the Kant-Laplace theory. At least one commentary on the symbolism of the Salt Lake Temple reads the Saturnstones in the context of Pratt's lectures.[68] I

67 Abraham 4:1.
68 Matthew Brown and Paul Thomas Smith, *Symbols in Stone* (Covenant

agree that Pratt's astronomical vision influenced Angell's architecture. Saturn, however, means little on its own in that lecture series: it has a section devoted to it, but so do most of the planets. It is written with scientific language and is only religious by extension. The symbolism on the temple walls seems more concerned with Pratt's description of the solar system's formation than it does with Saturn as such. This is especially true since Pratt mentions Saturn as a microcosmic image of the primordial nebula in the section devoted to solar system formation.

> When these two antagonistic forces [centripetal and centrifugal forces] becomes too great for the adherence of the matter, the ring will be circumferentially divided into two or more rings, as is the case with that of Saturn's. But that would take place at a very early stage of its formation, while the adherence was small.[69]

Saturn, which is a body with rings, both a center and a periphery, mirrors the nebula at creation's beginning.. The sun too was once like Saturn. Before order, there was chaos. Before light, there was darkness and warmth. Before the sun, there was a nebula or cloud. This cloud fails to distinguish the sun and its satellites. They are not yet distinct.

Angell's use of Saturnstones repeats this basic intuition: that the Sun is not ultimate or primary. What adolescent atheists tend to point out in Genesis—that light existed on the first day before the sun on the fourth day—is, in a way, a confirmation of this reading. As science expanded the universe for us from our solar system to a universe of many solar systems, both Smith and Steiner believed in a God who wrought many suns. There is not one beginning, and the beginning repeats. There are many Genesises, and Genesis must recur from age to age. Old Saturn and Kolob both point to this Genesis: the moment where timelessness becomes time, what every age must repeat to begin, the Beginning itself.

Communications, 2017): 153.
69   Pratt, *Wonders of the Universe*, 168.

WORKS CITED

Angell, Truman, "The Salt Lake City Temple" *Millennial Star* vol. 36 no. 18 (1874).

Anthon, Charles to William E. Vibbert, August 12, 1844.

Bīrūnī, Muḥammad ibn Aḥmad, *The Chronology of Ancient Nations: An English Version of the Arabic Text of the Athâr-ul-Bâkiya of Albîrûnî, Or "Vestiges of the Past"* Translated and Edited by C. Edward Sachau (1879).

Bishop, Francis Gladden, *An Address to the Sons and Daughters of Zion, Scattered Abroad, Through All the Earth* (1851).

Bradley, Don, *The Lost 116 Pages* (Greg Kofford Books, 2019).

Brown, Matthew and Paul Thomas Smith, *Symbols in Stone* (Covenant Communications, 2017).

"General Smith's Views of the Powers and Policy of the Government of the United States, circa 26 January–7 February 1844," p. 4, The Joseph Smith Papers.

Gurdjieff, G. I., *Beelzebub's Tales to His Grandson* (Harcourt, 1950).

Online Etymology Dictionary, www.etymonline.com.

Peters, John Durham, *The Marvelous Clouds: Toward a Philosophy of Elemental Media* (University of Chicago Press, 2015).

Pines, Shlomo, "The Semantic Distinction between the Terms Astronomy and Astrology according to al-Biruni", *Isis* 55 (3) (September 1964): 343–349.

Pratt, Orson, *Wonders Of The Universe: Or A Compilation Of The Astronomical Writings Of Orson Pratt,* Compiled by Nels B. Lundwall (1937).

Quinn, D. Michael, *Early Mormonism and the Magic Worldview* (Signature Books, 1987).

Smith, Joseph, "The King Follet Sermon," *History of The Church of Jesus Christ of Latter-day Saints* (Deseret Book Company, 1950)

Steiner, Rudolf, "An Outline of Occult Science IV: The Evolution of the Cosmos and Man."

———, *Anthroposophy in Everyday Life* (Steiner Books, 1995).

———, "Eurythmy as Visible Singing: Lecture III," February 21, 1924.

———, "Genesis: Lecture II," August 18, 1910.

———, "Health and Illness, Volume I: Concerning the Soul Life in the

Breathing Process," December 23, 1922.

———, "Human and Cosmic Thought: Lecture III," January 22, 1916.

———, "Occult Reading and Occult Hearing: Lecture II," December 4, 1914.

———, "Occult Reading and Occult Hearing: Lecture IV," October 6, 1914.

———, *Outline of Esoteric Science* (Anthroposophic Press, 1997).

———, "Speech and Song," December 2, 1922.

———, "The Child's Changing Consciousness and Waldorf Education," April 15, 1923.

———, "The Ego: Lecture II," December 7, 1909.

———, "The Festivals and Their Meaning III: Ascension and Pentecost," June 4, 1924.

———, "The Riddle of Humanity: Lecture VIII," August 13, 1916.

———, "The Gosepl of St. Matthew: Lecture VII," September 7, 1910.

———, "Toward Imagination: Lecture III: The Twelve Human Senses," June 20, 1916.

———, "Truths and Errors of Spiritual Research," February 16, 1913.

———, "Steiner's Words before the Eurythmy Presentation of the 'Twelve Moods' in Dornach," August 29, 1915.

Turner, History of the Pioneer Settlement, in Dan Vogel *Early Mormon Documents* (Signature Books, 2000): 3:52.

Webster, Noah, *American Dictionary of the English Language*, 1828.

Woolfson, Michael Mark, "Solar System—its origin and evolution." *Quarterly Journal of the Royal Astronomical Society* 34 (1993): 1–20.

Young, Brigham, *Discourses of Brigham Young*, compiled by John A. Widtsoe (Deseret Book Company, 1954).

King Solomon and the Fire of Azrael

Jack Chanek

There's a scene in Dion Fortune's occult novel *The Sea Priestess* that has always puzzled me. The two protagonists, Wilfred Maxwell and Vivien Le Fay Morgan (alternatively: Morgan Le Fay), are engaged in constructing a sea temple where Morgan is to conduct a lunar ritual in honor of the Goddess Isis. Halfway through the book, though, they pause building the temple in order to perform a divinatory ritual called the Fire of Azrael. The Fire of Azrael has always seemed odd to me, out of place with the rest of the novel's events, and the purpose of this passage in the book—lovely though it is—has never been clear to me.

In the ritual, Wilfred and Morgan build a bonfire and gaze into it to receive a vision of the mythic past: "She asked me if one day I would like to look in the coals of the fire of Azrael, and I asked her what it meant; and she said that one made a fire of certain woods, and gazed into the embers as it died down and saw therein the past that was dead."[1] According to Morgan, the Fire of Azrael must be built from three types of wood: Cedar, sandalwood, and juniper. The ritual itself is named after the angel Azrael, the Jewish angel of death, whom Aleister Crowley associates with the Path of Nun (Death) on the Qabalistic Tree of Life.[2]

---

1   Fortune, *The Sea Priestess*, 96.
2   Crowley, *Liber 777*, footnote to column XCIX.

The odd thing about this ritual is that it's unclear why those woods, specifically, should be required. Fortune was careful with the placement of esoteric symbolism in her novels, intending them to be used as a training guide for students in her Fraternity of Inner Light. She wrote that

> It is because my novels are packed with such things as these (symbolism directed to the subconscious) that I want my students to take them seriously. The 'Mystical Qabalah' gives the theory, but the novels give the practice . . . those who study the 'Mystical Qabalah' with the help of the novels get the keys of the Temple put into their hands.[3]

However, she is curiously silent on the significance and magical properties of the three woods in the Fire of Azrael. She gives no explanation for the cedar and sandalwood, and of the juniper she says only that "It is the tree of the old gods, more ancient than oak or ash, the Nordic hawthorn or the Keltic mistletoe, for it was a sacred tree to the people of the river-drift . . . they it was who worshipped the Mother Goddess."[4] Beyond this vague association of juniper with the Goddess, though, Fortune offers no insight into the woods being used in the ritual or why they were chosen.

This is quite uncharacteristic of her. As almost all of the imagery in the novel is overtly Qabalistic, we might be tempted to think that the three woods in the Fire of Azrael are chosen for Qabalistic reasons, but that line of thinking proves unfruitful. There is no mention of juniper anywhere in Fortune's own *The Mystical Qabalah*, nor in Crowley's *Liber 777*. Crowley does identify sandalwood and cedar as Qabalistic perfumes, but not in any way that meaningfully corresponds to the magical work being done in the Fire of Azrael ritual: Sandalwood is assigned to the Path of Daleth (associated with Venus and the Empress card from the Tarot), and cedar to Chesed (the Sephirah of mercy).[5] Neither of these has a magical association with death, the past, or scrying. In *The Mystical Qabalah*, Fortune herself mentions cedar and sandalwood only once, writing that they are examples of "Dionysiac odours of the

---

3   Fortune, *The Sea Priestess,* xiii.
4   Fortune, *The Sea Priestess,* 105.
5   Crowley, *Liber 777,* column XLII.

aromatic, spicy type" that "awaken the subconscious mind."[6] While this could plausibly make them useful for a divinatory ritual, it seems that any spicy-scented wood would meet the criteria; there is not a clear reason why it would have to be these two, in particular, used in the Fire of Azrael.

It turns out—or at least, I'm going to allege—that this combination of woods is Biblical in origin. Cedar, juniper, and sandalwood are the three woods used in the construction of King Solomon's temple, as described in the books I Kings and II Chronicles:

> Solomon sent this message to Hiram king of Tyre: "Send me cedar logs as you did for my father David when you sent him cedar to build a palace to live in. Now I am about to build a temple for the name of the LORD my God . . . Send me also cedar, juniper and algum logs from Lebanon, for I know that your servants are skilled with cutting timber there. My servants will work with yours to provide me with plenty of lumber, because the temple I build must be large and magnificent.[7]

The "algum" mentioned here is a Hebrew word, אלגומים, which has no clear English translation, and Biblical scholars are at odds as to what plant it refers to. However, a number of scholars have suggested that algum is the red sandalwood, and this view is widespread to this day.[8] The identification of algum with sandalwood was certainly already popular by the time of *The Sea Priestess*'s writing: An 1898 article in *The Expository Times* comments on "the opinion of 'the majority of scholars,' which inclines to identify 'almug' [*sic*] with red sandalwood."[9] While the exact identity of algum in its original context is still open to lively debate, we can confidently assert that Dion Fortune would have known the three building materials used in Solomon's temple as cedar, juniper, and sandalwood.

What's more, we know that this is a passage of the Bible that For-

---

6   Fortune, *The Mystical Qabalah* XXV, §39.
7   *The Bible*, NIV, II Chronicles 2:3-9.
8   *Encyclopædia Britannica*, "Ophir."
9   *The Expository Times*, vol. 9, no. 10, 470.

tune was familiar with and that she found esoterically significant. She considered Solomon a member the same tradition of Western mysteries to which she belonged, and she identified Solomon's temple with the temple spaces used by modern esoteric traditions like the Hermetic Order of the Golden Dawn or her own Fraternity of Inner Light. In *The Mystical Qabalah*, she writes: "When we read of Solomon sending to Hiram, King of Tyre, for men and materials to aid in the building of the Temple we know that the famous Tyrian mysteries must have profoundly influenced the Hebrew esotericism."[10] Although she doesn't mention the Fire of Azrael's three woods by name in *The Mystical Qabalah*, she directly references the Biblical myth that they were drawn from. We know, then, both that Fortune was aware of the woods used in the building of Solomon's temple and that this story informed her thinking about occultism and mystical experience. The inclusion of these woods in *The Sea Priestess* is no accident.

We have a link between the Fire of Azrael in *The Sea Priestess* and the occult theory of *The Mystical Qabalah*, the sort of link that Fortune had promised when she wrote that reading the two books side-by-side would give us "the keys of the Temple." Still, the question remains: Why these woods? We've identified where they come from, why they're in this particular combination, and that Fortune was aware of their origin. It's still not clear, however, why she should put Solomon's woods in the novel in the context of a divinatory ritual to see "the past that was dead." What's the connection there?

Here, I confess that I'm giving way to speculation, as I think there's no exact way for us to know Fortune's intentions. However, in *The Mystical Qabalah*, immediately before speaking of the construction of the temple, Fortune speaks of "The mysterious figure of a great priest-king, 'born without father, without mother, without descent; having neither beginning of days nor end of life' ... Generation by generation we trace the intercourse of the princes of Israel with the priest-kings of Egypt."[11] She suggests that initiates of the "Hebraic" mysteries (with whom she identifies herself) can only achieve their initiation through the aid of an outsider, a foreign priest-king who offers them exotic wisdom that they

10   Fortune, *The Mystical Qabalah*, I §10.

11   Fortune, *The Mystical Qabalah*, I §9-10.

must then incorporate into their body of existing knowledge. According to Fortune, "So it is with a tradition: that which is not antagonistic will be assimilated ... we shall equally judge the vitality of a tradition by its power to assimilate. It is only a dead faith which remains uninfluenced by contemporary thought."[12] For Solomon, she says, this figure was Hiram, who sent him the woods with which he built his temple; she likewise identifies the Egyptian Pharaoh as playing this role for Moses, and the Babylonian Magi for David.[13]

We can, perhaps, view the Fire of Azrael in *The Sea Priestess* as symbolic of this process. Like Solomon sending away to Hiram, Wilfred Maxwell and Morgan Le Fay must seek esoteric wisdom from a foreign land in order to complete their own magical initiatory experience. Burning the three woods of Solomon's temple in the Fire of Azrael connects them to the myth of Solomon. It allows them to solicit magical counsel from a spiritual contact beyond the sea, just as Solomon sought aid from King Hiram—and once they have received that help, they may complete the construction of their temple and the magical rites they intend to perform therein.

This spiritual contact is, in the novel, the Priest of the Moon: A political and religious leader from the lost continent of Atlantis, who had brought Morgan Le Fay to England in a past life when they fled the destruction of the continent. He is exactly the sort of shadow priest-king that Fortune describes in *The Mystical Qabalah*, an exotic initiatory guide for the seekers of the Western mysteries. To put an even finer point on the matter, we are told that the Priest of the Moon served at a temple in Atlantis that "was the prototype ... of the Temple of Solomon the King, and all other temples of the Mysteries take after it."[14] In the novel, the Priest of the Moon guards the lost secrets of Atlantis, and it is only through the ritual of the Fire of Azrael—by collecting the materials of Solomon's temple and seeking foreign aid as Solomon himself had done—that Wilfred and Morgan can obtain those secrets and complete their magical work. In short, he is their Hiram.

Though *The Sea Priestess* is most remembered for the extraordinary

12   Fortune, *The Mystical Qabalah*, I §8.
13   Fortune, *The Mystical Qabalah*, I §10.
14   Fortune, *The Sea Priestess*, 145.

lunar ritual at the novel's climax, most of the book is in fact dedicated to the building of the temple, creating a place that is fit for the mysteries to be performed. This process is both physical and psychic, not just a matter of erecting a building but also of refining Wilfred and Morgan's souls so that they can do the magical work they have set out to perform. Understood in that context, the ritual of the Fire of Azrael (and the choice of woods burned for the rite) makes perfect sense. It establishes a symbolic and thematic affinity between Solomon's temple and the sea temple of the novel, and between Solomon himself and the novel's protagonists. Like Solomon, they are yearning for a deeper wisdom, and they can only attain that wisdom through the aid of a priest-king from a foreign land. And so they call to him, as Solomon did, with cedar, sandalwood, and juniper.

WORKS CITED

"Contributions and Comments." *The Expository Times*, vol. 9, no. 10, 1898, pp. 470-480.

Crowley, Aleister. *Liber 777 and Other Qabalistic Writings: Including Gematria and Sepher Sephiroth*. Ed. Israel Regardie, revised edition, Weiser, 1986.

Fortune, Dion. *The Mystical Qabalah*. Weiser, 2000.

———. *The Sea Priestess*. Weiser, 2003.

"Ophir." *Encyclopædia Britannica*, 20 Jul. 1998.

The Holy Bible. New International Version.

Undoing The World: Parts 1–5 A Paratheatre Manifesto

Antero Alli

Part One: Culture, Verticality, The Asocial

The following five-part manifesto was written, updated, and rewritten over fifteen years of group paratheatrical research. It's included here to clarify the underlying principles, methods, and discoveries that occurred over this period, as well as, to share my reflections on the larger contexts of sociopolitical trends that this work often mirrors. This manifesto does not posit any absolute answers or final arrivals but rather the fruition of a work in progress. - A.A.

On Culture

One of my mentors, Christopher S. Hyatt, suggested that culture may be nothing more or less than the ongoing results of daily interactions between human DNA and geography. I came to understand his big picture vision as what happens when a given tribe dwells within any given bioregion where a distinct culture develops through its ongoing interaction with the native food resources, power fields, the land, and weather patterns sustaining them there. Mountain ranges, deserts, shorelines, valleys, and forests all carry distinct powers of influence shaping the daily lives and souls of the people living there—what they eat, the artifacts they create, and the technology (tools) they need to survive within this complex Planet/People weave we call "culture".

When we take pride in "our" culture or believe we can "create" culture, a delusional field is ignited obscuring the true source of culture. Nobody owns culture; we are more likely owned by the culture we live in. Culture as the ongoing interplay between human genes and geography develops organically. *Nobody creates culture.* We are more likely 'created' by culture. At best we can contribute to and maybe even advance a culture; at worst, we can corrupt and destroy it. Any culture corrupts when it becomes excessively anthropocentric and loses touch with its vitalizing sources in the geocentric pulse of the living earth.

We live in an era of dying cultures. Any culture or subculture that survives must turn to those rituals and traditions that sustain it. Any human culture achieves longevity by the success of its sustaining rituals, how well we are feeding the planet and how well we are being fed by the planet. Sustaining rituals return us to the primordial interaction with our immediate womb environment, through soulful communion and communication with the planetary entity. These sustaining rituals cannot be understood or proven by any empirical, literalist mindset. However, our primordial contact with planetary forces can be experienced firsthand through intuitive resonance with the Earth as a living entity *that has incarnated as our planet. The planet is not dying; the egocentric cultures feeding off of the planet are dying.*

Some geomantic power fields and planetary hotspots express innately charged conflict zones where highly volatile energies dwell and erupt without warning: earthquakes, tsunamis, volcanos, hurricanes, tornados, lightning strikes, landslides. The underlying causes of human conflict, violence, and warfare may run deeper than bloodlust for revenge, money, power, oil, and religion. In these conflict zones, we may be unconsciously acting as conduits, vessels, for the eruptions of feral geomantic forces innate to the region we live in. There are also geomantic leylines and electromagnetic fields expressing a deep harmony that supports the development of more harmonious cultures and the people that inhabit these regions.

We act on culture and are acted on by culture. Over time—decades, centuries, aeons—this genes/geography interplay crystallizes into symbols, languages, and artifacts that encode, encrypt, and transmit the characteristics of each distinct cultural identity. Cultures developing in the Himalayan mountains will differ from cultures stimulated along the shorelines of southern India or the Sonora deserts of Mexico or the lush Amazon river basin or the Cascadian forests of the Pacific Northwest. Each unique bioregion informs the nature of its tribe's religions, arts, mythologies, commerce, education, language, community rituals, and values. Though each culture maintains its own distinct signature and appearance by its unique sustaining rituals and traditions, all cultures are linked by the universal molecular language of DNA; we are all human beings living and dying on the same planet.

On Theatre and the Paratheatrical

Theatre acts as one of many sustaining rituals keeping a culture alive. As with any sustaining ritual, theatre must evolve and change over time to meet the growing needs and values of the era, the people, and their environment. Like a snake shedding old skin, any culture molts and grows by outgrowing itself. Any theatre that cannot outgrow itself ceases to function as a vital sustaining ritual. For theatre to remain vital, a kind of Paratheatre must be developed and implemented to dismantle stagnant work habits frustrating creative response. Paratheatre—*in the theatre but not of it*—provides a context set apart from theatre to experiment with excavating the internal landscape of autonomous forces in the Body for vital and spontaneous movements, gestures, vocalizations, actions, and interactions—in a kind of *archeology of the soul.*

This excavation process starts with releasing the pressure to perform and replacing it with self-created pressures to increase personal commitment to sources of energy, impulses, power, and grace within the Body itself. This redirection of commitment, from external to internal, opens the door to our innate verticality—*what can be experienced as energy/information flowing down from above and up from below, as a vertical column running up and down the spine.* Alignment with our innate verticality initiates receptivity towards engaging and expressing *the Body as the living embodiment of the so-called Subconscious mind.*

> *With verticality the point is not to renounce part of our nature;*
> *all should retain its natural place: the body, the heart, the head,*

*something that is "under our feet" and something that is "over
the head. All like a vertical line, and this verticality should be
held taut between organicity and the awareness. Awareness
means the consciousness which is not linked to language (the
machine for thinking), but to Presence."*— Jerzy Grotowski

Verticality, Asocial Intent, The Archetype of Self

*Groups create bonds of shared acceptance, support, and belonging
through community-building social events.* However these social bonds
can also inhibit or frustrate the expression of true feelings and spontaneous responses which frustrates creativity. When a given group becomes preoccupied with maintaining their social personas and meeting
their social needs—*for friendship, courtship, belonging, approval, security,
status, etc.*—this group begins feeding horizontally-oriented social needs
and the sense of verticality is quickly lost or was never established in the
first place.

The experience of verticality can be accessed in an asocial work climate.
Implementing an asocial intent starts with realizing our non-responsi-
bility to others in the workspace. This shift from external to internal
dependence replaces social considerations with an active discovery of
our most honest, spontaneous, and authentic responses. Without this
adjustment, the "default" conditioning of our local culture's socialization 'programs' can easily dominate the tone of any group interaction
and corrupts the quality of paratheatrical work with social cliches and
conditioned reactions. Actualizing an asocial intent naturally frustrates
social compulsions and needs to bind social agreements. Social needs
are obviously important but are best met outside of the workspace. By
relaxing our social agendas and motivations, we can begin sourcing the
internal landscape of autonomous forces in a somatic, visceral expression
of what Carl Jung calls Active Imagination *for making the Unconscious,
conscious.* This starts the process of Self-initiation through interacting
with the centralizing archetype of The Self.

> *The Self is a quantity that is supra ordinate to the conscious ego.
> It embraces not only the conscious but also the unconscious psyche,
> and is therefore, so to speak, a personality which we also are.
> The Self is not only the centre but also the whole circumference*

"Bardoville" (May 2017) performance ritual featuring poetry by Charles Bukowski. Directed by Antero Alli.

> *which embraces both conscious and unconscious; it is the centre of this totality, just as the ego is the center of consciousness.* — Carl Jung, Two Essays on Analytical Psychology

Part Two: Integrity Loss and Recovery
commitment, sacrifice, the impersonal culture

Self-Trust and the Force of Commitment

No such thing as self-improvement. You cannot improve who you are; you already are who you are. You are not some kind of apprentice to yourself who will someday, with enough "self-improvement", become the real you. It is too late for that. You can wake up to who you are and accept yourself or, keep trying to improve this thing called "self", whatever that is. Who are you beyond your beliefs, assumptions, self-images, and ideas of who you are? Certain habits and behaviors can certainly be corrected and "improved" but we'd be mistaken to assume identity there. You are not only more than you think, you are more than you *can* think.

The aim of paratheatrical work is to discover our firsthand experience as a source of authority, integrity, and autonomy. This inner work starts with increasing the force of our self-commitment. This means becoming fully accountable for our experiences, choices, actions, and their consequences. Before self-commitment can be increased, it may be necessary to expose any doubts, distrust, or negation of firsthand experience as an authority source. Perhaps we were raised by a family or schools that dismissed personal experience as too subjective to be relied on as a barometer of truth. If so, this dismissal of your own experience may have damaged the self-trust essential to even having an experience. Trusting firsthand experience as an authority source demands a time-intensive process of testing its legitimacy for ourselves. Once enough self-trust can be earned and established, we are more free to interact with others and the world from a greater sense of personal integrity. With enough self-trust, more reality-based relationships can develop free of wanting approval or acceptance for what we already know from firsthand experience.

Sacrifice; the Life & Death Wishes

Any act of true sacrifice unleashes torrents of creative and psychic force. Something can only be a true sacrifice if what we are asked to give up has become near and dear to our hearts. Releasing our attachment to cherished objects, possessions, relationships, jobs, dreams, and goals unleashes the torrent of forces invested in them. True sacrifice tills the ground of our being for seeds of new behavior, new ideas, new beliefs, new habits and new rituals.

This force of self-commitment is rooted in our survival instincts for how committed we are to being on the planet. If you are still alive and breathing, some part of you remains committed to being on the planet. Our daily lives are shaped by deeper unconscious forces that I call *the death-wish and the life-wish.* If you feel grave doubt or are deeply conflicted about being on the planet, the death-wish is winning. When you are more fully committed to being on the planet, the life-wish dominates. These contrary forces of regeneration and degeneration express the underlying existing conditions of our lives. Whatever we choose to align ourselves with determines the quality and nature of our fates. A metaphor comes to mind—*if fate is in the cards, destiny is how they're played.*

What makes our lives worth living, without which our lives would not be worth living? At some point in our lives, we face what we are living for: *life or death.* Until then, we are second-guessing our reasons for being. The death-wish and life-wish express contrary dynamics within the totality of our human nature; they are not separated at root. Each possesses a function in relation to the whole. Sometimes, we benefit when certain habits or behaviors are allowed to die off; the death-wish becomes relevant! Other times, certain productive areas in our lives suffer weakness or insecurity; committing to the life-wish can resuscitate them.

The Impersonal Nature of Culture

Integrity loss is not always a personal problem; it is not entirely our fault if we lack the power of follow-through. We live in an era where integrity loss expresses an impersonal cultural casualty common to any hyper-materialistic, death-ignorant consumerist society fractured by spiritual bankruptcy. Many of us endure this spiritual damage as a private burden we carry for the impersonal culture of society. Even though this damage may not actually be personal to us—*who can take credit?*—many of us mistakenly shoulder the burden of impersonal culture as a personal cause. *What a complete waste of time and energy!* The impersonal culture of society does not, cannot, care about the person. Society at large acts like a corporation that uses the person to advance its impersonal machinations and agendas. *The impersonal culture at large is not your friend.*

    Those who drop the impersonal burden of this cultural guilt do not become free of suffering. They become free of the impersonal social culture of suffering that depersonalizes the populace. Only after we embrace the honest burden of our own existence can we know the futility of trying to save the tragedy of the world. When we are fully accountable for our own suffering, we are less likely to believe we are accountable for saving the world. The world does not need saving. The world is full of people who need saving from themselves. Exceptions include those raising children who cannot be accountable for their own survival and those caring for the elderly, the sick, and the dying.

    Rejecting the impersonal culture of guilt does not mean shying away from helping others. It means becoming more aware of how we actually can and cannot help another. Not everyone needs or wants to be saved or awakened from their cocooning trance of impersonal cultural identification. Try breaking the spell of anyone resigned to the comfort of spiritual sleep and you may face the gnashing of teeth, the bearing of claws. Sometimes, naive gestures of helping others can be experienced as offensive, invasive, or annoying to those being "helped". If we are to actually assist others, we must first relax our personal agendas to discover more truth about their values, history, allegiances, and beliefs. Otherwise, we may be simply imposing our so-called help and alienate ourselves and others in the process.

Not all suffering is meaningful. Suffering becomes meaningless when it results in a more meaningless life. Meaningful suffering results in a

"Soror Mystica: Ritual Invocation of the Anima" (Dec. 2017) featuring poetry by Hilda Doolittle (aka HD). Directed by Antero Alli.

more meaningful life. How to tell the difference? Look to the results of your suffering to determine whether it's actually relevant or pointless. Self-created suffering—*over-thinking, courtship compulsion, self-pity, nonstop complaining*—can render our lives meaningless. Suffering that builds character, compassion, and strength renders our lives with more meaning. Meaningful suffering demands an honest confrontation with the existing conditions of our actual (not ideal) lives, i.e., not the life we wanted or believed we should or could have had, if only things were different. No—I'm talking about your actual life.

Respect existence or expect resistance. A living mystery pulses within the heart of existence—that we exist at all is a mystery! By exposing and surrendering ourselves to the existing conditions of our lives, a dimension of mystery can be penetrated and experienced firsthand. At some point, we may even become aware that we are this mystery and we embody it. *Become the mystery.*

Part Three: The Performer/Audience Romance
need for love, talent & skill, the total act, No-Form

Falling in Love with What

The torrid romance of audience/performer dynamics is fraught with mystery, anticipation, and insecurity. The tremulous rush of stage fright does not come from any promise of long-term relationship but the spine-tingling prospect of an eternal one-night stand. Theatrical conventions of distance (the fourth wall), talent, and skill naturally separate performers and audience, a separation sealed by post-performance audience applause. The audience/performer power dynamic tips and sways with fickle electricity; one night we're up and on, the next night we're down and out. As with any one-night stand, the audience/performer romance remains unpredictable and most performers would not have it any other way.

Can real connection between performer and an audience actually occur? Yes and no. Real connection between audience and performer may not be possible through any direct attack—presentational confrontations where the performer directly manipulates and/or emotionally assaults the audience. Whether it's via seduction, performer charisma, or the performers' "need to please, be liked, or to impress others"—or the more aggressive "in your face" assaults of Artaud's *Theatre of Cruelty* or Julian Beck's *Living Theatre*—direct attack theatre often fails to achieve any real connection beyond sledgehammer dents and crashes. Though this direct attack approach can sometimes prove effective as political theatre, historically it has consistently failed to achieve its social utopian ideals of "awakening the sleeping masses" or "saving or changing the world".

A Performer's Need for Love

No matter how great a given performance, the audience can only love the performance but not the person performing it, unless they are performing as themselves and not a character. Everyone needs and deserves love but that's not what the audience can offer. Confusing audience applause for love is like feasting on popcorn; you bloat and stay hungry for more popcorn. As a cultural entity the audience has been conditioned by centuries of tradition to act as a passive, receptive vessel for the stimulation of their own impressions, emotions, ideas, beliefs, and reactions to performances presented onstage or onscreen. The audience applauds a performance for arousing their own passions, thoughts, views, and sense of identification—in short, for arousing their own humanity. When any performance achieves this arousal, the audience responds with applause, praise, admiration, and respect. But not love. Oh, we hear them say, "I absolutely love your show" . . . "what an amazing performance" . . . "LOVE your work" and so on, but all these affects quickly fade. Audiences can be fickle; one night they're warm and responsive and the next night they're aloof and we never hear from them again.

Those who fall for "audience love" are fated to wander and chase the hungry ghost high of leap-frogging from production to production, from film to film, without taking any significant breaks to breathe, to live, to actually love and be loved. Attempting to meet your need for personal love in any audience-defined medium may be the worst reason to become an actor or a performer. Better to find someone to love (and to love you) and then, decide why you want to perform. If you can't find someone to love, love yourself like there's no tomorrow. Or if you are so graced, turn to God for the unconditional love no human can be expected to provide and then, share this spiritual presence with the world. Become the love that you seek. Love is never what we think. Love is the law, the crime that creates and breaks the law.

The Total Act—Capacity For Resonance

Why do we perform? If we are to make real connection with the audience, the will to perform must be liberated from all externally-driven considerations such as seeking acceptance, pleasing others, trying to impress the director, getting attention, love or approval, or seeking external acceptance for our talents, skills, and abilities. Only when the will to perform is emancipated from external social approval mechanisms can we become aligned with what Jerzy Grotowski calls *"the total act"*.

Performance of the total act requires development of an internal faculty of resonance, an intuitive capacity for knowing truth. Resonance requires no understanding, forethought, or plan. We either resonate with a given direction or state or we do not. When we lose this resonating capacity, we suffer indecision and can be plagued by vagueness of direction or over-thinking. Whenever we can fully commit to the visceral and spiritual resonances within us, a ripple effect occurs. Like a stone dropped in a calm pool of water, our personal resonances indirectly stir similar resonances in others and in the audience. This mutual interaction of resonances relies on the performer's total commitment to their own visceral and spiritual sources which, in turn, trigger audience resonances. In this way, the audience experiences an amplification of their own presence and not just the impact of a performer's force, or will, or charisma. After such a performance, the audience leaves exalted and amplified, as if they are leaving with more of themselves than when they arrived.

How can we cultivate a deeper capacity for resonance? A violin produces resonant tones due to its empty chamber; a violin stuffed with cotton becomes muted. To increase our internal resonating capacity,

"A Turbulence of Muses" (Dec. 2016) featuring poetry by Arthur Rimbaud. Directed by Antero Alli.

we must learn how to cultivate a kind of "empty chamber" within the instrument of the self. If we are stuffed with ideas, beliefs, techniques, and knowledge, our capacity for internal resonance quickly diminishes. The creation of internal space requires a process of "undoing" or emptying. There are many ways to initiate this process of undoing. The most direct and simple approach I have discovered and used in paratheatre is a method borrowed from Zen meditation that I call No-Form. In paratheatre, it's practiced in a standing posture, rather than traditional Zazen sitting meditation; one cannot move very far while sitting. The aim of this No-Form stance is to cultivate enough internal receptivity to detect and then, be acted on by autonomous forces in the body/psyche. By engaging and expressing these forces, we allow their presence to act through us as vessels in spontaneous movement, sound, gesture, and actions.

The Undoing Method of No-Form

Though No-Form represents a very direct and simple process, it can also be difficult and frustrating for anyone burdened by over-thinking, compulsive rationalization, and excessive self-analysis. The Inner Critic and the Ego Ideal naturally resist the prospect of being nothing. Other impediments to No-Form include: identification with self-images, preconceptions, ideals, beliefs, over-confidence, and excessive certitudes. No-Form can be experienced as a kind of intimacy with Void, a comfort around being nothing . . . of being nobody.

No-Form can be approached in any standing posture of balance resulting in a position of vertical rest—standing with minimal effort—and supporting a state of emptying or internal receptivity. The breath is focused on the exhale, allowing the inhale to occur by reflex. Mentally, we relax the desire to control and the desire to control the outcome or any appearance of our expression.

No-Form acts to charge a ritual to engage the body's vital forces and then to discharge these forces after each ritual or performance. In this way, No-Form serves a double function as a receptivity point to creative energy and then, as a discharging point to release whatever energies were engaged. It's like an on/off switch to our creative engines. Some performers seem to be "on" all the time, as if they never found the "off" switch. No-Form practice allows us to turn the creative engines on and off according to our needs. In this way, we are free to use our talents and skills as tools, instead of being owned by them. We no longer need to fear losing access to our creative sources or diminishing our talents when we know how to turn our creative engines on and off.

The W.N.S. (Wayne Newton Syndrome)

The audience/performer dynamic expresses an inherent imbalance. As performers, we're onstage because we exhibit, or should exhibit, more talent and skill than the audience that has paid to see us. The audience expects to be entertained and enlightened to some aspect of their lives and of their humanity. The audience arrives looking to be informed, stimulated, and amused. Performers are paid to control the communication in whatever medium they're working in; performers call the shots, must call the shots. When the actors take charge and do their job, theatre happens. There is a difference, however, between theatre that just gets the job done and *theatre that changes lives.*

Performers of theatre that changes lives must continually develop their craft in very specific and precise ways. Though these ways may differ for each performer, it starts with making choices on projects that stretch and expand our existing skill sets and talents. Without consistently challenging ourselves, performers can slip into plateaus of redundancy and stagnation by getting paid for repeating what they already know and what they do best. Without consistent challenges, artists can easily sink into a quagmire of inertia; existing talents wither, corrupt, fritter away. We become more tourist than artist, more mimic than creator, more spectacle than substance.

The Universal Patron Saint of Show Biz Glitz, Wayne "Mr. Las Vegas" Newton, demonstrates the fate awaiting those who only perform what they do best. Don't get me wrong. Mr. Newton is a wonderful and talented performer. He just does what he does over and over and over and over, again . . . and gets paid handsomely for it . . .

> *I'm still doing the kind of shows I've always done and I can tell you one thing: people may leave one of my shows disliking Wayne Newton, but they've never walked out saying, 'He*

didn't work hard for us' or 'He didn't give us our money's worth.' —Wayne Newton

Talent and Skill

Talent demonstrates a fluid capacity for gaining access and expression of the internal landscape in a spirit of constant discovery. Skill refers to a dexterity for articulating the internal landscape through externally recognizable forms, symbols, images, speech, and structures. Skill shows precision and clarity of form; talent shows spontaneity and "spirit" in action. Through talent we experience the presence and energy of creative force of an artist. With skill, we experience virtuosity, technique, and a clear sense of design and form. Artists and performers often demonstrate an imbalance between talent and skill. Too much spontaneity can overwhelm skill, just as too much structure can crimp talent.

Striking a dynamic balance between talent and skill is the aim of any committed artist and/or performer. The more exceptional the performer, the higher the integration of talent and skill. Though talent cannot really be taught, it can be nurtured by encouraging total freedom of self-expression. Skill, however, can be learned by consistent application of method and the refinement of technical dexterity. As talent and skill cohere at higher and higher levels, High Art occurs. Talent in paratheatre refers to an elastic capacity for accessing sources in the body itself, of mining the body for veins of autonomous forces, images, emotion, sensation, and the deeper complexes and numinous archetypes of the personal and collective Unconscious—*the inner actions of source-work or sourcing.* Skill in paratheatre refers to the precision of expression and articulation of source-work. Paratheatre skills can be developed by an ongoing practice of paratheatre techniques (see "The Trigger Methods").

Part 4: Self-Observation and Ego
identity, contraries, the emotional plague

The Mystery of Identity

Who are you, really? Are you your name? Are you the offspring of your parents and the genetic link to the future of your ancestral gene pool? Are you the collection of your habits, fears, desires, beliefs, ideas, and needs? Are you a figment of your imagination, a dreamer dreaming yourself into existence? Are you what you were hoping for? Beyond all these scenarios, parental and genetic influences, education, and philosophical ideas and beliefs, *who are you really?*

"Ego", as the term is used here, refers to any emotional investment and attachment to a self-image. Ego as self-image; big ego as big self-image. Can you distinguish an "image" of who you are from the experience of who you are—before any labels were imposed on that experience? A strong ego is not the same as a big ego that feeds on any inflated, one-sided idea or image of ourselves; big egos express brittle states of psychological rigidity. Strong egos are flexible and at ease in the heart of contradiction, openly embodying the contraries of our universal human condition.

Ego is subordinate to, and created by, The Self, what Jung calls the centralizing archetype of The Self. When the part (ego) is confused for the whole (The Self), the ego becomes "bedeviled". Ego is not the devil but identifying with ego can be vexing. Who has not experienced creative shutdown—*our so-called "creative blocks"*—after falsely assuming credit for what we never truly created or was never truly ours to claim? *We are all imposters!* Why not openly expose the Imposter within us and its social mask, the Poseur? No shame in confession; no crime in being unknown to oneself. Replace the antiquated adage of "Know Thyself" with: *Now Thyself.*

Allowing and embracing contraries within our human nature is an exercise in psychological freedom—freedom from the oppression of a one-sided self-image. For example, if we are enamored by the self-image of being strong, look to your weaknesses to balance your ego. If you are in love with the self-image of independence, are you independent enough to be dependent? If you covet an ego of intelligence, are you smart enough to confess ignorance? If you pride yourself as a "radical person", are you radical enough to be conservative? Embracing our contraries supports a more flexible ego structure.

When the ego is aligned with The Self, we start to experience ourselves as an expression of a larger, changing whole and can act as vessels for the expression of The Self. As the archetype of Self is accessed, sourced, and expressed, we encounter contraries innate to our human nature: we are weak and strong, stupid and intelligent, beautiful and ugly, good and

"Orphans of Delirium" (May 2004) featuring poetry by
Samuel Coleridge. Directed by Antero Alli.

evil. However, it may not be enough to continually expose more truth
about ourselves and each other. Truth without self-compassion can feel
like cruelty. As empathy for ourselves and for others develops, the narcissism trap can be minimized and sometimes, bypassed. A little narcissism
goes a long way and empathy keeps that in check.

The Emotional Plague

*During the 2020 Plague of Covid, another invisible plague spreads
across the land.* "The emotional plague", a term coined by Dr. Wilhelm
Reich, refers to the "irrational insistence on beliefs and ideas that depend
on dissociation of mind from body". This body/mind fissure has been
historically dramatized in any religion that maintains this dissociative
belief. In the modern era, the emotional plague is sustained by mass
projection of vital physical, emotional, psychic and sexual energy into
the absorbent mediums of the internet, VR technology, video games,
mass media advertising, and television. The emotional plague is sustained whenever the virtual is mistaken for the actual, when confusing
talk for action, when ideas and ideals are confused for the realities they
symbolize, when we are eating the menu instead of the meal.

*Two modern-day symptoms of the emotional plague in the current
Hypermedia Era: 1) an increasing trend towards de-personalization,*

homogenization and gentrification and 2) a steadily decreasing capacity for direct experience.

As we lose trust and faith in the legitimacy of firsthand experience, we can naturally become more vulnerable and compliant to the dictates of external sources of authority and its moral codes of obedience and punishment. Without enough trust in our own innate sensibilities, intuitions and instincts we lose touch with our own internal compass. We lose the capacity to distinguish the real from the illusory, the true from the false, and what's right from what's wrong. Without self-trust, we remain as timid children dependent on parental approval and guidance for how we live, work, procreate, domesticate, and die.

What is real and what is an illusion? Do you know? Do you care? If you don't know and can say so, you are probably waking up. If you don't know and/or don't care, don't bother; you are probably asleep. It doesn't care either and you will soon be assimilated, if you have not already been consumed by the toxic emotional plague. If you have come to know what's real in life, dare to live by the dictates of your truth. Your example acts as a beacon for those lost at sea struggling to keep their heads above water on the slow-mo shipwreck of the dying cultures at large.

Part 5: Initiation Never Ends
a bridge between worlds; restoring the dreaming power

On the Bridge Between Worlds

The most challenging aspect of paratheatrical work may be the integration of its results into daily life experiences. Insights, realizations, and epiphanies erupting in paratheatrical processes can disappear if they cannot find life *beyond the workspace.* Without the application of "Lab" insights into the daily, their rarified moments quickly dissipate like fading photographs. For this work to have any lasting influence and value, we must find ways to build and maintain a kind of bridge between worlds—*between the internal landscape of the soul and the external world of daily life*—between the infinite and finite dimensions of existence. How to arouse ecstatic moments amidst day to day toil and drudgery?

Can we find No-Form when we're snagged into someone else's soap opera melodramatics? Can we engage verticality in the face of political insanity and corruption? Questions worth addressing.

Us humans have always sought out and invented new ways to alleviate boredom and get high and attempt escape from the banality and tedium of existence. Many escape attempts often lead to dispersion and self-destruction, where no true escape happens at all. If this escapist compulsion is innate to the human condition, how can we actually escape? Escapism itself does not seem to be the real problem. The real problem looks more like a naive assumption that we can escape *from reality. Nobody escapes from reality.* To truly escape, we must find ways to shift *the context* of escape, from trying to escape *from* reality towards escaping *into* reality, *into the very heart of the human condition.* Escaping *into* the existing conditions of our lives, rather than away from them, we stand a better chance to tap the pulse of mystery beating at the very heart of existence itself.

At first, this escape into reality may seem impossible and even undesirable. Why would anyone want to pass into and through the wretchedness of mundane existence? This seemingly impossible task demands a certain kind of power, a power that does not originate in any Nietzschean personal "will to power" but a deeper power within our psyches, in our Body, that's drained by unconscious habits of power loss. Maintaining the bridge between worlds requires an exposure and knowledge of habits that drain *the power of dreaming*, a power emanating from the cosmos that we are expressions of.

When we wake up to how we are losing power, we are faced with the choice to minimize or eliminate the drainage points in our lives or keep suffering from power loss. Self-imposed habits of power loss can be self-corrected. Some sources of power loss are imposed on us by others and some come from the dominator culture at large and these require different strategies. Once our power drains are exposed and released, the power of dreaming returns on its own volition. *Nothing else has to be done.* Remove the drains and the dreaming power returns of itself. This power is not personal, it's not of our personal will; it expresses the cosmos itself. Restoring this dreaming power empowers the bridge between worlds. Maintaining this bridge between worlds must continue as an ongoing ritual of Self-initiation. Like any bridge, new cracks can appear

"Escape from Chapel Perilous" (Dec. 2018) featuring poetry by Sylvia Plath. Directed by Antero Alli.

and must be mended. Unattended, new power drains can weaken this bridge. We can fall back and get lost in our own worlds or fall out of ourselves and get eaten by the world.

How the Dreaming Power is Drained

Perhaps the two greatest drains to the dreaming power are: 1) The Poor Baby and 2) Courtship Compulsion. Both drainage points diminish and ravage the energetic body, the chief conduit for the power of dreaming.

The Poor Baby Syndrome corrodes the will. This power drain is maintained by self-pity and the immature refusal to accept one's flaws, shortcomings and inadequacies. It can manifest as self-denial, constant complaining and whining about feeling "not enough". *Poor Baby!* When afflicted by the Poor Baby Syndrome, we can become as emotional vampyres feeding off the sympathy of others while hosting pity parties in private or commiserating with other Poor Babies. This self-victimizing habit shrinks the decision-making muscle, resulting in the self-created anguish of indecision. The mass culture of advertising feeds and controls the Poor Baby Syndrome by appealing to the unmet needs of the emotionally immature consumer, i.e., *you are not enough without our product!*

Self-denial sustains the Poor Baby. Defusing the Victim archetype starts by learning to accept yourself, warts and all. As self-accountability increases, acceptance eventually replaces self-denial as a powerful foundation of self-support. However, this may be easier said than done. Facing the internal ravages of this power loss can be painful and embarrassing and may require professional therapy if the damage has become too overwhelming for Poor Baby's fragile ego structure.

Taking everything personally fattens the Victim. If you are easily offended, perhaps you suffer from excessive self-importance or delusions of entitlement. This can occur through positive or negative ego-inflation. Unless you're creating a Clown character for a theatrical performance (taking everything personally makes any clown funnier), it's a good idea to discover what is actually personal to you and what is not. Not everything is personal. Most of life, society, corporations, governments, the culture at large and the world at large doesn't give a fuck about the person - these agencies are all impersonal by nature. Distinguish yourself or be extinguished. Knowing what not to take personally means not taking most things personally.

Courtship, Compulsion, and Power Loss

Courtship Compulsion ravages the energetic body of the soul and its psychic home, the imagination. This complicated power drain occurs with any excessive emotional investment in an idealized image of the "dream lover", and/or any obsessive search for "The One", the "soulmate" or "twin flame". When these projections are imposed onto any external person who somehow matches that psychic image of the "dream lover" (what Carl Jung calls "the Anima" in men and the "Animus" in women), we can become as psychic vampyres merging with the energy of another in a misguided attempt at achieving "oneness" or some new-age ideal of "alchemical tantric unity". Give me a break; it takes two distinct individuals to sustain any honest interaction and relating.

This power drain also taxes the imaginal faculties that might find more productive and creative outlets through Art, Poetry, Music, Dance, Theatre, Cinema, etc. The power of Venus that's projected onto dream lovers is the same energy fueling Art projects. Without creative outlets, all that psychic energy projected onto dream lovers can backfire and implode into a downward spiral of self-destruction. Courtship compulsion takes tremendous psychic energy to sustain itself and leaves us emotionally drained, always wanting and always needy. It's not courtship itself, which can be a lovely ritual in budding romances, that drains our power. The problem is this one-sided obsession that occurs in our own heads with very little to show for itself beyond the power loss it creates. Courtship compulsion turns into a dumb-down spiral of diminishing returns.

Courtship Compulsion veils a sophisticated ritual of self-torment where love is always wanted but never truly found. The mass culture of advertising controls the Courtship Compulsion by the Beauty Myth oppressing every woman and man mistaking glamour for true beauty (see *The Beauty Myth* by Naomi Wolf). Glamour casualties are assimilated into a vapid world of appearances that drains the dreaming power with the negative spirits of Envy and Greed, the endless comparisons with others, and the endless hungry ghost search for approval, acceptance, and love.

Often times, this Courtship Compulsion mythologizes unconditional love. When we seek and expect unconditional love from another person, it places them under tremendous pressure to deliver the impossible. What flawed human person can love unconditionally all the time? This external projection of unconditional love may mask an unmet spiritual need for the love of God, perhaps the only true source of unconditional love. As this projection persists, we can easily fall into a Poor Baby life where any kind of love we receive or expect never measures up. We become snagged in a web of constant disappointments. If we can trace this projection back to the spiritual frustration, we may discover how we are love at essence. When we become the love we seek, the worldly search for love ceases. Realizing this spiritual truth, we can enjoy romantic liaisons and endure long term loving relations—*not from any desperate need or search for love but*—from an offering of *self as love* where being in love takes on new meaning—*to be love is to be in love.*

An Aboriginal Vision of Dreaming

As these habits of power loss are minimized or eliminated, we may notice a new kind of energy and feeling inhabiting our lives and relations. Calling this "the power of dreaming" was inspired by my 1986 encounter with Guboo Ted Thomas, an Aborigine Koori elder. Guboo views the planet itself as this massive dreaming entity that dreams all its inhabitants into existence, the birds, insects, animals, trees, flowers, fishes, and yes, humans. When I heard Guboo talk like this, my big white mind freaked out and threw up a wall thinking, this old guy's batshit crazy. But there was something about his presence that got under my skin and relaxed the mental grip I had on thinking I knew what reality really was.

Had I unwittingly stumbled into some kind of aboriginal initiation ritual? Looking into his eyes, I started feeling the presence of the dreaming power of the planet that he was talking about. And the longer he spoke, the more I felt the dreaming power. And then, he stopped and started singing. I don't remember the words he sang as much as how the energy or spirit in his song zeroed in on my heart, cracking it open. My tears flowed. He smiled and said, "The best is yet to come."

After meeting with Guboo (I interviewed him for a local paper in Boulder CO), I soon became aware of my habits of power loss, namely the Poor Baby and Courtship Compulsion. It wasn't until I diminished their hold on me that I was able to start realizing my dreams. . . writing books, creating theatre, making films. There was some start and stop over the next few years, including a painful divorce from my first wife, but once I got clear on these power drains my dreams started to come true. I won't bore you here with a list of my accomplishments (check my websites for that). I can say that the rituals and methods in this book were designed to restore the power of dreaming and the insurrection of the Poetic Imagination. When the imagination, the canary in the cultural coal mine, goes belly up the soul soon follows; *imagination death precedes death of soul.*

LIBER ZZZ: Hypnosis for thee Practitioner

Saul Mondriaan, Brother Stone his Booke
XI.XX.MMXXI 156:663

The boy in my lap had no idea who I was and didn't know why he was in a strange house, naked under a light blanket, surrounded by candles, but—perhaps because he was still in a light trance—he wasn't afraid. "Hi, Zack." I said. "You don't know me, yet, but you will in about ten years. My name's Saul, and I'm a magician. I've brought you forward through time."

I had just performed the most successful operation of my magical career, and for the next four hours my boyfriend's body was inhabited by a teenager I had never met, a person whose body language, vocal affect and vocabulary had unmistakably changed, who reminded me of someone I loved but who was definitely—so long as my enchantment, that thirty minutes of hypnosis, held—no longer the same. The operation had been simple: After a short induction I invited PJ to imagine moving through a pillow fort, picking up objects from their past as they went. They put on a backpack and an old hoodie, picked up a sketchbook, and emerged from trance as a stranger. He didn't know how to work the lightswitches in our house; he couldn't open his own phone. PJ had been immensely stoned when we began, barely able to keep their eyes open; when Zach came back from the past he was sober, energetic and alert. The weed pen he found in his pocket—which I had to explain to him—made his eyes turn red, something I'd never seen happen to the current instantiation of my boyfriend. I showed him the music he would make, the drawings, his room, his olympic-white Jazzmaster. "This is who you're going to be," I told him, "The kind of person you're already turning into. I wanted you to know it's going to be OK."

When he put his head back in my lap, I put an amulet around his neck and explained what was about to happen, that I would start counting backward from ten and he would sink back down, back to his own time. I said he might not remember what had happened, that it might be like waking up from a dream—but that even dreams we can't remember have the power to change us, to change everything. "I'm going to miss you," he said, and went to sleep.

Ten, nine, eight, seven, six, five, four, three, two, one. Another deep, deep breath. And you're back with me.

●●●

What I want to emphasize here is that I am not a master hypnotist and PJ is not unusually susceptible to hypnosis; I am, in fact, a rank amateur. The result I obtained wasn't dependent on surpassing magical or technical skill: This is the kind of thing any magically operant person can do with no tools and a few not-especially-sophisticated techniques you can learn in an afternoon. Although I am increasingly convinced that hypnosis *is* magic—and that many magical practices, from petitions to goetic invocations, operate by the same mechanisms as does hopelessly disenchanted clinical hypnotherapy—what I would like to do here is lay out a few hypnotic techniques from the perspective of a magical practitioner and provide enough material for you to attempt a few experiments of your own. I find that this stuff is a bit like astrology or Black Eyed Children: The more you think about it the more you will find, to your surprise, that you have evoked it into your instantiation ov Consensus.

I. Basic Hypnotic Techniques From a Magical Standpoint

The hypnotic operation is extremely simple and it is always the same. Hypnotists frequently express their surprise at how *many* things all seem to work, how little anything depends on the details but how much depends on the confidence of the practitioner; and I could rewrite this statement, of course, using the word "magical" and "magicians" instead. In fact, if you have made any advancement at all in the foundational techniques of magic—trance, the use of Names and barbarous words, sigilization, the writing of prayers and incantations, even the light flow-state we arrive at when working on craft projects or magical art—you have obtained, by other names, the essential skills of a hypnotist; even more excitingly, the hypnotist's skillset is exceptionally appropriate to the magical practitioner in her role as healer and wonderworker. The practice of magic *using hypnotic techniques* is a technical approach that brings easy and immediate power to an active spiritual life; the practice of hypnosis *as magic* is a way to openly and confidently practice thaumaturgy on others' behalf, since its techniques are the techniques of magic, wonderfully and cunningly disguised.

Induction. Every hypnotic operation begins with the breath, with altering consciousness through the slowing and regulation of breathing—this is the beginning of the ritual, immediately familiar to us. The client is invited to sit comfortably—which is a command, one of the first of many—and to breathe; the hypnotist begins to speak of relaxation, to direct the breath, to link the breath to *certain sensations*, and so on. The client expects that they will enter a trance, even not knowing what that means; so the hypnotist tells them that they will enter a trance. When something changes in the client's body, they recognize this as a trance, whatever that is, and they know that the hypnotist's voice will have a certain power over them in this condition. The Alexandrian who has sought the service of a hellenistic magician has very similar expectations: The practitioner will do certain things, they themself will experience certain sensations, and the magician's voice will have a certain power in that space. "ΑΒΛΑΝΘΑΝΑΛΒΑ," says the Hellenistic wonderworker. "Ten times deeper, twenty times deeper, entering a very warm, very comfortable trance," says the hypnotist.

To perform a hypnotic induction, control the breath. Slow it; name it; use language to describe and thereby command the body's relaxation, its change in state. Declare that these things mean that there is a change in consciousness, that a trance is coming. You are creating a charmed circle—the act of hypnosis begins as soon as the client has decided that you are going to hypnotize them. Everything you do contributes to this, in exactly the same way that candles and suffumigations, the use of lustral waters and the creation of magical circles contributes to the magical act in our paradigm. The client expects counting, so the hypnotist counts; they could as well be reciting a psalm or humming a bar of music—the result would be the same. For my part, I was furious to discover that it is actually very easy to enter a trance—that anyone can do it, often without meaning to—and that magical gnosis feels remarkably similar to being in a light hypnotic state. Worst of all: The recognizable, bodily trance that we induce this way may not even be necessary for hypnotic operations to work. *The confidence of the practitioner is, somehow, enough.*

Once the client has been inducted—and there are dozens of ways to do this, some as famously simple as a handshake[1]—she is ready to receive suggestions.

Hypnotic suggestion. It is immediately obvious that hypnotic suggestion only works because the subject has decided that the experience she is having *means* that some kind of change will occur; otherwise our dreams would program us, conversations overheard while dozing off on the couch would program us, we would be a mess of confused and conflicted internalized compulsions. The simplicity of delivering a suggestion teaches us something about magic: The hypnotist simply declares that something is so, or that it *might* be so, and—*as if by magic*—the client discovers that it *is* so, just as expected. There is absolutely no trick to this: It is artless. Advanced techniques involve embedding suggestions into shaggy dog stories, into analogies from the client's experiences, into wordplay and homophones and so on. A cynical magician might begin to think that all this is just a way to bolster the hypnotist's confidence in the same way that lengthy prayers and invocations are more for our benefit than for the sake of the angels or thoughtforms we address.

Here repetition is useful for its numbing effect, for its uncanny ability to convince by exhaustion, for the illusion of hard work to which contemporary humans are addicted. All of this is *exactly* analogous to declaring "By the burning of this candle I do destroy my enemies" or to deciding that an egg rolled over the body has removed an evil influence:

---

1   See, for example, Mark Carich and Mark Becker's "A Brief Review of the Key Hypnotic Elements of Milton H. Erickson's Handshake Technique."

Hypnotists and magicians alike believe in the fundamental, transformative power of language, of symbols, of the power to declare and decree a thing in full faith that reality will follow suit. During this process, the client passively accepts what she hears, following the language of the hypnotist in an unresisting, pleasant condition of belief; It seems clear to me that this is precisely the same kind of activity as we engage in when writing out a petition statement until the syllables become meaningless or holding a sigil in our minds without thinking about its significance—these are magicians' tricks to engender the basic and powerful *belief* that our activities depend on. Hypnosis demonstrates that this belief can be created just by informing someone that they will, for a certain time, simply believe whatever they hear.

To deliver a hypnotic suggestion, assert that a thing is so. To coöpt the belief of the client and distract her psychic censor, couple these assertions with rich sensory detail; draw from memory, engage the client in active imagination, repeat yourself in many ways. As in the construction of sigils, avoid negative statements.[2]

Returning to normal consciousness. In the same way that a practitioner needs to explicitly close a ritual and perform certain actions to return to normal consciousness—grounding and centering, by whatever name—the hypnotic operation needs to be closed and the client returned to a normal condition. Just as in magic, the close of the operation is significantly less elaborate than its beginnings; to simply count up from one to ten is enough. Again, direction of the breath is simple and effective: It became slower when she entered trance; in making it more rapid she is invigorated and returns to normal consciousness. These practices exist not because it is difficult to leave trance—god knows we've all had our magical trances ruined by a roommate or an unwelcome noise—but because humans find a lack of boundaries to be uncomfortable. By clearly demarcating the end of the hypnotic operation the client is able to participate in a transition from one state to another and is allowed to confirm, once more, that the hypnotist has exerted supernatural control

---

2   Presented as the transcript of a seminar, Grinder's *Trance-Formations: Neuro-Linguistic Programming and the Structure of Hypnosis* is out-of-print but regarded as an outstanding and comprehensive introduction to this material.

over her experience of reality.

To comfortably end a trance, declare that the client will soon return from her trance state and return to normal consciousness feeling refreshed and alert. Then direct a change in the breath, describing the sensations of returning from trance as you do so. Counting upward is an easy way to provide a structured return to normal consciousness, but this, again, could be done any number of ways.

Posthypnotic triggers. The magical name, the word of power, the reality-warping gesture: These are the archetypical possessions of the magician, and hypnotic techniques can be used to give them an immediacy, a reality, that confirms and empowers our participation in an enchanted world. Although the hypnotist may choose to focus on the use of narrative and internal ritual to create long-term change, the design and arrangement of posthypnotic triggers—words or gestures that cause an immediate response in a client who is no longer in trance—create resources for deployment in particular situations such as relaxation in the face of anxiety, a burst of energy, or an erotic response. These look, from a magical perspective, exactly like charms and words of power—which they are.

To create posthypnotic triggers, describe them while the client is in trance. Declare that a particular thing means that another thing will occur. Play through it while the client is in trance; assert that this will be the case even once she has returned to normal consciousness. In my experience, posthypnotic triggers are most dramatic for five to twenty minutes; afterward their effects begin to fade.

II. Hypnosis for thee Practitioner

Experiment one: Invoking trance states. If you are struggling to reliably enter trance states when your practice calls for it, here is a weird trick from the hypnotic repertoire: A standard hypnotist's technique is to draw the subject's attention toward the sensations in the body that *happen to arise* while she is experiencing an induction and to assert that these are both the signs of *and* gateways into trance. Notice that my wording is intentionally vague: Not sensations *provoked* by the induction but any sensations at all. This chicanery is the mechanism of the standard script: "You might notice certain sensations in your arms and legs, perhaps a lightness, perhaps a warmth on the skin; and as you experience these sensations you fall more deeply into a very comfortable, very deep trance . . . " This is bog-standard chaos magic, very Alan Chapman, deciding that one thing means the same thing as another.[3]

This becomes exceptionally useful once you have experienced trance on your own terms enough times to know what it feels like for you *specifically*, meaning that you can both recognize *and remember* those sensations. When they are present you can name them and thereby deepen them; when they aren't, you can name them *and thereby cause them to occur.* Trance can be invoked—exactly like a spirit—in exactly this way; silently assert that you are experiencing in your body what you would experience if you were entering a trance and, lo, you will discover that you are soon experiencing them—and entering a trance. For me this looks something like this:

> There is a lightness in my hands as I feel warmer and more liquid. As my hands and arms grow lighter and warmer I notice certain sensations in my body and I enter trance, going deeper into trance with every breath, breathing in as my hands feel lighter and warmer and as my legs begin to feel different than they did before, becoming very comfortable, very light, and as I enter a deeper state of trance I notice certain sensations in my body, a certain skewing of all things to the left, a certain warmth and displacement and lightness in my head . . .

. . . and so on. You might observe that this is effectively a kind of patter, a babble that doesn't need to be true in order to work; because it is so banal it requires no effort and its flatness, its artlessness, is itself effective in obtaining the result.

I find that using facts about my actual experience of trance, such as that sensation of skewedness, uses my memories of successful trance inductions to create more of the same in a very easy and productive feedback loop. If this feels offensively unaesthetic, that's because it is—fortunately, with a little practice, I can knock off the verbal noise and accomplish the same goals by silent attention to the sensations

---

3   My thinking about the core mechanism of magic is lifted more or less entirely from Alan Chapman's *Advanced Magick for Beginners.*

themselves in the same way as I direct attention to my breath.[4] This can *absolutely* be performed with much grander language: *Behold, the breath ov Hoor-Pa-Kraat, or whatever, riseth up in my thews; open are the double doors of the horizon, unlocked are its gates, I am a very serious magician, abracablahblahblah...*

Experiment two: Arm levitation. The fact of the matter is that I need to be constantly, emphatically reminded that magic works; the arm levitation induction is a standard part of the hypnotist's repertoire because it provides a sledgehammer-to-the- head demonstration that *something is happening.* This sort of thing jingles keys in front of the practitioner loudly enough for magic to occur without our interference, which, I find, is the core mechanism of all our most arcane and thunderous techniques. This is one of those cheap tricks I mentioned: When you feel your body begin to behave strangely you will begin to believe that anything is possible—and then it will be.

This has been written up in a hundred ways by a hundred hypnotists so I will not exhaust you with instructions.[5] In the standard version you will enter a light trance and talk to yourself about how there is a balloon tethered to your fingertip, asserting that you can feel it tugging upward, that your arm is becoming lighter and lighter etcetera; and then, to your great delight, all of this will happen. Similar techniques involve the hands joining as though there were magnets in the palms; and so on. Please feel free to imagine instead that VII The Chariot is tied to your fingers by the reins or that our friend Baphomet has you by the wrist—have fun with it.

I have recently been working on enchanting an Air tool, a banishing bell, using exactly this mechanism: As I work on it the bell becomes

---

4   Relatedly, I don't think that it's clear to occidental magicians why, specifically, the Gyan mudra is so useful in meditation; since I haven't seen this explained in the sort of media we consume, here's a secret: The sensation of your fingertips pressing together is a point of focus, a distraction of the same sort as "return your attention to the breath." If you meditate while seated in a chair you can do something similar by focusing on the point of contact between the soles of your feet and the floor.

5   Detailed and useful instructions for techniques of this type are given in Anthony Jacquin's charmingly amoral *Reality is Plastic*, which at the time of this writing can be easily found online.

lighter and lighter, eventually seeming to levitate in my hands, pulling my arms into the air as I blast it with invoking pentagrams and what-have-you. I have found this especially rewarding because *it will not do so* unless I'm doing a good job: Whatever deeply-buried part of me actually knows when magic is happening has weaponized the cheap hypnotic trick to give me a reliable sense of my own progress. Interestingly, when I am not in a trance state I can still feel cool air swirling around the bell when I touch it, which strikes me as a nice illustration of the blurred boundary between posthypnotic suggestion and effective object-level enchantment.

Experiment three: Thee Cheapest Trick[6], with corollaries. When the body enters trance the eyes have a tendency to roll back in the head. In a very similar vein to experiment one, this can be exploited in reverse: To rapidly enter trance, alter your breathing as you ordinarily do. For the sake of distraction, vividly imagine a scene, a tone, or some other sensory detail that you can sustain and use as a misdirection while your body does what it needs to do. On the inbreath, roll your eyes from left to right, strenuously enough that it's a little uncomfortable. While at the top of the breath, roll them again. When releasing, roll them a third time. Then, as you take another breath, roll your eyes as far back as you can—enough to cause yourself fatigue—and hold them there through the top of the breath cycle, counting down from five to one. At one, give yourself whatever command you like—"Sleep!" for instance, or "Float!" or "EI IEOΥ ΥΠΝE"—exhale—and let your eyes relax. If you are already in a tranquil state this will reliably knock you into a light trance.

What aggravating nonsense like this demonstrates is, again, that bodily sensation is a useful tool when altering states of consciousness; but more interestingly it points toward use of *voces magicae* as hypnotic triggers—or vice versa—as shortcuts to mind control and metamorphosis in the sense of Pete Carroll.[7] Setting up trigger phrases is immensely rewarding, and it's hard to feel more like an actual pointy-hatted Wizard than when those hypnotic triggers are also magical words in their own right—verbal sigils, god-names or words of power. I absolutely decline

---

6   I learned this from the hypnotist Alan Nerenberg, who demonstrates his "Float Induction" on YouTube.
7   As described in Peter J. Carroll's *Liber MMM*.

to draw a distinction between hypnosis and magic here: I just encourage you to try hypnotic programming to the effect of "When I vibrate *ARARITA* I will notice certain sensations, and as those sensations intensify my hexagram will blaze with power . . . " in order to supercharge your *experience* of magic—and therefore your ability to *execute* that magic.

Experiment four: Shaggy Dog Stories. Milton Erickson—a hypnotist who was primarily a wizard in exactly the way that Jung was a psychiatrist who was primarily a wizard—was known for telling meandering, symbolic stories at the beginning of client sessions; he would finish telling the story, the befuddled client would ask when the hypnotism would begin, Erickson would explain that the session was over and the client would walk out of the office cured. As practitioners, this behavior looks immediately and obviously familiar. In my opinion, having read demonstrations of this technique, it is *obviously* the case that this doesn't work because of precious manipulation of the language into a kind of subtle code; no, the story itself is magic and draws its power from symbolic manipulation rather than cheap neurolinguistic tricks. These stories can be crude allegories or as cryptic and Borgesian as you like: It doesn't seem to matter. This is, for us, an aesthetic jackpot—your opportunity to create a hypnotic experience that feels like magic, your magic. Mine are a bit cottagecore, a bit fairy-story, but you should absolutely go nuts: treat it like a sigil, start from *this story means that I will receive a message from my HGA* and go from there. *One time in Seattle I watched a frog watch itself in the dewdrops on a watch-face . . .* The details don't matter—you'll know what you need to say in the same way you know how to set up an altar or what your daily card pull means.[8]

Experiment five: Thee Voice. If you find yourself with a friend or

---

8   Once you have gotten into the habit of designing these stories for your own use or use on others, try entering a trance with your result in mind but no particular plans for the shaggy dog story: Begin telling yourself your stupid little yarn and let it just unroll however it likes. Passively allow yourself to carry the story to its turgid conclusion without judgment or intervention; see what you produce. Then, carry details of the story back with you and manifest them somehow—through art, for instance, or cunning arrangement of circumstances. Play with symbols. Symbolize symbols with other symbols. Consider all of this the content of your operation and, as they say, record your results.

partner that lets you experiment on them, you might eventually discover that you can give them suggestions simply by changing the tone of your voice. I *absolutely* have a Hypnotist Voice—distinct, that is, from my normal affect—which is a lot of fun in domestic situations. Why should "vibrating god names" be any different? Try cultivating a specific tone of voice that makes it clear that what appears to be a run-of-the-mill Thunderous Invocation is actually, in fact, self-hypnosis: Make a subject of yourself. The delight here is that, again, it doesn't matter *at all* what is actually going on: Is it hypnosis? Is it "vibrating" the syllables of a prayer? Who cares! Nothing is true, everything is permitted—and it works. Do this with your magical practice for a little while, then try doing it for mundane things: **I feel like getting started on my taxes**, you say into your coffee, casually. **It'd be very easy to get that done today**. And look at you, off to the tax prep software. OK, so your hypnosis-magic is working—now what? Flip the context again. Apo pantos kakodaimonos, you roar, doing that thing with your throat that you do—and suddenly it hits different. Success!

III. On Trickery

The charlatan-magus spectrum, with Le Bateleur on one end and The Magician on the other, has recently[9] been under reëxamination in the circles I move in—that mundane illusion and flimflam not only contributes to belief in the client but engenders power in the magician herself; that moreover high strangeness itself is attracted to trickery, that thaumaturgy might *require* fraud as the price of admission into a more magical world. In this spirit, let me exhort you toward the virtues of self-deception for the sake of Thee Great Work.

I am told that in New England spiritualist circles the most obvious and hackneyed parlor tricks are still deployed at the beginning of séances. These rituals are held and attended by true believers who have repeatedly experienced the visible manifestation of spirits. Notice that I say *the beginning* of the séance—because after the conclusion of these formalities

---

9   Uncle Ramsey, of course, **anticipated the trend** by about thirty-five years. Ramsey Dukes, "The Charlatan and the Magician," (1984), thephilosophers-stone.com.

comes the inexplicable. Objects are apported; ectoplasm spills from the mouth of the medium; impossible knowledge is transmitted. No, the charlatanry is not there in place of occult power—it is there to produce it. For some reason—ridiculously, insultingly—trickery *is* a ritual act. As such I invite you to consider hypnotic techniques as a means by which the practitioner may knowingly deceive *herself* in the pursuit of magical attainments.

I am increasingly convinced that a kind of insane, cretinous confidence is the necessary spiritual perfection that magic requires of us. When the practitioner exhausts her own desire to distinguish between magical result and coincidence she has created the charmed circle in which the power of consensus reality is broken; I speak, I suppose, less of a lack of judgment than a sustained and effortless *yes*, yes to magic, yes to the will, yes to the unseen world. So this, then, is my proposition: Accept that hypnosis is a set of ridiculous tricks, that it is a cheap and insipid exploit of the human hardware, that it bypasses the sick stupid demiurge-poisoned security system of the personality and produces result without attainment, magic without insight, behavior modification without wisdom—that it is rightly the purview of extremely divorced men with pinky-rings and a certain raw-scrubbed grindset earnestness. Yes, good—and it works, just as magic works so effortlessly when we stop applying our little notions about Truth to our experiences; and the most absurd trick of all is to allow magic to creep up behind you as you manipulate the brightly-colored trash on your conjurer's table. Here, then, is trickery: Use it fortunately, friend.

Works Cited

Carich, Mark and Mark Becker, "A Brief Review of the Key Hypnotic Elements of Milton H. Erickson's Handshake Technique," Erikson-foundation.org.

Carroll, Peter J., *Liber MMM* (1987).

Chapman, Alan, *Advanced Magick for Beginners*, (AEON Books, 2008).

Dukes, Ramsey, "The Charlatan and the Magician," (1984), The-philosophers-stone.com.

Grinder, John and Richard Bandler, *Trance-Formations: Neuro-Linguistic Programming and the Structure of Hypnosis*, (Real People Press, 1981).

Jacquin, Anthony, *Reality is Plastic! The Art of Impromptu Hypnosis* (Revised Edition, 2008).

Nerenberg, Alan, "Hypnotized in 10 Seconds. Float Induction. New Self-Hypnosis Technique," Sept. 13 2020. Youtube.com.

Interview With Ina Auderieth

Introduction

Ina Auderieth is a hermetic practitioner and artist residing in Austria. She graciously allowed me to use her artwork on the cover of this issue. She's also the creator of The Conjunction Tarot deck, which is absolutely gorgeous. As someone with very little artistic ability, I was curious how she created her drawings and whether they were merely inspired or if there was something more to it. I did not realize the sheer amount of effort she puts into them, the amount of her soul that is poured into it, and how integral it seems to be in her life. This really is practical magic at its best.

How does magic or the occult play a role in your work?

I've been interested in these topics my whole life. When I initiated my hermetic studies years ago, it was about the same time as when I started drawing. My art is influenced by my interests and is simply an expression of my occupation with the metaphysical realms and my spiritual work. My symbolic and Tarot art is defined as "path working" for me. That means that during the time of drawing a piece, my focus is entirely on the subject I'm working on. Art is always an invitation to the current, or archetype I'm occupied with, to form a relationship with me during this process. This is sometimes really difficult, like walking through water or clouds, and at times really easy with a quick opening of the veil—it depends on my own experience and characteristics. I learned to approach these themes on different levels and my visions are getting clearer as I move from drawing to drawing.

I think that every artist does the same thing in a way, sometimes without even knowing it. By choosing my focus in an active manner, the path gets clearer and mistakes can be avoided more easily. Drawing a certain current/tarot card lasts about one to two months. During this time it reflects in my physical life as well, often accompanied by challenges and trials, so the process is a real life experience every time. Usually by following this process I learn about the current firsthand and then by finishing the drawing close the veil actively. This ritual repeats itself continuously with every tarot card or symbolic drawing, so the process really occupies my whole life.

And what is the role of art in magical practices or in ritual?

The process I describe is basically a standard ritual. It elapses during a specific time period, has defined borders, rules, operations, and is themed in a kabbalistic structure. I guard myself by following the basic rules of the hermetic laws and keep the "ritual of drawing" safe from outside influences. What I call "currents", others call gods, archetypes, forces, etc. For those who are new to Tarot I'd like to explain this in short.

Each Major Arcana can be connected to a path in the kabbalah. There are three elements (water, air, fire) bound in one (earth), seven planets, and the twelve zodiac signs = 22 major arcana. There are 56 Minor Arcana cards, 14 cards connected to each set. The sets are connected to the four elements and to the worlds of the Kabbalah:

> Wands – Atziluth – the world of emanation – element: fire
> Cups – Briah – the world of creation – element: water
> Swords – Yetzirah – the world of formation – element: air
> Disks – Assiah – the material world – element: earth

Each of these sets is composed of cards from one to ten (connected to the 10 planets/spheres) of the Kabbalah and four royal cards, again connected to the elements.

So, when I draw a card, I am able to focus on one specific idea which the universe expresses itself in. These basic ideas can be explored by the practical ritual of art, which is much more effective than by just reading about them. Any art can be the key—drawing, painting, music, acting, writing, etc. Without this key, an explorer of magic, hermetic teachings or the occult often is helpless in approaching these matters practically.

The explanation is as simple as logic. Symbolism is the true and innermost language of all things and the expression of the deeper layers of existence. By drawing them in different compositions a connection to this language is made like a link to the great opus itself. With more art, more connections are growing and an access to the deep, the subconsciousness, and to that we call the "occult" develops naturally.

What's the inspiration behind your art? Or where does it come from?

I was talking about forming a relationship with the current I'm drawing. So, the inspiration flows during this gate. Unlike a medium, I'm not possessed or used by the force behind this, nor do I invoke it completely. The outcome of the creative process is rather a magical child between us both.

To be clear—these currents are not completely outside forces or entities separated from us. Those entity-like forces exist too, but they are not what I'm searching for. Rather, what I'm doing, path work is meant to open oneself within, for the purpose of discovering inner aspects of the self which are unknown and were hidden before. This inner pass that opens up *can* be a gateway to the original and universal aspects, with time and an ongoing practice, but initially the personal process and progress is the most important thing when following this path. However, each of these aspects can be called or channeled like a universal melody one is joining. The terms of this "mutual melody" or relationship between the current and my conscious self are always the same. I vow to honestly and without preconception involve myself in the process of creating, without becoming an exclusive representative of the current I'm working with.

This is usually a very honest and explicit designed relationship. After a specific time, we depart again and I'm walking on to the next aspect. I gain a lot from these experiences since I'm getting to know myself and my different aspects much better. This connection won't be as deep as working with one specific archetype for years, but it is often more candid and not as unilateral influenced. Also, it keeps the mind stable and I avoid one of the greatest dangers of occultism—letting too much of one specific force flow through the nervous system over a longer period of time. In my opinion our physical bodies are quite sensitive to those streams of energy and have to be trained. By opening a door wider and wider without limitations the body and the psyche can be truly harmed—I experienced this myself, so these are no hasty threats, I'm just relating that I've learned one should be careful of what you work with.

What themes do you find yourself returning to?

I do circle back to certain themes. My interest is naturally about the core aspects of existence. The relationship between the creator, the sustainer, and the destroyer. This often leads me to the complex aspect of the creator and the gnostic theme of Jaldabaoth [Yaldabaoth] and the architects/engineers. The triple goddess which is the custodian of veils and her elusive nature is another aspect I'm very deeply involved with and interested in. The dual concept of the child and the liberator, gatekeepers, gateways and rifts in space time are of general and personal interest to me too. I probably will always circle around these deep interests of mine.

Many of my pieces are influenced by these core themes which are always present in my mind. By exploring them further I learn a lot about myself and my surroundings at the same time. I also try to include keys which helped me along the way. They can't be too plain in sight but are hidden within my pieces. That's just the law of these things. Not to be secretive and mysterious, but, because it is almost holy for each and every one to lift the veil on his/her own, to throw directions and revealed mysteries around casually can restrict the experience as a whole.

Since much of your work has to do with Tarot, how do you view the Tarot? What's your relationship to it and why do/did you gravitate towards Tarot as a structure for your art?

I view Tarot a bit different than most, I suppose. I rarely read the cards and never tell the fortune with them, especially not to others. For me, Tarot is not the key to outside forces or to know more about my surroundings, but a key inwards and to get to know the subconsciousness and the inner self better. By exploring the different aspects, I learn about myself and develop my character—which is the ultimate goal in life. We all circle our lives in recurring spirals which often lead to the same decisions, outcomes and behaviors. Day after day, year after year, life after life and so on. To get to know the own self, means to get closer to the sources of our choices. By unveiling the decision-making process, which keeps us in our circles it frees me step-by-step from my own prison. This is true for everybody, but there is no universal truth to be told to others, because each path is different. The practice of introspection can never be taught or assumed by a guru or teacher but has to be worked out by each and every one of us on his/her own. However, the teaching of the "how" is a torch and can be passed from one person to the other, so the symbolic light bearer is a principle which I experience to be true nevertheless.

Tarot is such a torch. It describes archetypes as well as an inner process, it can be the key to solving various situations in countless life cycles, and is connected to recurring universal symbols. To get deeper into its mystery means to learn that a structural design is not only the basis of the universe with all its dimensions, but also of our own life's. The process of getting to know Tarot better, ideally with a practical approach like (in my case) drawing leads to an overview of this design and may guide to an active handling of this blueprint.

A famous example would be if one was the captain of a ship which randomly crosses the sea of life itself. This ship will be a passive vessel and exposed to all the dangers, concurrences, and outside forces which there are. It may discover a single island by luck, but it will also be likely to sink fast and never achieve a goal, which hasn't even been set. To get to know Tarot in all of its aspects is the same thing, as discovering not only a map of the sea, but to study also it's deepness, its borders, the weather, the islands, its inhabitants, and so on. The captain of this ship, the captain who studies Tarot, will increase the ship's chances of finding what they are searching for, but even if they don't find that, it will actively guide them through the sea and allow them to learn much during the journey. So Tarot is not simple cards with symbolic pictures for esoteric purposes, but so much more It is impossible to discover all of its secrets in one life.

Is there any particular style of art that you are influenced by?

I'm very much influenced by the artists of my youth but also by the art of some of the high crops of this world. I started with black on gold Tarot, because of an album artwork by metastazis I liked when I was younger. When I discovered Peter Proksch and fantastic realism it definitely opened a whole new chapter in my art. I like to be influenced by books, series, films, exhibitions, but also by nature and my own visions. It's a mixture of it all. I try new art styles to get better technically with every drawing, but I never considered technique to be my biggest strength.

I remember when I was only in elementary school and I was furious that I wasn't able to express what I had in mind artistically. When I reached the goal of being able to express myself in my work, it became less important to draw perfectly. Although I have technical ambitions, I focus more on content then on learning and combining new styles and methods.

How should the average magician think about the art they showcase in their home, the art on their tarot decks or their altars? What impact might it have on their practice?

First of all, I'd like to speak out about a thing that should be discussed more, which is showing the altar (or any magical work) on social media. Back when most of the hermetic books were written, this wasn't an issue, so not much has been said about this new approach on the occult and magic in modern days. I'd strongly suggest not showing your altars on social media. The altar or ritual room should be marked of a "place between the worlds". It is the most sacred room or place a magician or practitioner could have. To show it around like it was a new piece of clothing or any physical item, may lift its energy and degrade it to just a "decorative place" with no more usable energy—also it may close the gate for you at this point. The altar should be veiled and be the most personal space one has. In many religions the sanctuary is shrouded for the same reason, which is the following. As anyone who practices spirituality on a certain level will notice, there are steps on the path which are marked by trials. The sephirah of hod for example can only be passed by resigning to vanity and shallowness. Yesod is still all about illusion and a certain publicity isn't harmful when approaching this mystery. Following the path further to hod, showcasing the magical work won't get one very far. It is absolutely alright to show the outcome to others, to compare experiences and to be social about the work which has been done, but at this point there should already be a layer been established, that is symbolic for "the veil" in personal life. In a world where almost nothing is hidden any more, the altar must be the last thing which is revealed. Everyone who has studied the mystery of the goddess of the veil will have learned about (or experienced) why, in detail. If you haven't so far, take your time before showing around your work/altar—the reasons will reveal themselves with practice and time.

The altar can have multiple forms; not everyone has the space or the facilities to decorate it in a fancy way, and this isn't necessary at all.

One single piece of art, an item of personal value, a little statue, a necklace, or an unfolded cloth can be more effective than an expensive room, full of decorations. If a drawing provided a gateway for you, it would be a valuable asset to your altar, but if it was a film or some song, a blue ray disc or a CD wouldn't be wrong either. My whole flat is full of occult and spiritual art and items—I simply like to live this way and feel well, surrounded by these things. But I can tell you, my altar misses all of this stuff.

I have some handmade things and items I specifically bought (or better, made) for the purpose of my practice. These items are attached to no specific label, story or memory—they are almost free of any influence. I don't need distractions from outside while trying to find and keep my focus. I made the experience that beautiful things distract the ego from being uplifted into a higher state. The goal of a ritual is mostly detachment from the physical self to experience the topic of research from a different state of consciousness. And I can tell you, my higher consciousness isn't interested in pretty things at all, although it can help coming back from this state to be surrounded by something familiar and pleasant. But an old cuddly toy or the favorite comic figure from your childhood serves this purpose better than a huge statue of some god, figuratively speaking.

What might the average occultist be missing by not incorporating art of any kind into their practice?

Symbolism is art and vice versa. By not using symbols the practitioner won't have anything to mark his/her steps on the journey. When I look at the art I've created, each piece reminds me of certain steps and each line I've drawn is a key to a specific memory on the way. Written words mean nothing, where symbols mean everything. To those who are versed in kabbalistic terms, a symbol works on the level of briah [beri'ah], where logic and words fail the practitioner completely. To establish an artistic anchor on your own on an emotional level is the strongest suggestion I can give. It would be a failed experience if I wouldn't be able to remember what I learned on an emotional level. Words in a journal will serve the purpose of transcribing an experience to others, but they will fail in transcribing it to yourself after some time has passed. My drawings never fail me. They keep me connected to my journeys and are so much more worthwhile because of that reason than anything else I could create logically.

You mention that "My art should provide a gateway to different realms, currents or steps on the path" what do you mean by this? How do you view your art as gateways and what sorts of realms do you envision they lead to?

All art is a gateway; therefore, art is much more important to society then we consciously think. It leads to inspiration and may influence even the behavior of people. While advertising, propaganda art, and perfectly drawn sceneries often depict illusions and lead deeper into this beautiful but illusionary physical reality, some art is made to decouple the observer from it. My goal is to do that.

Since every single one of my drawings is a result of my occupation with different realms, subconscious realities, dream or visionary states of mind, these matters are bound into the particular drawing. I view them as being recaptured in my pieces. Often it is, that people, (myself included) can't change their routine or unveil things hidden from them, without a certain and specific input. If one of my drawings provides this input that a person is looking for, it serves its purpose. Because of my interest and engagement in metaphysical objectives most drawings are charged with those experiences as well. Each one who took a spiritual journey will know, that the key, as well as the gate are not always as easy to find.

So, each symbol can be the key and each drawing, song, film, or other artistic object is a different gate. Often it is that our favorite films or music provided such gateways to us during our life's—each uniquely specific, but different to each person. Only by accessing this gateway, can one be reminded of the experience and find the red wire to this specific state of mind again. Most people do not really know why they have a favorite film, song, or book. The reason is, that the first time, we consummate a piece of art it creates a marker to this special feeling. Those feelings are the doorways the practitioner is learning to pass through. Even a random person who can't pass this gate completely will be reminded of its nature. So, if there wasn't any art, our reality would be completely separated from any metaphysical realm. Art transcends these borders of reality and makes it initially possible to access other states of mind in the first place.

Your piece "The Magus" is the cover for this issue, can you tell us more about it? What inspired it? What is the significance behind it?

This is easy—I inspired it. It is truly visionary work without much outside influences. It marks the beginning of my "Tarot" journey, and it will close it one day. That means that it is the first Tarot drawing I made (which is still in the deck), and it will be my last when I finish the Conjunction Tarot process. So, in the end there will be two drawings of the Magus. The one, which is the cover of this issue is the one, which started my journey and the other one will be the Magus who ends his journey and circles back to the beginning. Each good work begins at the end and ends at the beginning. That's also the reason, why this is the only drawing I won't give away or sell the original. It was also the magus who led me to most of my huge projects. It is a drawing which radiates from energy and although it was an early drawing it is still the most popular one so far.

It was a pleasure to talk to you and thank you for your interesting questions, for featuring my work and publishing the interview in this journal.

Whoever wants to get in contact with me, please do so without hesitation. I'm happy to help with any questions, regarding the spiritual path and pleased to have philosophical discussions about symbolism as well.

Contributing Authors

Antero Alli
Inspired by the vital visceral theatre of Polish director Jerzy Grotwoski in 1977, Antero developed his own group paratheatre medium over the next forty-two years. His work has been documented in numerous videos, two books (*Towards an Archeology of the Soul* in 2003, *State of Emergence* in 2020) and by Nicoletta Isar, Professor at the Institute of Art History, Copenhagen University. Alli's personal experiences in this transformative ritual process inspired the creation and production of his many feature art films since 1993. An astrologer by trade, his recent book *Experiential Astrology* presents his embodiment bias for horoscope interpretation. Antero resides in a forest near Portland, Oregon.
Follow Antero at: verticalpool.com

Ina Auderieth
Ina Auderieth is a hermetic practitioner and artist residing in Austria. If you want to follow her artistic process, it can be found on her Instagram: @Ina_Auderieth or by visiting her website: https://www.inurath. com. If you have questions about her art or wish to discuss the spiritual path or symoblism she can be contacted at ina.auderieth@inurath.com.

Chris Bennett

Chris Bennett has been researching the historical role of cannabis in the spiritual life of humanity for more than a quarter of a century. He is co-author of *Green Gold the Tree of Life: Marijuana in Magic and Religion* (1995); *Sex, Drugs, Violence and the Bible* (2001); and author of *Cannabis and the Soma Solution* (2010); and *Liber 420: Cannabis, Magickal herbs and the Occult* (2018). Bennett's research has received international attention from the BBC, Guardian, Sunday Times, Washington Post, Vice and other media sources.

Jack Chanek

Jack Chanek is the author of *Qabalah for Wiccans* and *Tarot for Real Life*. He is a Qabalist, Gardnerian Wiccan, Tarot reader, and Slavic polytheist. Jack lives in New Jersey, where he works as an academic philosopher researching Immanuel Kant's philosophy of science.

Alex Criddle

Alex is an independent researcher, writer, editor, and gardener. He has a BA and MA in philosophy. He has written for *Psychedelic Science Review* and *Blossom Analysis*. You can find his writing and research at alexcriddle.com.
Twitter: @alexkcriddle

Saul Mondriaan

Saul M. (@saul_mondriaan on Twitter) is a queer chaos magician operating out of a little eggplant-colored house in the desert southwest.

Sadalsuud

Sadalsuud (after the fixed star) is a software programmer, architect, manager, and astrologer who builds astrological research tools with a long term goal of making astrology obvious and accessible to as many people as possible.
Twitter: @sadalsvvd
Resource and info website: https://publish.obsidian.md/sadalsvvd/
Readings website: http://readings.sadalsvvd.com/

Christian Swenson

Christian Swenson is a professor at Utah Valley University, where he teaches philosophy. He is a graduate of Brigham Young University's Comparative Studies MA program, and he was Westminster College's Outstanding Philosophy Graduate. He is enthusiastically interested in Rudolf Steiner and Anthroposophy, and he was a founding board member of Mountain Sunrise Academy, a Utah Waldorf K-8 charter school.

Becca Tarnas

Becca Tarnas, PhD, is a scholar, artist, and editor of *Archai: The Journal of Archetypal Cosmology*. She received her doctorate in Philosophy and Religion from the California Institute of Integral Studies (CIIS), with her dissertation titled *The Back of Beyond: The Red Books of C. G. Jung and J. R. R. Tolkien*. Her research interests include depth psychology, archetypal studies, literature, philosophy, and the ecological imagination. She teaches at both Pacifica Graduate Institute and CIIS, and is the author of the book *Journey to the Imaginal Realm: A Reader's Guide to J. R. R. Tolkien's The Lord of the Rings*.

Hereward Tilton

Dr. Hereward Tilton is a religious studies scholar who has taught on the history of Western esotericism at the University of Amsterdam and the University of Exeter. A past fellow of the Alexander von Humboldt Foundation, he has conducted research on the magical employment of plant-based entheogens in Europe and the synthesis of psychoactive forms of the Philosophers' Stone in the early modern alchemical laboratory. In recent years he has dedicated himself to the study of the 'serpent's path' in Western esotericism, a broadly gnostic tradition related both historically and psychologically to Indo-Tibetan tantra. In his books *The Path of the Serpent* (2020) and *Chaoskampf* (2022) he integrates historical and neuropsychological perspectives on this tradition's symbolism and techniques.